DATE DUE

DE10'98			
OC2 0'99			
NO1 0'99			
DE 1'99			

DEMCO 38-296

Women of Lebanon

WOMEN OF LEBANON

Interviews with Champions for Peace

by NELDA LATEEF

McFarland & Company, Inc., Publishers

Jefferson, North Carolina, and London

to Walt A. Barrage who inspired this **book.**

British Library Cataloguing-in-Publication data available

Library of Congress Cataloguing-in-Publication data available

ISBN 0-7864-0329-2 (softcover; 50# alkaline paper) ∞

Manufactured in the United States of America

McFarland & Company, Inc., Publishers
  Box 611, Jefferson, North Carolina 28640

ACKNOWLEDGMENTS

It is with profound gratitude that I thank the valiant women in this book for the privilege of delving into their lives. I especially appreciate the support and encouragement of Mrs. Mona Haraoui, the First Lady of Lebanon — a truly eloquent champion for peace.

I am indebted to the Lebanese Ministry of Tourism, Middle East Airlines, and Hilda and Khalil Nassar for their unstinting assistance whenever that was needed. Aouni Abdulrahim for his cultural insights and introduction to artisans, artists, poets, writers, musicians, and a few gurus as well! Sona Jendi for invigorating games of tennis in the most delightful of settings and reminding me what it means to "never give up!" Georgette Gebara, May Menassa, Houda Al-Naamani, Emily Nasrallah — women of enormous personal generosity, for their friendship. I want to express my appreciation to Aida Farha, Nada Halwany, Selma and Selwa El-Hoss, and Houda Kassatly.

Personal warmth, optimism, and generosity are qualities I will always associate with the Lebanese people. During the six months I spent in Lebanon researching this book, I experienced unparalled kindness and hospitality, which in spite of so many years of civil war is still Lebanon's enduring hallmark. I specifically want to thank Wafic Barrage who personifies so genuinely these qualities and who contributed immeasurably to this project. Teta Ihsan Barrage for dreaming up the most delectable of Mediterranean menus, leading invariably to cozy, piquant conversations that carried into the wee hours of the night. Mike, Nada, Aboudie, Kazim, Najwa, Maya and Dala for their thoughtful advice and unflagging support. And Nizar Kalaaji who did not live to see this project completed but whose memory, along with his family — Tante May, and sons, Amer and Maher — helped carry it through.

Last, but certainly not least, my bedrock — Dad, Mom, Noel, Nora, Ned, and Sage, for personifying what it is to be "all for one and one for all."

CONTENTS

INTRODUCTION

For seventeen years, Lebanon experienced an orgy of violence as civil strife engulfed this ancient land. Provenance of the seafaring Phoenicians, who at the dawn of civilization established colonies on distant shores of the Mediterranean and whose trading and business traditions are sustained today by over nine million Lebanese expatriates scattered on every continent, Lebanon was the birthplace of the alphabet that codifies the most exalted thoughts of Western civilization. Yet, for seventeen long years, Lebanon was gripped by such stubborn bitterness and savage anarchy that civilization became a thin veneer. Timeworn suspicions and misgivings were exposed and turned to grist for promoters of violence both within and without the polity. A murderous cycle took a horrific human toll, leaving 150,000 dead, 425,000 injured, causing 875,000 to flee abroad as refugees, and almost 1,000,000 — one-third of the population — to become refugees in their own country.

Milco Manchevski demonstrates in his powerful film *Before the Rain* that, in a charged environment, any act of wanton violence can be the match that sets off a powder keg; "that violence escalates organically and mysteriously, in ways that suggest there can be no innocent bystanders in an explosive, hair-trigger world." Like the Macedonian hilltop setting where *Before the Rain* unfolds, the mountains and coastal plains of Lebanon bear sad testimony to the "mind-forged manacles" of ancient divisions. In the absence of a societal commitment to an inclusive community, differences have the potential to ignite fires that burn out of control.

The Lebanese women in this book paint a syncretic picture of violence. The savagery of the civil strife encroached upon their lives in different ways, always demanding concessions that challenged inexorably the will to carry on a "normal" life. And yet, in the end, numbing though the violence was in its intensity, its real limitations — indeed, its impotence — in the face of a people's refusal to capitulate to fear came as a revelation. I sought, therefore, in my interviews with these accomplished women, to plumb their lives contextually — as mothers, wives, sisters, daughters, career women — and not simply to abstract causes and effects of seventeen years of bloodshed.

Laura Nader, a proponent of "studying up," believes that "understanding the culture of the elite in a society should be of no less worth and importance than understanding the masses." Many of the women interviewed are accomplished professionals, fluent in Arabic, French, and English, with the economic wherewithal and educational background to lead prosperous, productive lives

1

outside of Lebanon. Instead, they chose to remain and see their country through good and bad times. The affection that these women have for their country has united them and spurred them to action. As poet Houda Al-Naamani has said: "We are all part of the same circle and the ripple created by every stone that is cast in hatred affects us all." These women, as one, reject violence in the belief that "an eye for an eye leaves everyone blind."

What emerges is a remarkable confidence that triumphs over recent experience and holds that the golden years of Lebanon, when it was known as "the Switzerland of the Middle East" and when tolerance and civility were practiced as high art forms, can be regained anew, with a stronger, if sobered, conviction. That the banishment of parochialism is the *sine qua non* of progress on all fronts. That people of different cultures and faiths need to engage each other in dialogue and confront the debilitating hobgoblins they may entertain about their differences. That people can and should revel in humanity's diversity.

A healthy, multicultural society fosters values that recognize the supreme worth of the individual, tolerate diversity and respect human dignity. Such a society does not permit different codes to apply to different groups. Laws are applied equally and grievances, no matter how unassuageable, are vented in courts of law. There is justice for all. These are some of the obvious but painful lessons to be learned from civil conflicts all over the world.

Johnnetta Cole has observed that social scientists have some important things to say about differences among human beings. These observations, she says, need to be expressed so that society may come to terms with diversity "until difference doesn't make any more difference." This exhortation applies *a fortiori* to the Lebanons of this world where, frequently, upon closer observation, difference is not so different. The women in this book speak to us about differences, but also about commonality. They urge us not to make false comparisons or to reach superficial conclusions. Indeed, they expose the futility of stereotypes — of what Flaubert called "la rage de vouloir conclure."

This book is about human endurance. The Lebanese women who speak to us about their trials during seventeen years of war were at once witnesses to the destruction of their society and the glue that prevented its total disintegration. Culture is of prime importance to many of the women in this book. Samia Saab traveled throughout the world setting up cultural exhibitions to remind Lebanese expatriates about their rich historical and cultural heritage. May Arida, president of the International Festival of Baalbek, routinely drove to Baalbek, in central Lebanon, to exhort the townspeople to protect the Roman ruins and stayed in contact with performers all over the world in anticipation of the day the festival could be brought back to Lebanon. Leila Badre, curator of the American University of Beirut Archaeological Museum, kept the museum open to remind the Lebanese people of their past. Nora Joumblatt, wife of politician Walid Joumblatt, opened an art gallery to display the works of contemporary artists and thereby help to reestablish Lebanon's historic role as a cultural center. Sculptor Saloua Raouda Choucair and artist Juliana Seraphim continued to work, channeling their anguish into art. Poet Houda Al-Naamani, among the first to return to her old neighborhood, poured out her feelings about her beleaguered country in spirited poetry and fiery works of art. Novelists Emily Nasrallah and Leila Osseirane, through their writings, gave voice to the trauma of those forced to leave and the suffering endured by those who stayed.

The disastrous impact of the civil war on the economy and social services was mitigated by the efforts of women who rolled up their sleeves and went into action. Judge Arlette Jreisatti established a free clinic in her neighborhood and founded vocational schools for boys and girls. Rhanda Berri, wife of parliamentary speaker Nabih Berri, established a center to rehabilitate the handicapped. Zahra Bissat founded a home for the destitute elderly. Bahia Hariri, who heads the Hariri Foundation, annually awards hundreds of academic scholarships to qualified Lebanese students. And first lady Mona Haraoui raised funds to build and operate a medical center.

Then there are those in interfaith marriages, who during the harshest fighting tried to bring the Lebanese people together by their selfless example. Interior designer Rima Shehadeh, a Muslim, decorated and opened up her house to the public for Christmas. Nimat Kanaan, director general of the Ministry of Social Affairs, worked tirelessly to help those in need. Hala Maksoud, professor of political science, toured the United States speaking out against the war and, by her example, helped destroy age-old stereotypes of Arab women. And television journalist Sonia Beiruti, in spite of lucrative offers to work outside the country, stayed, boosting morale throughout Lebanon.

The raw courage of these women is epitomized by journalist May Menassa, who, as she covered the war, fearlessly berated fighters to put down their weapons and stop fighting. Popular singers Fayrouz and Sabah led protest marches, singing patriotic songs. Pediatrician Majd Ariss-Timani lost her home and all her possessions, yet stayed on to save lives as young victims filled pediatric wards. Lamia Shehadeh continued to teach even after receiving a kidnapping threat. Hilda Nassar not only kept the American University of Beirut Medical Library up to date but automated it as well. Raymonde Abou and Mishka Mojabber, principals of elementary and secondary schools, kept their schools open at great personal sacrifice. Leila Khoury, the first female pharmacist ever elected president of her profession's board, took on the task of insuring that pharmacists are held accountable to the public.

Many of these women lost family members to the war. Attorney Laure Moghaizel, whose daughter, a Sorbonne-educated Ph.D., was killed, founded the Nonviolent Movement in Lebanon as well as the Lebanese Association of Human Rights. Historian Nina Jidejian wrote a four-volume series entitled *I Love Lebanon* so Lebanese children could learn about their cultural heritage, and dedicated the series to her late husband, a noted surgeon, who died during fierce fighting that prevented him from obtaining necessary medical treatment. Anissa Najjar, who founded the Village Welfare Society to educate rural women and train them to be self-sufficient, lost her daughter, a summa cum laude graduate of the American University of Beirut, in a bombing raid. Nayla Moawad, whose husband was assassinated after seventeen days as president of Lebanon, founded the René Moawad Foundation, a humanitarian organization, and chose to pick up her husband's fallen banner and run for a seat in parliament.

What surprised me most about these women was that rather than being embittered by the horrors of war, many spoke of gaining understanding, compassion and an acceptance of human weaknesses. Choreographer Georgette Gebarra described a new awareness and tolerance of human differences. Journalist May Menassa spoke of becoming "more spiritual" and having a "need to be overwhelmed by God." Many said they had gained a deeper faith, an awakened love for humanity, a release from fears of death, and a greater appreciation for the simple things in life such as the pleasure of tending a garden or watching a sunset. Former first lady Nayla Moawad said, "I have learned that you can survive even your worst fear." And Houda Al-Naamani ended our conversation with a question: "Is love too great a price to pay for the salvation of humanity?"

It is fitting that Lebanon's Education for Peace Program, designed to counter the effects of violence, fear and stress imposed on children by the war, and to spread the message of tolerance and commitment to peace, is now serving as a prototype in a number of countries. In a world enmeshed in a growing number of conflicts, the women in this book firmly believe that they must shape succeeding generations' capacities for tolerance and understanding.

The women come from a range of backgrounds, reflecting the mosaic of modern Lebanon, which comprises a confederation of sixteen national communities, each of which claims the ultimate loyalty of its members. This system, which recognizes the primacy of religious communities vested with political authority, is known as "confessionalism." The political system is underpinned by confessionalism, perpetuating the power and influence of traditional religious figures. The allocation of parliamentary seats on a sectarian religious basis insured the continued preeminence of communal leaders. The inbuilt conservatism of the system inhibited the rise of modern politics based on broad socioeconomic interests. Lebanon's parliament emerged as an institution mirroring the complex web of relationships between the traditional centers of power and patronage centered around clans, regions and sub-regions.

What makes these women special is that they have all risen above the pull of confessionalism and embraced humanity. They are Lebanon's salvation. With their considerable contributions, what is happening in Lebanon today is nothing short of the rebirth of a nation, reclaiming what it lost during the period 1975 through 1990. These women are determined to defeat the intolerance and narrow-mindedness that resulted in such massive death and displacement. These women, in the words of Mona Haraoui, "attach great meaning to Pope John Paul II's statement that Lebanon is not only a country but also a message to the rest of the world." They are champions for peace.

*   *   *

While the circular quality of history is sadly evident in many contemporary conflicts, time moves forward. Indeed, the last words in Mr. Manchevski's film are "The circle is not round." The need to examine critically received assumptions has never been greater. Too frequently, the pull of historical biases can cause good people to become lost in their own undergrowth. And in the words of Edmund Burke: "The only thing necessary for the triumph of evil is for good people to do nothing."

A better world must be underpinned by a foundation of respect between individuals. And it is individuals like the women featured in this book, working to foster tolerance and respect for human dignity, that have made it possible for Lebanon to weather the storm. As poet Andre Lorde said, "It is not difference which immobilizes us, but silence. And there are so many silences to be broken." Now, hear, in their own words, the voices of those who will not be silenced.

Arts
and
Literature

MAY ARIDA

PATRON OF THE ARTS

In Lebanon, the name May Arida recalls the glamour of the pre-war years, when Beirut was the "Paris of the East." As the last president of the International Festival of Baalbek, Arida, with her immaculate good looks, is widely considered the high priestess of Lebanese society. Self-described as "someone who loves to do good things for her country," she is especially admired for her tireless efforts to preserve the Roman ruins of Baalbek, keeping alive the dream of restoring the festival back to Lebanon.

Since its inception, Arida has been actively involved in the International Festival of Baalbek, perceived by many as a symbol of peace and prosperity, hearkening back to the days when it attracted to Lebanon the world's best symphonies, ballet companies, and performers. Fluent in Arabic, French, English, and Spanish, Arida is married to international financier Carlos Arida. She is the mother of four daughters and is a talented sportswoman. For many years, she was Lebanon's ski and water-ski champion. Educated at Beirut's Protestant College, Arida is a board member of the Lebanese National Conservatory of Music and has received numerous honors, including France's Legion of Honor and Jordan's "Al-Kawkab" Order.

In person, Arida lives up to her reputation. She is charismatic and disarmingly unpretentious. We met in her tastefully decorated apartment in Hazmiyeh, a suburb of Beirut, where she is surrounded by cherished mementos and photographs of herself with royalty, heads of state and family members. Impeccably groomed, with every strand of blond hair in place, she wore a classic navy blue suit. Her accessories included an honorary ribbon bestowed upon her by the Lebanese government for her philanthropic work. As we sat in the drawing room, with its panoramic view of Beirut, the sun broke through the afternoon clouds and the face that graced Vogue, Town & Country, *and so many other magazines around the world shone with radiance, hazel eyes sparkling.*

*   *   *

What was it like to attend a performance at Baalbek?
It was extraordinary! The music, the lighting that lit up the ruins, the canopy of stars above and the stars on the stage were almost equally brilliant. Whether

it was an evening of music with the Berlin Philharmonic Orchestra with Von Karajan conducting; an evening of dance with The Royal Ballet; or an evening of song with Oum Koulsoum, the most famous Arab singer of modern times, it was always memorable. I have been everywhere — the Acropolis in Athens, the Colosseum in Rome — but never have I felt the way I feel when I am attending a performance at Baalbek and the orchestra is playing full-force and the flood-lights are on the ruins. I remember, as though yesterday, Rudolph Nureyev leaping across the stage and Margot Fonteyn dancing like a swan. It was always unforgettable. When the first astronaut landed on the moon, we were at Baalbek that evening for a performance given by the American dance company of Alvin Niko-lais. During the performance, the American ambassador received a message and immediately interrupted the performance to announce that American astronauts would be landing on the moon in minutes. The whole audience, three thousand people, looked up at the full moon and, as though it had been choreographed, we stood up as one, and started a spontaneous countdown. It was extraordinary!

How did you become involved with the International Festival of Baalbek?

I started working at a very young age for the National Conservatory of Music and helped create a "Friends" support group to raise funds for the conservatory. When President Chamoun in 1956 wanted to create an international festival at Baalbek, he invited a group of us to the Presidential Palace to form a committee to organize and raise funds for the festival. The president wanted the festival to be international in scope and to include music; dance; English, French, and Arabic theater; and traditional Lebanese folklore. In fact, the festival, in time, became renowned for its excellent coverage of so many artistic areas. Unlike, for example, the Salzburg Festival, known for opera, we had it all. Because of my connection with the conservatory, I was asked to head the music committee which included: opera, symphonic, philharmonic, and chamber music. We decided music would represent four of the six weeks of the festival. At the time, not a person among us had any experience in organizing a festival. We were all amateurs driven by a mandate from the President of the Republic to introduce the Baalbek Festival to Lebanon seven months from the day we met. Each of us went in a different direction scouting for talent. Because France is like a second home, and we are French-speaking, I went first to France. I knew I could find help and advice there. Sure enough, in Paris, I encountered a man who represented several world-class orchestras and that, in essence, is how the festival made its debut!

How was the Baalbek Festival publicized?

We did not have sufficient funds to publicize the festival, but we had something better: word of mouth among the performers! They loved the Baalbek Festival because they received the red carpet treatment from the moment they arrived at the Beirut International Airport to the time they departed. Everything was taken care of. They were greeted by a welcoming committee, whisked through customs, and never had to waste a moment on luggage or travel formalities. We organized parties, trips to the beach, sightseeing tours, and allowed

May Arida between Sviatoslav Richter and Mstislav Rostropovich.

the performers to rehearse whenever they wanted. When you have an orchestra of 120 people from Germany, Italy, America, or wherever, and they continue on their world tour, you can be sure that when they encounter other musicians they will spread the word of the marvelous time they had at the festival. No other festival in the world pampered their performers as we did and that is what contributed to the fabulous reputation of the Baalbek Festival. In addition, from a professional standpoint, the accoustics at Baalbek at the Temple of Bacchus, were nothing short of extraordinary. In fact, the Temple of Bacchus has the reputation of being the best open air theater in the world. Soloists like Jean-Pierre Rampal, Rostropovitch, Richter, Michelangeli preferred to perform there without a microphone because the accoustics were so marvelous.

How did the festival do financially?

The first year President Chamoun, with our help, raised the necessary funds for the festival. After that the government provided a small operating budget and, to tide us over, we would borrow money from the bank. Then in the summer, as soon as we sold tickets, we would pay the bank back. We had very good credit because our ticket sales were always dependable. All the great festivals lose money and we were no exception, but after several years we did something very simple. To attract the young generation, we decided to bring great American classical jazz performers like Ella Fitzgerald and Miles Davis. It was due to this decision that we started making money. For example, when the Royal Ballet came, they would come not only with their ballet troupe, but with a full orchestra. So even though they had sold out performances, their expenses were so enormous we would still lose money. In comparison, Ella Fitzgerald would come accompanied only by her pianist and saxophonist and we would sell just as many tickets.

As the president of the International Festival of Baalbek, you must have some wonderful stories to tell!

[laughter] There are so many stories! Some funny, some inspiring, some exasperating — none boring — I assure you! For me, I have always enjoyed attending rehearsals because it is by watching a rehearsal that you can really appreciate the achievement and the effort behind a flawless performance.

Do you play a musical instrument?

I used to play the piano when I was young, but when I started working for the National Music Conservatory and the Baalbek Festival, I no longer had the time nor the inclination to practice. I have been spoiled where good music is concerned! [laughter]

Did the occurrence of war in Lebanon come to you as a shock?

Yes, totally! The year the war began was the year we were planning to celebrate the twentieth anniversary of the Baalbek Festival. That year, we had extraordinary talent lined up. The performers were all scheduled to come to Baalbek in two to three months. Then fighting erupted in Sidon. I thought nothing of it. I flew to Paris as scheduled and announced the festival's program for the coming season. Shortly thereafter, former President Camille Chamoun, who created the festival, sent for me. He said, "May, you have to return to Paris and cancel the festival. Then forget about it for seven years." I said, "What do you mean, cancel the festival? The fighting is not serious! It will end in several weeks." He shook his head and said, "You are all little children. You don't realize what is happening." He was right, but he was also wrong. The war lasted a full decade longer than even he had predicted.

How did you survive the war years?

Not easily! There was nothing to do but to try to figure out where to flee to avoid the shelling. Throughout the war, to keep up our morale, members of the various committees would meet as often as possible to keep alive our hope of bringing back the festival to Lebanon. Today, if there was security in the country, we could launch the festival six months from now. I have stayed in contact with all the artists that came to Baalbek. Wherever I went, I would contact them. I visited Jean-Pierre Rampal in Paris and Mstislav Rostropovich in Washington, D.C.

I'll tell you a story that took place in London. I went to see Rostropovich perform. During the intermission, I sent him a note informing him I was in the audience and that I wanted to come back stage to congratulate him on his performance. That evening, he had seventeen curtain calls! By the time I got back stage there were more than fifty people ahead of me. Rostropovich saw me from far away and he called out: "May-ishka! May-ishka, come!" Everyone immediately cleared the way to make room for me. They all wanted to know, "Who is this lady?" Rostropovich simply said: "This is Miss Baalbek!" I said, "What do you mean, 'Miss Baalbek'?" He said, "Okay, this is Miss Baalbek, May-ishka." [laughter] Wherever I go I try to stay in touch with all those who have performed at Baalbek. Many of these artists are booked solid four to five years in advance. Rostropovich, for example, is booked six years in advance, but he has told me: "Give me one month's notice and I will come during the month of August, my vacation month, because I love Baalbek." Many of the musicians have said the same. If the Festival of Baalbek resumes, we will have a marvelous festival beginning with the first year.

You have held on to the hope of bringing back the festival for so long, how have you maintained your sense of optimism all these years?

Beirut has always been my home. I would travel for one or two months a year to visit my children. I have three daughters in Paris and one in Washington, D.C. Even when the airport was closed, I would come back. Sometimes, I would return through Jordan and then take a car through Syria, or I would come back by sea. We spent most of our time in the basement of this building. Sometimes, when we could, I would take my mother (she died last year at age 92) up to the mountains. But most of the time I stayed here. I thought if everyone left Lebanon there would be nothing to return to. Look what happened to the Palestinians when they left Palestine. My mother did not want to leave Lebanon. Like all the elderly, her desire was to die in her own country. My children left. I had no right to force them to stay and endure the bombardments. Many Lebanese left, but many of us stayed, and that is why I am certain Lebanon is going to return to the way it was before the war because we Lebanese have faith in our country. Every time a house, a shop, a factory was destroyed, it was immediately rebuilt. I can't tell you how many times this apartment was destroyed, and look, I am still here!

What was the worst time for you during the war?

All seventeen years of the war. They were the most difficult years of my life. There were some terrible moments when I was alone without my children or my husband. But during all those years, I never stopped going to Baalbek. The great Temple of Jupiter has been there since the beginning of our era when it was one of the wonders of the world. I wanted to make sure it would still be standing when the war was over. I want my grandchildren to enjoy Baalbek as I and my children have. I did not want to have happen to Baalbek what happened to Tyre and Sidon, where so much of the ruins were vandalized. When I visited Baalbek, I would organize reunions with the local people, many of whom had worked for the festival for over twenty years. I would talk to them and urge them to guard the ruins. I visited Baalbek several days ago and police are now guarding the grounds. There is no reason for me to worry any longer. During seventeen years, it was like a fifth child to me, I visited it at every opportunity to make sure it would survive the war.

What were your aspirations when you were growing up?

I married very young, two months short of my seventeenth birthday. I wanted to become a doctor, but I didn't have the opportunity. I come from a family of doctors. My father and uncles were all doctors and two of my daughters are now in the medical profession: one is a biologist; the other, a cardiac intensive care nurse. But my husband, at the time, said: "Finish! There is no school, now. You have to raise our children and receive our guests." I married into a family that received a lot of guests. I married Ibrahim Sursock first and we had three daughters. Then I married Carlos Arida and we have one daughter, Maria.

You are known for your sense of style. How did that develop?

Style is a matter of knowing what looks good on you and what doesn't. Then achieving a look that makes you feel good about yourself. It takes time and a bit of experimentation. I believe, when you feel good about yourself, you look good. It is really as simple as that. Sometimes, of course, it's also a question of whether you have it or you don't! [laughter] When I married for the first time, I was very young. It was my second husband, Carlos Arida, who gave me the opportunity and encouragement to develop my personality. I was a woman who was excessively timid. I was so bashful, I could not even walk across the hall, if people were there, without my face turning red. Carlos always assured me that I could do anything. It was his belief in me and his support which gave me confidence in myself.

When I married my first husband, Ibrahim Sursock, my godmother was Madame Catroux who was the wife of General Catroux, the High Commissioner of Lebanon during the French period. The first time I went to Paris, Madame Catroux accompanied me. I was young and I fell in love with Paris. I would walk through museums all day and never get tired. I attended fashion shows and viewed the latest haute couture collections. Madame Catroux introduced me to Christian Dior and I always remember what Dior told me. He said, "You have to wear what looks good on you. Don't ever wear something just because it is in style." My fashion doctrine has always been: *Prend dans la mode ce qui te va.* [Take from fashion what suits you.]

That same year Christian Dior was introducing the "New Look" and I was fortunate to be in Paris and possess the means to afford it. I was going to New York and Christian Dior said to me [this was in 1947], "I am going to make you a magnificent wardrobe so that you will be my ambassador in New York." I arrived in New York on the *Queen Elizabeth* liner. It was perhaps the first or second time the ship had docked in New York so there were a lot of curious journalists waiting to see who was arriving. Dressed as I was in Christian Dior's "New Look," the journalists immediately assumed I was a celebrity and started taking photographs. I told them, "Really, I am no one special." But that didn't stop them, and soon I was in all the magazines!

I understand that you are a very active sportswoman and that you were the president of Lebanon's Water-Ski Federation for many years.

I did a lot of sports. I still do. The question of the hour was always, "May, how can you work, do sports, and take care of your four daughters?" I have always believed it is a question of organization. I was the ski champion of

Lebanon for many years. I would work on festival matters until Friday evening, then go up to the mountains and practice Friday night and all day Saturday and Sunday. I didn't have the time to train like most world ski champions, but three days a week of training was sufficient to maintain my title in Lebanon! Eventually, I lost my title to my daughter, Maria, but I didn't mind it terribly as long as it stayed in the family. I then took up water-skiing because my brother, Simone Khoury, was a world champion in the sport and he trained me. He spent several years performing at Cyprus Gardens in Florida. I came in second at the European/Mediterranean Championship. The person who beat me was Maria Dora, who became the future daughter-in-law of the king of Italy.

What is your secret for always looking so good?

I sleep. I must have eight to nine hours of sleep a night. If I don't have anything scheduled in the morning, I sleep. Sleep is a great healer. When I am depressed or sad, sleep revives me. There were so many times when I was deeply discouraged because I always had the hope that this war, which started in 1975, was going to end right away. Until two years ago I used to swim 1000 meters, three times a week. Now, I have reduced that to 600 meters because I worry about my heart! [laughter] I still ski the slopes alone and I do gymnastics. I am always the oldest one in the group! All my life I have been a very competitive sportswoman; my brothers are great sportsmen: Rene, my older brother, in tennis; Simon, in water-skiing.

What accomplishments are you most proud of?

First, my four daughters, not because they are my daughters, but because they have fine, thoughtful personalities. Some children are indifferent to their parents, mine are the opposite. My daughters are all that a mother can hope for and because of them I don't fear my old age. I know that I will always be embraced and encircled by my children. Second, I am proud that I did what I could to assist the south of Lebanon. The South was deprived of everything. I saw women wash their laundry and drink from the same basin of water. In schools, children were crowded thirty-five to forty students in a tiny classroom; and the working conditions in the factories were terrible. With the help of friends, I created a committee to assist the South. Every Tuesday and Thursday, we would go at six o'clock in the morning to see what was needed. Entire families would work all day carrying water to irrigate their fields. So our principal focus was working with the government to bring them water. Also, instead of cultivating their fields by traditional methods, as they were doing, we bought tractors and olive presses and taught them how to use the equipment. We worked very hard for a number of years until the government took over. After that, all my time was devoted to the International Festival of Baalbek.

What do you think differentiates Lebanon from other countries?

The answer is very simple: the Lebanese people. In Lebanon, we have extraordinary human relations. The Lebanese are not selfish. They adore receiving and entertaining people. Everyone and their friends are always welcome. You will not find the same hospitality anywhere else in the world. We are a people who enjoy the pleasure of other people's company.

When you travel outside of Lebanon and people learn that you are Lebanese, what is their general reaction?

They tell me, "You don't look Lebanese." I tell them, "Make no mistake, I am Lebanese on both sides, entirely!"

SALOUA RAOUDA CHOUCAIR

SCULPTOR

One of the Arab world's foremost sculptors, Saloua Raouda Choucair is credited with being the first abstract artist in Lebanon. She says of her work: "I look upon it as the mirror of our age." Born in Lebanon, in 1916, she graduated from Beirut College for Women in 1938 and attended courses at the American University of Beirut (AUB) and the École Nationale des Beaux Arts in Paris during the late forties and early fifties. She received art certificates from both the Pratt Institute in New York and the Cranbrook Academy of Art in Detroit.

Islamic art inspired Choucair and steered her inventiveness to abstract art. Her work is distinctive for its architectonic purity. She concedes, were she to begin again, she would be an architect. As a student at AUB, she excelled in science, mathematics and physics. As an artist, her work reflects the mathematical precision and clarity of thought of her academic interests. Art critic Helen Khal explains, "Saloua perceived the foundations of the design structure of Islamic art as being essentially rooted in a mathematical source and thus she devised a new universal expression founded on geometrics, pure color, and form that goes beyond language barriers and sociocultural differences."

On a visit to Paris in 1948, Choucair was introduced to the works of Europe's pioneer abstractionists Picasso, Mondrian, Kandinsky, and Vassarely. She was astounded to learn that their ideas reflected her own independent findings. Inspired by the artistic milieu in Paris, she remained there for three-and-one-half-years, working in various ateliers, and attending lectures and discussion groups. In 1951, she held her first Paris exhibition, prompting one critic to write: "The walls of the Collette Alendy Gallery are about to burst with the force of the paintings hanging there this week!"

In 1974, the Lebanese government held a retrospective of her work, covering a time span of thirty years — the first exhibition of its kind ever held for a Lebanese artist. The following year, the Lebanese Civil War broke out, and throughout the long stretch of turmoil, Choucair continued to work with a singularity of purpose.

I met Saloua Raouda Choucair at her family's spacious villa, with its orange tile roof, situated on a busy street in Beirut. The villa, divided into separate apartments, is shared by Choucair and her husband, her 102-year-old mother, and her sister, Anissa Najjar. We chatted in a cozy, inner-room of her studio, located in its own separate wing. Her distinctive artistry is everywhere: paintings, sculptures, carpets, throw pillows, and woven straw mats; evident even in the distinctly designed sweater and brooch Choucair was wearing and the exotically decorated homemade delicacies set before us on the coffee table. Choucair's enthusiasm for her work and sense of wonder and pleasure in art is contagious.

*   *   *

Tell me about yourself?

I come from a family of doctors, lawyers, engineers and historians. My mother was widowed early and she had to raise three children by herself under difficult circumstances. She was well-educated, an excellent orator and, until now, recites poetry beautifully. All her life, she was very energetic and belonged to many different women's associations. She was presented a medallion from Broummana High School, two years ago, when she turned one hundred. She is the only living graduate from her class!

How did you decide to pursue art?

For me, art is innate. When I was very young, I did a lot of handicrafts. I would sketch classmates and professors, and draw caricatures of visitors. I was always better than my art teachers! I used to roam freely around the classroom talking to my classmates and assisting those who needed help in drawing. For my sociability, I spent most of my time out in the corridor! [laughter]

When did you realize that you were a "real" artist?

When my brother-in-law, Fouad, had to go to Paris on business, I joined him. I had been working at AUB for three years and I had saved up some money. I wanted to see what was happening in the world. Paris to us was always some-place special. At that time, I only knew post-impressionism. I had seen works by Picasso, Klee, Miro, Van Gogh, and Gauguin. These were the artists I read about in the news from France. To my amazement, I discovered while in Paris that many French people had never heard of these artists! We stayed in a beautiful hotel, The Normandy, on Rue de Louvre. Fouad would leave to attend to his business and I would roam the city visiting art galleries and museums. I saw abstract art for the first time! It was something incredible. I decided I had to remain in France.

To stay in Europe by myself was a big step! I took the underground for the first time and went to Cité Universitaire in search of student accommodations. I discovered one meal at The Normandy cost as much as a month of meals at the student dormitory. I could afford to stay! I told my brother-in-law of my plans and when he left, in spite of my desire to stay, I broke down into tears. Suddenly, Paris, with all its people became empty. I thought, if he were here and I were sick, he would at least be able to come and check on me. If I needed

Saloua Raouda Choucair

money, he would be my banker. There were so many "ifs" pounding in my head. Finally, I pulled myself together. I had to get my *carte de séjours* to stay in France and to do that I had to attend school so I enrolled at the École des Beaux Arts.

Did you have any formal art training before going to Paris?

When my sister, Anissa, was at AUB, I was still in high school and I would go with her to the university every Saturday to audit an art course taught by the artist, Farroukh. I also took art lessons with the Lebanese artist Omar Onsi. And that, at the time, consisted of my art training! I really learned by myself. I joined an Arab cultural club which featured literature, music, and philosophy lectures. I was given carte blanche to schedule every month a lecture by an artist and an exhibition of the artist's work. This was in 1947. There were no galleries in Lebanon. Artists exhibited their work in the hallways of Parliament!

In 1943, I was in Egypt during World War II and all the museums were closed. I wanted to see art. I went into the streets of old Cairo and visited the mosques. It was thrilling! I thought this is real art! It endures. We live in a high-tech, modern age; we have electricity, radios, television; we travel by jetliners and, yet, I found the art in those mosques timeless. I wanted to recreate this art from the perspective of a woman living in the twentieth century. Consequently, some of my sculptures use the principles of static dynamism. I have read so many books on architecture. It is my second love. I started out as a painter and then moved to sculpture.

When I returned to Lebanon from Egypt, I happened to attend a philosophy lecture. The professor was complimenting Greek art by saying it represented "the apogee of artistic achievement," because Greek art glorified the human body while Islamic art was second-class because it was simply decorative and forbade the drawing of the human body. This statement infuriated me! I was full of admiration and wonder for Islamic art and here this professor was saying our art was second-class! I went and read the Koran from cover to cover and discovered no reference in it that forbade the drawing of the human body. In fact, in the autobiography of the Prophet Muhammad, *Sirat el Nabi*, there are three people drawn in the manuscript riding camels on their way to Mecca. The Prophet, himself, is shown riding on his horse! Yet, nobody cut off the hands of the artist or burnt the books!

What I find fascinating about your sculptures is that they are like puzzles: the pieces can stand on their own or interlock together to form a whole new sculpture. What is the inspiration behind this connectiveness?

My art is inspired by Arabic calligraphy and music. In my art you see the proportions of long and short notes, especially quarter tones, as opposed to syllables. I sculpt poems using different proportions, different measures, and different rhythms. In school, we were taught that if we memorized any five lines from a one-hundred-line poem, each line is complete in itself and can stand on its own. My sculptures are the same way. They are made of five, six, seven pieces, measures if you will, and they can be put in various combinations together or apart. Whatever the combination, each is complete. I call these sculptures "solutions" because everyone can come up with their own combination — their own solution. But when the pieces are fitted together, as I had originally sculpted them to fit, it is then called a "poem."

So your sculptures are carved poetry. How do you begin?

The true believer in mysticism tries to get rid of all the vices within himself: absolve himself of greed, envy, jealousy and all negative feelings. He must only keep within himself virtuous qualities such as being generous, good to people, and believing in God. In sculpting, you employ the same principles. You begin with a block of wood (I prefer wood because it is light and you can work with it on your lap) and as you sculpt you take out all the negative things. Sculpting, for me, is a form of meditation. It is like repeating the name of God while threading worry beads or participating in *Halakat el Zikker* (Circle of Thoughts — a Sufi ritual — where a group forms a circle and repeats in unison over and over again: Allah, Allah, Allah.) The idea is when you don't think of anything but God, you reach.

Who has had the greatest influence on your work?

My inspiration comes from Arab art, mosques, decorations, buildings. My art is Arab art. It is very precise and geometric and my geometry uses the proportions of the circle. Arab artists used the circle, point and line, long before Kandinsky. The essence of Arab art is the point — from the point everything derives. The point and circle is the environment of God. One cannot escape God. God is the point. In my art, I employ geometry and the Golden Rule that was used to build the Parthenon. The influence is Arabic poetry and music and the Arabic language which is so rich. A word can begin in the past tense and have so many different meanings. You begin with the root and you add. I have sculptures that are like words, I call them *kalimat* [words].

I very much enjoy reading about science. I used to borrow books from a nuclear physicist, Selwa Nassar, who was a professor at AUB. I would read about new inventions and technology, and incorporate it into my art. For example, Nervi, the Italian architect, has done some wonderful new things in architecture. In my paintings, you will see evidence of Nervi. You will also see something from Buckminster Fuller and Eero Saarinen as well. One of my favorite trips was a visit to the United States at the invitation of the U.S. State Department. I asked to see the Ford Manufacturing Center in Detroit, Michigan. I remember when I walked into the plant, it was like entering a church or a mosque. It overwhelmed me. I thought how amazing God is to have given man such strength of mind. I saw a twelve meter long block of iron, one meter high and one meter wide, brought out by a wench from the fire. It was bright red hot and before my eyes it was cut and transformed into the body of a car. It was miraculous! I love to observe a printing press at work — machinery and modern technology fascinates me.

What is it you wish to communicate through your art?

Beauty! Beauty is God. The happiest person in the world is the one who believes that this earth is not the only place for us. We are different from Occidentals. Their art reveals their true selves ... they are afraid of life! They are terrified of nuclear war, the destruction of the ozone layer, over population, and so many things. Their art reveals their daily life. I went to a gallery, once, and in the entrance, in the space of a triangle, were empty gallon containers lined up next to each other — the very same containers we used here, in Beirut, when we had to store water. Is this art? Is this beauty? Is this what life is — so monotonous, so insignificant? Another gallery showcased everything the artist had that he had no use for: an old toothbrush, pencil stubs, wasted batteries. Everything was put on the floor and that was the entire exhibition. How empty such a life must be.

What do you think accounts for this "fear" in the Occident?

It is the result of living without a cause — in a vacuum — and being inundated by technology. The airwaves are full of television, radio, computers. The daily expenditures of an individual are so great that money is the focus of concern. There is no time to think of others. I think there is something degrading about such a life where the only thing that counts — the only thing that can fill that vacuum — is money. One sleeps thinking how can I earn more and wakes up thinking the same.

Wouldn't you say the same concerns apply here in Lebanon?

I don't believe that applies to the majority of the population here, yet. We believe the happiest person is the believer. We believe this earth is transitory and that a better life awaits us if we do good. For many of us, our life is lived guided by this belief.

How did the war affect you and your family?

My husband is a very independent man. When he was young, he was always the main draw in social gatherings. If he went to visit someone in a village, the rest of the village would hear that Youssef was in town and everyone would come to see him because he was so witty and full of fun. Now, because of the bombs, he doesn't hear well and his walk is old.

This villa we are sitting in was shelled so many times I've lost count. Much of my art was destroyed. This war was dirty! There was never a real reason for it on the part of the Christians or the Muslims. Kamal Joumblatt, the late leader of the Druze community, my community, was not prepared for war. Those who were fighting did not shoot to advance and take land. No! They were shooting simply to shoot. Now, for ten more years we will suffer trying to regain the life we had before seventeen years of war. They made certain everything was destroyed. "They" who hid behind their barricades shooting innocent civilians and claiming: "We are going to liberate Lebanon." From whom?

I went to a minister in the government and I told him I want two things: I want you to arrange for an exhibition of my sculptures outside of Lebanon and I want a visa for my daughter to leave the country. My sister Anissa's daughter was killed during the war. I have only one child. At the beginning of my marriage, I did not want to have children but I changed my mind. I wanted to experience motherhood. When my daughter was nineteen, I sent her to Paris to study film making. For our traditional society that is too young an age to be left alone in Paris, but I thought it was safer there than keeping her here with us in Beirut with the civil war in progress. My husband wanted her to study literature or law, but she told me: "Mother, art is in my genes. I cannot do anything but art!" I told her, if I were a young woman, today, I would take cinema and not art, because cinema is the pen and chisel of today's society.

Is art a struggle for you?

No, it is love. It is hope! It is through art that we can show the best of our culture — our civilization — and it is through art that we must overcome the cruel and inhumane attitude of western societies towards Muslims and the Arab world.

I don't like anybody near me when I am in a creative mode or starting something new. Even when I have an assistant, I say: "Please go, take a break. I don't want any distractions."

What really matters to you?

The success and happiness of my daughter matters a lot to me. Also, I would like my government to support my work by offering me commissions to do sculptures for public buildings or spaces. I am a Beiruti by birth. My family has lived here for centuries. I was decorated many times by the government, but decorations belong in a box hidden in a closed drawer. As a sculptor, what is important to me is to see my work exhibited and appreciated. I am seventy-seven years old and I am very much thinking of old age. My brother died at seventy-five. I am now trying to organize my life. My daughter tells me, "Please, write your memoirs. Don't leave that task for me." There are so many things that I need to do. I need to get a commission to do something big. In the Arab world, I am the first to do the kind of work that I do. I did this kind of work before ever seeing the work of other sculptors. When I exhibited my work in Paris, in 1947, I had never studied sculpture.

What quality do you cherish most?

Honesty! I once received an invitation from a London art dealer to exhibit my work in her gallery. Apart from painting and sculpting, I do tapestries, ceramics, jewelry, fountains, ceramic tiles for swimming pools and building murals. I also work with iron, glass, wood, bas relief and other media. The art dealer thought it would be exciting to have an exhibition of all my work at her gallery in London. She told me: "We will insure the works while they are in our gallery, take care of all exhibition costs, make posters, advertise, and send out invitations. We only ask of you that you transport your art to London." As a postscript, she added: "Abstract art is very hard to sell in England. Unfortunately, I can't promise you any sales." This, I appreciated more than anything I've received in my life, because it told me she was willing to spend money and time promoting my art without the hope of gaining anything. She wanted to exhibit my work only out of appreciation of what I had done!

What do you enjoy doing for relaxation?

My work takes time ... it is so precise. Any free time I have from housework, I come here to my studio. Free time to work has always been very precious to me. Even though it is my work, I relax when I am doing art. During the war, when there was shelling, I would come here to my studio and forget everything that was taking place outside. I had a friend from America who came to visit me and she asked: "How can you work with all these shells exploding everywhere?" I told her, "what I am doing here has value. When I am in the kitchen cooking it is torture but here, in my studio, I feel I am doing something of worth." When I am sandpapering a sculpture, it is such sweet pleasure! I don't care how long I stay doing it. Art for me is everything that is wonderful!

FAYROUZ

SINGER AND ACTRESS

Fayrouz laughs! In spite of an aloof public image, in private, the great chanteuse of the Arab world is an attentive and gracious hostess with a lively sense of humor. Seated on adjacent sofas casually covered by white sheets and a colorful assortment of throw pillows, we chat in a cozy alcove of her comfortable home in Rabiya (a resort area in the mountains of Lebanon overlooking the Mediterranean), surrounded by informal family photographs, mementos from her performances around the world, and a plethora of magazines and books featuring herself and members of her family.

With a grin, I read aloud the unexpected message written in large bold letters on a plaque hanging on the wall: "I hate people who sing in the morning!" and look at Fayrouz inquisitively. She laughs and admits that her day rarely commences before two o'clock in the afternoon.

Fayrouz wears a long, white, flowing abaya and her dark hair falls loosely around her shoulders. She wears no make-up, with the exception of eyeliner dramatically highlighting expressive dark eyes; nor is there any sign of nail polish on her neatly trimmed fingernails. Her jeans-clad daughter, Rima, who has her mother's brown eyes, joins us to act as an interpreter. As it turns out, Fayrouz's comprehension of English is proficient. Fayrouz's handicapped son, Haly, who was the first member of his family to greet me, remains in the outer room where there is more maneuvering space for his wheelchair.

In this family setting on a brilliant, late Sunday afternoon, Fayrouz is very much at ease and there is an air of contentment about her. Throughout the interview we are interrupted only once. It is a telephone call from her eldest son, Ziad, heralded by many as Lebanon's most innovative theater director. Ziad, like his late father, is also a talented composer who is currently reviving some of his mother's old songs.

Born, Nohad Haddad, in 1935, the famous chanteuse was conferred the name "Fayrouz" by poet and composer Halim El-Roumi who compared her voice to the rich, tranquil color of turquoise (fayrouz). Her debut as a singer began, at age five, in the chorus of the Lebanese Radio Station. It was there that she met Assi Rahbani (whom she married in 1955) and his brother, Mansour. Together they formed a musical triumvirate. Fayrouz's velvet voice and the Rahbani brothers' distinctive music, combining strains of East and West, would become an integral part of the musical repertoire of the Arab world. The passion and devotion Fayrouz inspires is well illustrated in an observation made by well-known Syrian writer, Sihan Tergeman, who concludes one of her books with the statement: "I am glad I live in the age of Fayrouz."

Dubbed Lebanon's "Ambassadrice aupres des etoiles," Fayrouz served as a voice for tolerance and a beacon of hope for all Lebanese living at home and abroad, as she continued to sing patriotic songs about Lebanon throughout the long, bleak war years. She has received countless honors and awards, including the Key to Jerusalem; a stamp issued in her name by the Lebanese government; and, in 1995, the French magazine L'Express named her among "the one hundred women who move the world." She is especially revered for refusing to do command performances or sing in praise of any head of state, maintaining that her allegiance is to the people, alone.

The voice that is omnipresent on Lebanese radio is now insisting that I have something to drink. I accept a soft drink and my long awaited interview with Fayrouz begins.

* * *

Do you think music has a healing effect on society?

Yes, of course! When I sing patriotic songs like, for example: "I Love You, Lebanon," I have seen Muslim and Christian militiamen, who days earlier were fighting each other on the streets, standing up in the aisles with tears streaming down their cheeks, hugging each other and singing the words to the song along with me. If people spent more time singing and listening to music, there would be less fighting in this world, I am sure!

When you sing patriotic songs about Lebanon and your audience becomes emotional, what effect does that have on you?

I feel very much with the audience and therefore I try not to get entangled in their emotions. I try not to look directly at the audience but rather above their heads. It is very moving when you and the audience are one. It is hard for me to explain the feeling I get when that happens.

Were you not fearful for your life when you took to the streets, along with other marchers, to protest against the war?

No, not at all. I was much more angry than I was afraid. I wanted to stop the war: the senseless killing and the uncontrolled violence. I wanted Lebanon to be safe for those of us not carrying guns and flouting the law. I wanted Lebanon to return to the way it was before the war. Peace is worth risking one's life for. I don't think you really appreciate peace unless you have lived without it. Those

Fayrouz

who have peace in their country should never take it for granted. They should guard it well.

What was the worst point for you during the war?

There was no one worst point. It was the entire war. I feel that I have become a reincarnation of myself. I am not the same person I was before the war. Watching my country destroy itself, bit by bit; seeing innocent people killed; living without water, electricity and the basic necessities was not easy. We used to live in a beautiful, civilized country often described as "the Switzerland of the Middle East." That is why it has been so terrible to see it crumble before our eyes; why it is so difficult to see it now as it is today.

Did you ever consider leaving Lebanon?

Never! During the war, I traveled, but I always returned to Lebanon whenever I could. There is no place in the world like one's own country. I am proud of my heritage and very proud of my country.

What changes would you like to see occur in Lebanese society?

I would like people to be less concerned with appearances and more concerned with substance and character. There should be no differences among Lebanese. What affects one Lebanese, affects us all. There should be no discrimination. We are all Lebanese. That is what is important.

You are idolized by so many. What are some extraordinary examples of devotion shown to you by your admirers?

There have been many who have given me lavish gifts and flown around the world to see me perform. But, for me, the most extraordinary example of devotion is when I am in a crowd. No matter how emotional or excited the crowd is they always part to make room for me. It is almost magical when it happens. It is as though I have a protective halo around me. No one touches me. I can see and hear the crowd's excitement, but rarely does anyone penetrate that invisible shield around me. That, to me, is always extraordinary!

During your entire career was there any one performance that stands out above all the others?

No. Every time I appear on stage there is a certain excitement in the air. I always give my audience, whether there are 1000 or 10,000, the best performance I am capable of giving that day. They come to hear me and I don't want to disappoint them. Every audience is special. I can feel the electricity generated from their anticipation the moment I step out on the stage. The excitement is something you can almost touch.

What don't you like about your success?

Success is a prison. The more successful you become the tighter become your prison bars. If I go out and I am casually dressed the next day I find myself in the paper with a story about me that I am not well or some other fantastic fabrication. Success also breeds jealousies from unexpected sources: from people you know and from those you've never met. It is a double-edged sword.

Have you tried wearing a disguise when you go out in public?

It doesn't work for me because if people don't recognize me, they still recognize my voice. Then if they recognize me and I am dressed in disguise I've compounded my problem! [laughter]

Your voice has been written about by so many music critics, what are some of your favorite descriptions?

If I tell you I will appear immodest! [laughter] But there have been some very nice descriptions.

Would you describe yourself as shy or timid?

Yes, I will agree, I am timid.

Many have said that you are depressed and unhappy, is that true?

Those who say that don't really know me. They see me on stage and I don't usually laugh there. It is inappropriate to laugh when you are singing love ballads or patriotic songs. I've had my share of unhappiness though: a daughter who died; a son who was born handicapped. My husband's death affected me very much, even though we were separated, we still shared many years together. My country has been at war for seventeen years. There hasn't been much to be happy about. But in spite of all that, I've had much to be thankful for in my life.

Was your life made more difficult or easier having your husband in the same business as yourself?

In some ways it was easier in other ways more difficult. I liked working with my husband professionally because it added another dimension to our relationship. We were not just husband and wife, we were colleagues, as well. It was especially nice when I was performing. He understood the pressure I was under because we were both in it together: I on stage; he off stage. But it was difficult because in sharing our professional and personal lives, we could never entirely get away from the business. We were constantly discussing the score, the music, the performance, et cetera. It was never easy to turn it off entirely.

Who was more of a perfectionist, you or your late husband?

We were both perfectionists. We wouldn't quit until we were both satisfied. We never compromised when it came to music.

If you never compromised and you were both perfectionists, your household must have been quite lively!

[Fayrouz and Rima look at each other and laugh in agreement.]

What sort of things did you compromise on?

Things that husbands and wives need to compromise on in order to stay married. [laughter] When we stopped compromising we separated.

Who would you say is your best music critic?

In general, people who don't know me personally. Those who do know me are more protective about my feelings and therefore tend to be less honest with me. They tell me what they think I want to hear.

How do you protect your voice?

You saw the "No Smoking" cartoon on the front door. It was put there for a purpose. I don't like people to smoke around me. I don't like to go anywhere where there is cigarette smoke or, for that matter, any other kind of smoke!

Did your husband ever wake you up in the middle of the night, or you him, to discuss an idea for a song?

[laughter] We were never in bed in the middle of the night!

How do you go about selecting a song?

There really is no special formula, I either like the song or I don't.

What have you learned that has made a difference in your life?

I have learned that if you want to be heard in this life, it helps to be able to sing! [laughter]

*   *   *

The interview completed, Fayrouz leans back smiling and invites me to join her for a cup of her specially brewed Turkish coffee. We chat about her dislike of cooking, her upcoming concert in England, and the current musical her sister, Hoda, is starring in. As I prepare to leave, she accompanies me to the top of the interior staircase. I reach the first landing, when Fayrouz calls after me to come back. She disappears and returns with a silver bowl cradled in each hand: one filled with chocolates; the other, sugar-coated almonds. Descending once more the flight of red carpeted stairs, I leave with a sugar-coated almond nestled in the palm of my hand, the sweet taste of chocolate melting in my mouth, and the voice of Fayrouz echoing good-bye in the fading distance.

GEORGETTE GEBARA

CHOREOGRAPHER

Founder and director of the Lebanese School of Ballet, Georgette Gebara is a petite, vivacious woman with an engaging smile and a keen sense of humor. The first time I met Gebara was at her book-lined apartment in the Beirut suburb of Hazmiyeh. She was preparing to go on a two-week cruise along the Turkish coast, her first vacation in twenty years.

Born September 3, 1937, Gebara, a talented dance instructor and choreographer, has directed and choreographed countless musicals, plays, and films in Lebanon as well as France, Italy, Syria, Iraq, and Ethiopia. In 1970, she helped found the International Center of Traditional Music and Dance in Tunisia. She is on the board of the Dance Committee of the International Theater Institute of UNESCO and a founding member of the cultural movement "Dar al Fan."

A gifted linguist, she speaks Arabic, English, French, Italian, Greek and Spanish. Gebara studied ballet in Cairo and traveled to Yugoslavia on a dance scholarship provided by the Yugoslav government. She was founder and choreographer of "Les Soirées de Ballet," the first professional dance group in Lebanon, which she financed from earnings from her dance school. For eighteen years, she was a professor of dance at the Lebanese University's National Institute of Fine Arts. Since 1974, she has been a popular member of a panel of judges on a highly-rated television program, "Studio al-Fan," which discovers and encourages new talent in the performing arts.

For the interview, we met at her ballet school, on the top floor of a building in East Beirut. In spite of a broken toe, she had been conducting a ballet class and was looking relaxed and radiant, having just returned from her long overdue vacation.

*   *   *

It is said, when you dance or choreograph, you bring your own special life experiences on to the stage. Recognizing this, how have the last seventeen years of war influenced your work?

The war kept changing its face. It dashed a lot of my dreams and hopes. It dispersed my students. As an individual, I found it very difficult to understand its various aspects. My final sentiment was a total rejection of violence. Dancing for me became a quest for something uplifting, something that would relieve thoughts of the war. I created a ballet, "The Good Lord Loves You," which was inspired by Neil Diamond's song of the same name. It's a plea to the politicians, the soldiers, the militiamen, telling them: God has not abandoned us, it is we who don't know how to find Him. I also did a ballet called, "Night Visit," and choreographed it to Lebanese music. A young man is on watch. He is a fighter. There is no indication what side he belongs to. He wears a typical militia outfit: khaki trousers, black T-shirt, and carries a machine-gun. He is on watch, at night, dancing alone. He hears someone approaching and freezes, his gun pointed toward the sound. A pretty girl steps out of the shadows wearing a soft, diaphanous dress, made of chiffon, and a long floating scarf. She throws her scarf on the gun, which is still pointed at her, and catches it as it falls. Softly, she places the gun on the ground. A relationship develops between them. The idea — a very simple one — is that tenderness and love can overpower hate and violence.

Another dance I created was called *Al Intizar* (The Wait). I did it as a homage to Lebanese women who have endured so much during this war. It is a tribute to women who are condemned to spend their lives waiting for a man to propose, a child to be born; waiting for a child, a husband, a brother to come home. A woman's lot is essentially a commitment to waiting for something or someone else. Rare is the woman who is free to take her own destiny in her hand. I have been very lucky to have been able to do that. Many women can't because they live in a family context that forbids or makes it very difficult for them to do what they want to do.

During the beginning of the war, in 1975, there were Kuwaites who lived in a furnished flat nearby. In those days we referred to the fighting as "the event" because we didn't know that it was an actual war. For us, it was outbursts of violence, and loss of electricity. Today, we take everything in stride, but then it was a terrifying experience because we didn't know what was happening. I remember, in this terrible darkness, while the sounds of bullets and bombs were coming from every direction, the Kuwaites next door would invite gypsy dancing girls over and they would dance until three or four o'clock in the morning to the accompaniment of a very lively rhythm played on the *derbeke* [a drum]. Imagine how nerve-wracking such a sound can be when you are cowering in a corner of your apartment in an absolute state of terror!

This sound became a source of revulsion and terror for me. I hated the lack of respect these people had for us and our country. I used this same music in "The Wait" to accompany a woman dressed in black on the stage. As she dances, she rids herself of a succession of veils but in the end she is still not completely free of them. The powerful rhythm of the music is what carries the idea through. The woman thinks about the confined state of her life. She thinks of revolting, and then she cowers back because she fears what society will do to her if she does. She takes one of the veils, wraps it around her, and the dance ends with her in the light swaying like a person who is wondering what to do next.

You have choreographed so many works, do you have a favorite among them?

There is a piece that I danced for the first time in America. It's called *Al-Tareeq* (The Way). It is only about five minutes long. It is a dance — actually a study — based on the prayer movements of Christianity, Islam and Judaism. It took me two years to work out the movements and to find the right music. Finally, I chose a piece of very pure music performed on the *bouzok* [a very

Georgette Gebara

simple string instrument with only two double chords, played by desert Bedouins.] It is very difficult music to perform to, because even though it is recorded, it is improvisation and there are no regular rhythms. But that specific music helped convey exactly what I wanted: the feeling that we all pray towards something. The Muslims pray toward Mecca, the Christians toward the alter, and the Jewish people have their own symbols. The symbols in the last intention represent God, and the idea is to reach God. The challenge of this piece of choreography was for the dancer to move in a single diagonal created by a ray of light. I refused to use any other kind of prop. As the dancer moves towards this light her movements reflect the various religions. For example, a very stylized movement for the Christian sign of the cross, then the dancer moves into a series of Muslim movements: kneeling down to pray, reading the Koran, the call to prayers, the special way Muslims have of counting the sublime names of God on their fingers and rosaries.

As a child, I had a Muslim nanny who used to pray five times a day. My sister, who was then a little toddler, thought she was playing when she bent down to pray and she would climb on her back. She didn't know the nanny was doing something very serious. My mother would become very upset with my sister and tell her: "No! No! Get off her back!" The nanny would make a silent sign indicating that it was all right. Then after she would finish praying, she would tell my mother: "Don't be upset with the child, when she comes to me and I am praying, she is like an angel sent from God." I grew up close to many religions. I had Jewish neighbors whom I used to see perform certain movements when they came out of their house. They would kiss their finger tips and then touch the Masouja, a holy inscription, which hung at their door. These religious rituals were part of my childhood. So this dance was a very profound form of expression for me.

I was invited to give a lecture in Wichita, Kansas, for the American Dance Symposium. I told the audience, "I come from a part of the world where the three great religions were born and instead of talking to you about peace, I am going to dance for you a dance of peace," and I performed "The Way." The dance ends with a ray of light. I reach up towards the light. I think I have made contact with God, I bring my arms down, open my hands, and they are empty. But I look up again because I still have hope. Then the lights go off.

Walter Terry, one of the great dance historians in America, was in the audience as were many other important dance teachers who were taking part in the symposium. I stood there for a few seconds and there wasn't a sound from the audience. I was preparing to fly off the stage in distress, when suddenly there was a burst of applause. I couldn't believe it! The president of the symposium rushed up and hugged me and said, "You gave us something very special." The next day at breakfast Walter Terry came over to me and said "Georgette, thank you for yesterday. I was in the Middle East as a young soldier and you brought back many memories. What do you call the piece?" I told him I was still searching for a title because I wanted a title that would communicate the fact that we all pray toward one direction — toward God. He thought about it and said, "Why don't you call it 'The Way' in Arabic?" And that is how the piece was named.

What does dance do for you?

It is my life to begin with. I had a creative streak from an early age and dance was my expressive outlet. I am a very dramatic dancer. When I dance I am very expressive. The most important day of my life as a child was the day I went to dancing school. I was not as young as I should have been. I was eleven. I will never forget that day. Dance also complements another aspect of my life which is very important to me and that is music.

As a choreographer, does it help being a dancer?

Absolutely! You feel the lack of dance in a piece if the choreographer does not know how to dance. As a dancer, your body acts as a melting pot for many different techniques and styles. When you choreograph, it's helpful to watch yourself in a mirror and see the movements come out. If you have not had the feel of what it is to dance on stage, your ideas and the movements you try to communicate are transmitted in a way that is more cerebral than emotional. Dance should combine both, but especially feeling.

What do you look for in a dancer?

Stamina and talent. The capacity of never being tired is very important to me. I work the heck out of my dancers. I've had quite a few dancers quit on me, which woke me up to the realization that not all people have my energy. I like dancers who learn quickly, who bring a part of themselves to the role, and who feel what I am telling them and can express themselves. I don't want photocopies of myself. When I choreograph, it's a two-way process. An expressive dancer can help enrich the choreography. Of course, I like dancers who are motivated and enthusiastic and who have a sense of rhythm. I hate people who have blank eyes. It drives me crazy.

How did you become a choreographer?

My connection with dance was a very profound one from the beginning. I felt there was something in me that had to come out and it could only come out through dance. Dance allowed me to dream. I used to read and listen to a lot of classical music as a child. In school, I remember, I was constantly reprimanded for being "up in the clouds." There was this creative streak in me. I wanted to create and to express things. So when I became involved with dance, I was deeply committed from the very beginning. The average dance student attends class twice a week, but I used to go almost every day and take several classes. I advanced very quickly as a result.

Do you still dance?

On my fiftieth birthday I offered myself the luxury of performing one last time. I decided this is it. It's hard to decide when that last time should be. It's a terrible decision to make, but you have to make it. One should exit with grace. The body changes after a certain age. It becomes heavier, the bones set, and you realize anything you can do well, someone younger can do better. I think every age has its time. If you don't have the lucidity to accept it, you haven't learned much in your life.

For my last performance, I created a ballet which I called, "The Last Rehearsal," where a teacher/choreographer is conducting a last rehearsal before performance day. As she works with her dancers, she experiences a flashback. She finds herself dancing her leading dancer's role. At one point, she picks up a pair of toe shoes by the ribbon and dances with them. Then she looks at them, puts them down at the bottom of the stage, and moves away. As the teacher fades into the background, the young leading dancer appears and performs almost the same movements as her teacher. It becomes obvious that the teacher has handed over her role to the next generation. It was a very simple statement and those who knew me well understood. I was very moved after the performance when people started coming up to me with tears in their eyes to ask: "Are you really going to retire from dance?"

What is it like to watch a piece you've choreographed performed on opening night?

Terrifying! I stand somewhere in the wing and whenever I know a difficult part is coming up, I hide my face against the shoulder of the person closest to me. It is agony! You never feel the dancers have rehearsed enough or the choreography is perfect. Never! You always feel that something could be expanded, or cut, or tamed. It's agony, but an exhilarating kind of agony, to see something which was an idea — which began with the feeling you have when you must write an important letter and you think, "Oh my God, what should I say?" — materialize into a full-fledged performance. It makes you think: "I did that? Not bad!" [laughter]

What distinguishes a piece choreographed by Georgette Gebara?

I am Lebanese, therefore when I choreograph, the Orient comes out instinctively in my work. I live in an Oriental environment. I am an Oriental woman. I think certain movements come out that reveal this side of me without my even being aware of it. Also, our bodies are different. The Occidental body is much leaner than ours because our way of life, our climate, our food, our environment are different from that of Europe or America. I always have themes in my ballets: an idea which has to come across, an argument, a problem solved, a story told. I don't like dance just for the sake of dance.

Which dancers inspired you when you were growing up?

When I began dancing as a child, I lived in Cairo, Egypt, and every season the Marquis de Cuevas Company from Monte Carlo would come. When I watched them dance, they would make me dream. They released a certain joy in me. Marjorie Tallchief was one of those dancers. I saw myself in her and I hoped to dance the type of roles she danced. I identified with her lyrical style of movement because even at that young age I knew I was not a technique dancer like many of the Russian dancers.

Tell me about your background.

My father was a great lover of classical music and he owned a broadcasting station. My mother began as a journalist and then went on to create a very popular radio program for children, which was the first of its kind in the Middle East. I have a younger sister who works in statistical and marketing research. In 1960, I received a dance scholarship from the Yugoslav government. In Yugoslavia, I had a wonderful dance instructor who invited me to join her in America. But my father died and I had to change my plans. My sister was still a student and I needed to help support my family. I taught ballet at a cultural center in Beirut and my classes became very popular. I was occasionally invited to perform for television. Once a year, we would put on a school performance, which I would choreograph. Unfortunately, the head of the center wanted to increase the center's profits by enrolling more students in my class regardless of their talent, so I quit.

And opened your own dance school?

No, that was quite by accident. I had reached a point where I had to make a decision. I couldn't go on indefinitely being a dance student, a dance instructor, and working at the United Nations during the morning to supplement my income. My former students and their families kept hounding me to open a school. I had studied ballet for twelve years, taken classes in the United States with the Joffrey Company and the Martha Graham School, and worked with countless dance teachers. I studied modern dance; tap dance; jazz; and Russian, Spanish, Egyptian and Lebanese folklore. So I thought, why not? I can do it! I never thought I would enjoy teaching but I discovered it opened up for me a whole new world. When you teach, you learn so much! Most of all, you learn to articulate what you are thinking. I opened the school with the aim of creating a ballet company so I could choreograph and perform. I was able to do that for several years and then the war broke out in 1975.

How did you manage to persevere during the war?

For me, the past seventeen years have been a kind of hell because of the population movement. I had so many talented students whom I invested so much hope and work in, who had to move to safer areas. Also, I experienced the terrible grief of having students die in the fighting. So the perpetual challenge was, and still is, to continue to create and choreograph. It takes eight years to form a dancer. I feel I am always having to begin again and train new dancers. There is also the problem of not having enough male dancers, which is a problem experienced by all major companies but even more acutely here.

Did you ever consider leaving Lebanon?

Never! Although I was offered a teaching position at a university in the United States. I could have lived very easily in America because America has so much to offer in my field. What is more, I am very adaptable, but I did not want to abandon my country. Sometimes, during the worst of the fighting, I used to ask myself: "Did I do the right thing? What have I accomplished here?" Those are difficult questions to face when so many years of your life have practically gone to waste — not complete waste — but as a dancer, I should have danced more. I didn't dance enough.

Having lived and studied ballet in Yugoslavia, how do you feel about the war in progress there?

I am torn apart for Yugoslavia because the things happening there are so similar to what we've gone through. The Yugoslavs I know are good people. They are warm, friendly, loving, and caring. I have never seen people sing so much as in Yugoslavia. I once took an eighteen hour train ride and there was singing from one end of the train to the other, the entire trip. I feel as hurt for what is happening there as I am for my own country.

Was there any one incident during the war in Lebanon that really affected you?

There were many. Two sisters were killed by the same bomb. Both had been my students since the day they were old enough to take ballet lessons. They were like my children. Their mother is a very dear friend of mine. We were both ballet students together. I had so many friends who were killed violently. There were certain atrocities I witnessed that happened to people I didn't know, but which affected me greatly. I developed a very severe stomach problem. It started one night when I had to identify a close friend lying dead on a mortuary slab. Her father is one of our great writers. Buildings, you can build again; objects, you can replace, but precious lives.... Lebanon used to be a cultural and intellectual showcase for the entire Middle East. The war destroyed that and left scars that will never heal. There are certain things that stay with me: a bus burning with children screaming inside. If I think about it, I go crazy.

Has it been an uphill battle pursuing dance as a career?

One of the things that has been very hard for me to accept as a serious artist is that dance, in this part of the world, is still often considered a light and frivolous profession. Also, being a woman does not help because Lebanon is still going through a macho phase where men and their activities are considered "what really matter." As a woman, you have to steel yourself against this attitude. You have to be strong and, sometimes, even tough. In the beginning, for example, renting a theater for my performances was like undertaking Ulysses' voyage!

I find that I have to constantly make men understand that when I ask for something, I want it because I know what I want; not because of some feminine whim. When I hear, "Oh, you women are always whining, always grumbling." I accept it once, twice, and then that's it. At a certain point, enough becomes enough. I've reached the point where I tell men: "If you want to work for me, you have to get rid of your complexes. Forget I am Georgette. Think of me as George."

When I decided to build my school on this roof, I reviewed the area with the owner of the building and an architect. At the end of our meeting the architect looked at me and said: "You really feel this is what you want to do? Are you sure you can pay for it?" I told him, "I am mortgaging my house to pay for this school. I am not wasting your time. It's not a joke." But it took him several meetings to understand that I mean what I say. This attitude is very frustrating when you are under pressure and you need quick action. People still have old-fashioned, cliched views about women that is programmed into them from childhood.

I was talking to a friend the other day, and she was telling me how her daughter can afford to be lazy and not study because, according to the girl's father, he's not worried about her future. Why? Because she will get married one day. But his son, on the other hand, is expected to work and study from morning till night and make a success of himself. It is this condescending attitude; this false sense of security that we are up against as women.

Do you have any regrets that you didn't marry and have children?

I would have loved to have children. For the past seventeen years I have had a wonderful relationship with a man, but we never got married and I don't know if we ever will. My friends tell me that's why our relationship is so good! [laughter] We both understand each other. What attracts me tremendously to him is that he understands me; he encourages me.

When I began building this school, I was terrified because bombs were falling all over the place, people were running away, houses were being destroyed and here I was mortgaging my home to build a dance school next door to the Christian militia headquarters, an area that was perpetually being bombarded. Sometimes, I would almost breakdown and wonder what am I doing? He would say: "Don't worry. You are doing the right thing. If you don't do it now maybe when the war ends you won't have the will or the stamina to build a school." I would say, "But this is sheer madness," to which he would respond, "Okay, you have to be mad, then." Not all men are capable of this kind of support.

He has a calming effect on me, even when I have stage fright! It is a disease for which if I live to be one hundred, I won't find a cure. It's terrible! But the secret is once you begin, stage fright is like a horrible piece of clothing that you shed. It takes a few moments and during those moments you think: Why am I on stage? What am I doing this for? Why did I think of doing it in the first place?

I should be hiding in the farthest corner. But once you start and you've created a bang, you can relax. But to reach that bang, my goodness, it is horrible! Your feet are cold and your hands are hot; then your hands are cold and your feet are hot and you begin to perspire in all the wrong places! (laughter)

I am a member of a panel of judges on a television program called "Studio al-Fan," which is like "Star Search" in the States. Each week we judge contestants in a range of categories including: singing, dancing, poetry, and music. I have been part of this jury since 1974 and every time I pick up a microphone and give a critique, I feel my hands trembling and my heart pounding away. It always takes me a few moments to calm down!

Why do you expose yourself to such stress?

It's part of my work, and as a pioneer in my field it's exciting to feel that I can help young people along in their careers. This year is the thirtieth anniversary of my career. My assistant came to me this morning and said, "Do you know the class I am about to teach is made up largely of the children of your former students!"

What do you think accounts for your enduring popularity?

A good friend of mine, a journalist, once told me, "You know, Georgette, there is one thing which will always amaze me about you. Even though you are well-known, you are always wide-eyed when somebody talks or writes about you." It's true! I often forget that I am known. When I am driving and someone cuts in front of me or honks without a reason, I become furious. I roll down my window and holler at them. Their reaction always disconcerts me. They smile and say, "Oh, it's Georgette Gebara! How are you?" I then have to undergo a complete shift in attitude.

When you travel, what is the reaction of people when they learn you are Lebanese?

Before the war, when I traveled abroad, people would say, "Ah, you come from Israel." I would say, "No, Beirut is not in Israel, it is in Lebanon which is an Arab country." During the war, we became known as the ultimate role models for terrorists. We were all considered terrorists until proven otherwise.

How do you feel about your country, today?

I've lived in Lebanon through the shelling, the bombing, the Israeli invasion, the terror, and the embargo. I've lived without water, food, sleep, electricity and I can tell you, without any reservation, I am proud to be Lebanese. Every time I land at Beirut International Airport, I have tears in my eyes because I am so happy to be back home. I love my country. One of the happiest moments for me was when Flag Day was made official. I put the Lebanese flag up in my school and assembled the children and told them: "This is your flag!"

VÉNUS KHOURY-GHATA

POET AND NOVELIST

"Writing is my source of oxygen," says writer Vénus Khoury-Ghata,
author of ten books of poetry and ten novels, one of which, Bayarmine, has
been translated into seven languages. Although, she currently lives in France,
and writes in French, her subject and source of inspiration has always been
her native Lebanon. In addition to being a full-time novelist and poet,
Khoury-Ghata is editor of the literary magazine, Europe, and hosts a daily
radio program, "Un Livre des Voies" (A Book of Voices), on contemporary
writers and their work.

A widely acclaimed poet, she has received France's most coveted poetry
awards, including the prestigious Apollinaire Prize, Mallarmé Prize, and the
Grand Prize of Poetry from the Société des Gens de Lettres. In France, Khoury-
Ghata is a member of twelve literary juries and, in many instances, she is the
only woman on the jury. In 1993, she received a series of honors: she was
elected an academician in the Quebec Academy; Jacques Toubon, French
Minister of Culture, nominated her to be a Chevalier des Arts and Lettres;
and the Museum of Modern Art in Paris commissioned the great Chilean
artist, Matta, to illustrate her poetry.

I met Khoury-Ghata, a tall, willowy woman with high cheek bones and
expressive dark eyes, at her sister's house on a late Sunday afternoon in
November. She was in Lebanon on a ten-day, whirlwind visit, chock full of
book signings, television appearances, poetry recitals, receptions, and dinner
parties, to celebrate the publication of an anthology of her entire work of
poetry. Attired in what she described as "Stendhal colors" (red cape and black
knit dress), and speaking in a strong, melodious voice with dramatic
inflections, Khoury-Ghata chatted with me in her sister's garden, under the
shade of a grape trellis.

* * *

How do you feel about having your anthology published?
Anthologies are usually published after a poet is dead. So I feel twice blessed:
It is published and I am alive! [laughter]

Who is Vénus Khoury-Ghata?
I am Lebanese. I was born in Lebanon. I left Lebanon at the age of thirty
to marry a French doctor, a brilliant researcher by the name of Jean Ghata. The
first few years away from my fatherland were very difficult. I missed Lebanon:
the sunshine and the warmth of the people. I was very unhappy. But when the
war broke out in Lebanon I learned to appreciate France. My husband was
very absorbed in the artistic milieu in Paris. He was the doctor of the Maeght

Vénus Khoury-Ghata

Foundation, which supports the arts. Consequently our house was always filled with an extraordinary group of people: Miro, the painter; scientists, Nobel prize winners, poets, and writers. Those were wonderful years. I used to say, "Happiness is having all my children under the same roof and a house full of brilliant and creative people."

How many children do you have?

I had three children in three years from my first marriage. I divorced my first husband after thirteen years of marriage and married Jean Ghata. My ex-husband did not want to give me the children but, when the war broke out in Lebanon, he consented to send them to live with me in France. I had a daughter with Jean Ghata and the house was filled with the laughter of children, and the discourse of scientists and artists. This was true happiness. Nine years later, my husband died of a heart attack at age fifty-two. My happiness turned into a terrible depression. I lived a nightmare. During that same period my ex-husband demanded my three older children be sent back to him. I suddenly found myself a widow, alone, with a baby in a house that was much too big. It was a cold winter; the temperature fell below freezing in Paris. The house was glacial. Even the dog abandoned us to find a warmer place. I wanted to die but I had a daughter to care for.

Why didn't you return to Lebanon?

I did not return because my career was the only thing I had left. To continue publishing, I needed to be near my editors. I had published six books during the nine years I had lived in Paris. I had established a name there. My happiness has always been connected to the happiness of my children and the quality of my work. The day I write half-a-dozen pages, or a poem or two, is a day I am happy. When a day goes by and I don't write anything, I feel that there is a disequilibrium in me. Once, a woman asked me, "What are the names of your children?" Without thinking, I gave her the titles of my books!

How did you raise a family and write at the same time?

I never sacrificed my children for my writing. The first few years in Paris, I had four children [two boys and two girls] at home. After the children went to school, I would vacuum, clean the house, put everything in order, and then settle behind my typewriter. An hour before they returned, I would put away my work and start cooking. At the end of the evening, after the children did their homework, they would watch television, and I would slip away to write in bed. I did not allow myself television or films. For many years, I only slept four or five hours a night. When I felt tempted to join my family and watch a film, I would remind myself that I was lucky to be in Paris and that I should make the most of it.

I wanted to do something with my life. When my first novel received good reviews, I followed it with another novel, then a collection of poems, then a novel, then a collection of poems. I never stopped writing. It was exhausting. I wanted to be, like my mother, a great housekeeper, but she had nothing else to do but to keep her house clean! I wanted to be the ideal mother, a successful writer, and a femme fatale at dinner parties. [laughter] I wanted to succeed in everything!

Do you remember the first time you were published?

Ah, yes! I remember very well. I was twenty years old at the time. I gave my manuscript to a French writer, who was going to Paris. A month later, she wrote me and said she had shared my poems with Pierre Segasse, one of the greatest poetry editors in France, and that he had offered to publish my next collection of poetry. I was so thrilled! I locked myself in my room that summer and in three months I produced a book of poems, which won the "Gens de Lettres Society Prize." It was my greatest joy.

When you are writing a novel, are you in a similar frame of mind as when you are writing a poem?

No! When I write poetry the language is very strict and rigorous. Afterwards, I need a change. I need to write something ample and large, where I encounter and create many personalities. So I plunge into writing a novel. It's like working in a factory. I sit behind my typewriter at eight o'clock in the morning and I finish at six in the evening. My friends come to visit me and they say, "It's unbelievable how changeable you are! Sometimes, we arrive in Paris and you tell us come and share a meal and you regale us with your stories. Other times, you barely have time to talk to us on the telephone!" It is true. I am a totally different person when I am writing poetry as opposed to when I am writing a novel. When I write a novel I become reclusive. I forget the whole world. But when I write poetry — I write my poems at one o'clock in the morning and I rewrite them in the afternoon — I am just the opposite. I love to see people and to have long chats on the telephone. Poets are generally urbane and civilized people. They have the time to live a social life, while novelists don't. A novelist has to become totally immersed in his characters' lives. When I write a tragic chapter, my face becomes somber and everyone who sees me asks: "Are you okay?" I cry and I laugh all by myself. I become my characters. When they are happy, I am happy. I even laugh at their jokes!

In my novel, *The Dead House*— this book was my psychotherapist after my husband's death — I wrote about a woman who lost her husband and has this great need to be near him again. To do so, she goes back into his past, into his childhood — a time she did not know him. She goes to the town, where he lived as a child, and meets his friends and his old teachers. Walking on the street, she thinks she sees his back among the people. Sometimes she thinks, "That's him driving!" She always has this expectant feeling that she is going to encounter him around the next corner. I was in the midst of writing this chapter when I had to get into my car to run an errand. Along the way, I saw a man driving who resembled my husband. I followed him, even driving after him through red lights and stop signs. I was finally parallel with him, when he turned and looked at me.... He wasn't my husband! At that moment, it was as though I had lost him all over again.

What makes your style of writing uniquely yours?

According to the critics, what differentiates my writing from others, is that I transform tragedy into a peculiar sort of comedy. Also, Lebanon almost always appears in my books. It's a tragic country, but at the same time things happen here that are incredibly humorous.

Do most of your novels draw from real life?

It has been my experience that writing and life blend so much that, sometimes, I don't know where one begins and the other ends. My novels draw from reality: the war in Lebanon, the death of my husband. A Lebanese friend of mine came to visit me in Paris and I told her, "It's marvelous, Jeannette, that we finally have peace in Lebanon." Her response stunned me, she said: "I detest peace! Peace for me is boredom. During the war all of us in the apartment building were like one big family. We would gather together in the shelter and share our troubles and our happiness. We had a life together! We ate together, we laughed together, and we were afraid together. Now, everyone stays alone in their own apartment and I am bored to death. I prefer war." Based on this conversation, I wrote a novel about a building located on the border of a divided city, and I describe how everyone is bored in this building. They feel that peace is death. They are nostalgic for the good old days when there was a war in progress. They imagined that history had created this war to entertain and distract them! I dedicated the book to Jeannette.

Do you write only in French?

Yes, and my writings are translated into many languages. My first poems were written in French and published in France so I was committed to writing in French. But for a very long time, Arabic and French swirled in my head. My rough drafts were written almost always in the two languages. I would write in French but there were certain words that I found more attractive in Arabic. My rough drafts were written right to left in Arabic and left to right in French and the two languages would merge in the middle. But after ten years of living in France, my use of Arabic became more and more infrequent. Then one day there was no longer any Arabic words in my writing. That was the day I went into mourning for my maternal language.

What language do you dream in?

I dream in both French and Arabic. But when I am surprised or cry out-loud in anger, fear or love, it is always in Arabic. The cry from my heart is in Arabic; the rest is in French.

Having spent so many years in France, how do you identify with your Lebanese heritage?

I consider myself an Arab writer, who happens to write in French. The form and feeling behind my words is Arab; French is the instrument I use for writing. But everything I write about is always related to Lebanon and what is happening in Lebanon. I never write about France. It doesn't interest me. For me, Lebanon is my home and France is my office.

What is the source of your attachment to Lebanon?

My mother's village, Bécharre. You can't imagine what poetry it evokes in my soul. It is a very special village with a river running through the valley. When we were children, they used to tell us the sounds coming from the river were the voices of fairies laughing! Khalil Gibran is buried there, up in a rocky crag. There are a lot of churches and parish priests, and probably more goats wandering about than people! It has always evoked for me an Edgar Allan Poe kind of feeling. This village made me a poet. For me, Lebanon is Bécharre.

Who are the poets and writers who have influenced you?

In France, Charles Baudelaire. In Lebanon, I like the old poets that I studied in school and who taught me the meaning of poetry: the Abbasside poets and the Ommiad poets from the time of Gaheliya — three hundred years before Christ — such as El Moutanabi and Ibn El Roummy. I like the poets of our time like Adonise and Ounssi El Hajj, a great Lebanese poet, who was the first to write astonishing, modern poetry.

What made you turn to poetry?

There are certain things one cannot say in a novel to express the thunderstorms within the soul. Certain emotions find release only through poetry. The other day, I was telling my sister, May, that writing a novel is like climbing a mountain, you place one foot in front of the other. It is a conscious effort that is thought through. Writing poetry, on the other hand, is like skiing down a mountain slope; there is no time to think. Thinking stops the process. It arrests the magic.

Are you superstitious?

Very! I check my coffee cup ten times a day! [laughter] I reverse my cup and I have a friend, who is an extremely lucid clairvoyant, read it for me. She often visits me and together we imagine ourselves in different circumstances. She tells me I was a great dramatic actress, in another life, and I acted in plays written by Sophocles! [laughter]

When you were young, what did you want to be?

I was what you might call an exalted child. I was the eldest of three daughters and I had an older brother whom I adored. He was a poet. I was nine years old and he would read his poems to me. They were wonderful poems and they moved me deeply. Sometimes they made me cry and I didn't understand why. Then my brother suffered from mental illness and he was placed in a sanitarium. It was at that time that I started writing seriously because he could no longer write. I was sixteen and I felt he was dictating his poems through my hand.

Do you remember the first serious poem you ever wrote?

Yes, it was a love poem! I was sixteen years old and I wrote about a nocturnal embrace. For that poem, I earned two slaps across the face from my father! It was many years later before I dared write such poetry again. I kept a diary from age twelve to seventeen, a very romantic diary! It instilled in me the habit of writing. Then I had the good fortune to study literature. I started out as a poet. I wrote three collections of poetry before writing my first novel. One day, in Paris, my editor said, "Why don't you write a novel?" I said, "I have never written a novel." She said, "I am asking poets to write novels and now is a good time for you to start."

"Vénus Khoury Ghata" sounds very much like a nom de plume. Who named you "Vénus"?

The source is my mother's megalomania! She wanted to give me a very powerful name from Greek mythology. In her search, she discovered Venus was the goddess of beauty and love. In time, when I am a little less youthful, I shall have to put a bullet through my head. It is not possible to live past a certain age with such a name!

What other names run in your family?

My brother is Victor; then there was Victorine — she died young — and myself, Vénus. Later, my parents tired of the letter "V" and named my two younger sisters May and Leila.

How would you describe your poetry to someone who is unfamiliar with your style?

It is surrealistic poetry. I write fables. For me, poetry must tell a story and have a conclusion like the fables of La Fontaine. I have written a lot for children. My writings are often assigned material in schools.

What was the worst time for you during the war?

It was the death of my husband. The worst thing that can happen is for death to enter your house and take someone away forever. You feel violated. The vacuum that death creates never goes away. It is always there. Often, after my husband's death, I found myself dialing his telephone number at the hospital where he worked. Then, I would remember he was dead.

What have you learned that has made a difference in your life?

I have discovered that the only thing in life that is insurmountable is death. When I have problems I tell myself: Laugh! It's not important because it is not death.

PAPOU LAHOUD

FASHION AND COSTUME DESIGNER

As I wait for Papou Lahoud at her atelier in Ashrafieh, her assistant hands me a stack of photo albums featuring Lahoud designs. I am barely halfway through the first album when a neat, stylish woman, steps briskly into the room, wearing crisp, white slacks with a navy blue and white striped blouse (her own design), sparse make-up, and shoulder-length brown hair, swept back and held in place by a velvet blue headband.

There is no mistaking Papou Lahoud. She exudes flair combined with cool efficiency. Lahoud studied fashion design in Paris and Milano. At age fourteen, she designed costumes for the International Festival of Baalbek. She has designed costumes for over forty plays, ballets and operettas as well as a dozen major international festivals, including performances for the Shah of Iran's coronation, and King Hussein of Jordan's fortieth birthday and silver jubilee. Aside from costumes, wedding dresses and evening gowns, Lahoud has designed uniforms in Lebanon for traffic police, Lebanese Republican Guards, hotels, and Middle East Airlines (MEA). Outside of Lebanon, she has designed uniforms for the national airlines of Sudan, Iraq, Sierra Leone, Jordan and Brunei.

Without wasting a moment, Lahoud provides me with a copy of her résumé, and settles behind a simple wooden desk that has been quietly vacated by her assistant.

*　　*　　*

Did you always want to be a fashion designer?

When I began there was no such profession in Lebanon or in the entire Middle East. I always liked to draw. When I was young, I attended a very strict Catholic school and I loved to draw pictures of the students and teachers. It helped me concentrate. One day, I was angry at one of the nuns so I drew her wearing only a wimple and a bikini. Unfortunately, she discovered the drawing and didn't have much of a sense of humor. I was expelled for three days! But I had a very supportive mother. Instead of taking the side of the nuns, she accused them of curbing my creativity and told them that they had no reason to complain since I was always first in my class. [laughter]

My father was a Member of Parliament representing Byblos. He was also a writer and a journalist. He had many friends in the publishing world. When I was fourteen, one of my father's friends was visiting and he saw me designing a dress for myself. In those days, it was the custom in Lebanon to hire a dressmaker to come to the house to make clothes for the family. I was explaining my design to the dressmaker when he said, "I am going to give you four pages in my magazine, *Hasna'a*, to design dresses and give women fashion tips." I was so proud he had such confidence in me! I accepted the offer and shortly thereafter my brother Romeo, a musical theater director, received a contract to do a folkloric show using traditional costumes for the International Festival of Baalbek. Romeo asked me to design the costumes. In the past, it was done on a very informal basis: the president's wife invited a group of women, who liked to sew, to the presidential palace to do the costumes. A professional costume designer was unheard of until I came along on Romeo's coattails. He had studied cinematography in Milano and Paris and was full of Occidental ideas. It was his first production and he began at the very top — the Baalbek Festival.

One of his ideas was to use a fashion designer to design costumes, but he settled on me, a fourteen-year-old girl still in high school. I had no idea where Baalbek was, what was folklore — nothing! But I liked to design. He took me by the hand and showed me Baalbek and Beit Eddine, where there was a small costume museum so I would have a better idea about our traditional clothes. He showed me lithographs done by David Roberts and other Orientalists. He had me watch his troop practice and told me what he did not want. He did not want the costumes to be ordinary. He wanted them to be rich and ornate reflecting our patrimony. Before Romeo, the ears were more important to please for an Arab audience than the eyes. Don't get me wrong, we had some great dressmakers in Lebanon but not fashion designers because they were not designing but rather copying the dresses made by the coutures in Paris. There were many articles written in newspapers about how I had introduced fresh ideas regarding traditional Lebanese costumes, such as: reintroducing the *tantour* [a long conical shaped headdress], the *tarboosh* [a tasseled red cap] and embroidery on velvet. I wanted to show the world that Lebanese women are not just "femme de menages," but that we have a rich and glamorous tradition.

At the time, I didn't consider myself a fashion designer because even though Romeo was producing huge spectacles, I was working for my brother and so I didn't take myself too seriously. I finished my studies: a baccalaureate in French and philosophy. The latter, I took in both French and Arabic. After that, I told my family: "Now, I want to do what I want to do. I am through with books! I want to be a painter." I studied under a well known painter and one day he told me I was more of an interior designer than a painter. I couldn't accept that. I did a show of all the paintings I did that year and sold everything except for one painting which I kept for myself at my father's insistence. It turned out to be my one and only art exhibition. I then went to Paris and studied architecture and interior design for five years. But even as I was studying in Paris, Romeo continued to send me scenarios regarding the popular year-round musicals he was staging at the Phoenicia Theater, and I would sketch costumes for him during my free time. I was studying interior design during the day, which I considered to be my real profession and, at night, I would take courses in fashion design for fun.

When I returned to Lebanon from Paris, I opened an interior and architectural design office. But I couldn't stop theater directors from asking me to design costumes for them. I had established a reputation, because even though I had been in Paris, the newspapers would always write about the costumes I designed for Romeo's musicals. So when I returned to Lebanon I was known for designing costumes. I was asked to design costumes for play after play. After a few years, I had to choose between interior design and costume design. I chose what in my heart came naturally to me. From there, I went into fashion design because women would see my costumes on stage worn by famous actresses and singers, like Sabah and Fayrouz, and they would ask me to create dresses for

Papou Lahoud

them. I began with wedding dresses because, like theater costumes, they embody fantasy and require imagination. Then I progressed into evening dresses. Now, my business consists of three divisions: costumes for the theater, haute couture made up of evening and wedding dresses, and uniforms for men and women.

What distinguishes a Papou Lahoud design?

In the beginning, my designs had an oriental motif and then when it was practical, I went into a more modern look. I like simplicity. It makes a dress more chic. I don't like too many ideas in one dress. I enjoy working with clients and that is why I do more *haute couture* than *pret-a-porter*.

Where does your inspiration come from?

Sometimes, I relax by dreaming. I like to dream. Sometimes, I stay lost for one, two, three weeks. Nothing comes into my head. I panic. I become depressed because people are waiting for my designs and nothing is happening. I talk to my sister, Nay, who is my right hand and best advisor. She helps me stay calm when I am under pressure. Then suddenly, from nowhere, an idea comes and I start working, enlarging upon it, changing, improvising. I think about the project constantly. For me, it is worse than an actor about to go on stage. I suffer at the beginning of every major project. Every time I sign a new contract I feel that I have placed myself in front of a firing squad. I must create something new, something completely different from everything I've done before. I feel I have to surprise myself, surprise others and do it, of course, in good taste because it is very easy to surprise with bad taste!

It must be very gratifying to board an MEA flight and see your uniforms worn by hostesses and pilots.

It's wonderful! Although sometimes, without thinking, I catch myself straightening scarves and then I get these curious looks! [laughter] I replaced the bright yellow and orange uniforms, which MEA personnel had been wearing for the past twenty-five years with more serious colors, taking into account the years of war we have lived through. I chose navy blue for the uniforms and bright red, white and green stripes [the colors of the Lebanese flag] for the shirts and blouses to remind passengers that Lebanon is a sunny, colorful country. It was a very patriotic design.

What is challenging about being a fashion designer in Lebanon?

The challenge is having my clients overcome the complex they have towards the Occident. While many Lebanese designers sew "Made in Italy" or "Made in France" labels on their clothes, I have always been proud to put "Made in Lebanon." I struggled to continue working during the fighting and for many years I was alone in the fashion business. Now, I am proud to say fashion is a booming industry in Lebanon.

Have you ever felt that you were discriminated against in your profession because you are a woman?

Not at all. When I competed for the contract to do the uniforms for Royal Jordanian Airlines which was then known as ALIA, I competed against well known French and Italian male-designers. I was just beginning my career and it was not the Jordanians who contacted me but rather officials from Pan American Airlines whose company at the time operated ALIA. They thought an Arab fashion designer would understand more the spirit of the airline than an Occidental designer. It was my first attempt at designing a uniform!

I completed my designs and went to Jordan. Much to my surprise, all the designers brought along tall, professional models to wear their designs. I didn't know that was the way it was done. To give myself courage, as I modeled and explained my designs, I rationalized that at least, being petite, I was more the size of an ALIA hostess. The room was filled with dignitaries. Queen Alia and all the top officials of the airline were there. I didn't know anyone. It was the first time I had been to Jordan. After I finished my presentation, I left, convinced I hadn't done well. I was packing my things in my room when the telephone rang and I was informed my design had won! They asked me if I would come down and sign the contract. I had never signed a contract in my life! I told them I couldn't because I had to travel back to Lebanon right away. I had a lawyer friend and I thought he would advise me. Surprisingly they agreed! In preparing me for the contract signing, my lawyer told me, "Don't even agree to change a comma." After the contract was signed, I heard several senior vice presidents of the airline say to each other: "My God, what a tough business woman she is!" [laughter] Several years later I was asked to do another design for them and it received a prize for best airline uniform.

When you go to see a film or attend the theater do you focus on the wardrobe?

Yes! I have what the French call a *"déformation professionnelle."* [laughter] I adore historical films and plays with beautiful costumes. I like to see things that make me happy. I don't like misery. I've seen too many sad things in Lebanon. I stayed here and continued to work during the entire war. But all my major work came from commissions from outside because there was not much work here except to design wedding dresses because, in spite of the war, people continued to get married. And Romeo was crazy or brave — I'm not quite sure which one — because he continued to produce and direct plays and I designed all his costumes. I was always traveling. But even if the airport was closed, I would return by sea or by road from Jordan or Syria. I always came back as soon as my work was completed, no matter what the situation was in Lebanon. I lived here throughout the seventeen years of war and I even got married here during the war.

How did you cope during those years?

I was never afraid. God gave me strength. I have something in me that says: if you want to live, you have to keep going. Death does not frighten me. My profession also helped me escape from the horrors of the war by allowing me to dream. In order to design, you have to dream. You have to let your mind take flight into a fantasy world especially when you design theater costumes and wedding dresses. In your head you can travel into the past, the future, to other countries, other worlds. But the last two years of the fighting, when the Christian forces fought against Syria and then against each other, I could not design. I could not touch a pencil. It was terrible. Life seemed so futile. It was the worst period for me.

Why didn't you leave the country at that time?

I couldn't. I am married to a surgeon, Dr. Bachir Saade. I met him, during the war. I am very proud of him. Everyone tells me he is one the real heroes of the war because he had so many offers to leave the country but he chose to stay. At one point, he spent four years living in the hospital. He lost his house, his clinic, everything. If it wasn't destroyed by the shelling, it was stolen. He never had time to go home to save things even when his house was burning. His only concern was for his patients. His specialty is heart and vascular surgery and there were so many people who suffered from heart conditions during the fighting. Many doctors left the country. During several extended periods, he was the only one in his specialty at the Hotel Dieu de France where he practiced. All through the war with the fighting ranging around him, he drove from hospital to hospital. So even during those terrible two years of fighting, I never thought of asking him to leave and take us somewhere safe. I couldn't. I knew what his answer would be.

Do you have children?

Yes, we have a son and a daughter. During four months, I was alone with the children. I didn't know where he was. Everything was cut off. Thinking of that time even now upsets me. We had no telephone, no electricity, no water and because of the constant bombing, we couldn't go out. One day, after four months had passed and I was in despair, I heard a commotion outside. The concierge was shouting: "*Hakim, hakim!* [Doctor, doctor!] My God, it's the hakim." Everyone in the building came rushing down to see my husband. It was a scene filled with emotion. The concierge was hugging him and everyone was shaking his hands and kissing him; some just wanted to touch him. I was crying. Many knew him by reputation only because I had moved into my mother's building. We had been staying in a shelter when our apartment was destroyed and I had to run with my two children to my mother's apartment. Everyone in the building had grown very close to each other because, with the constant shelling, we lived together in the shelter in the basement. We all supported one another by sharing our thoughts and worries. Everyone was concerned about my husband. "Dr. Saade, where is he?" They would ask. And I was praying that he wasn't driving from one hospital to another because the fighting was so crazy and he can be crazy himself. When a patient needs him, he doesn't think about the danger to himself. During this period, I couldn't design. I couldn't concentrate.

What have you learned that has made a difference in your life?

I think I am a very lucky woman. When I was in school all the girls in my class were dreaming about Prince Charming coming along. I never had such dreams. I dreamt that I wanted to be a working woman. I had it in my head that there was no difference between a woman and a man where work was concerned. I never understood why girls were only expected to marry and have children and not realize themselves. I wanted to realize myself and I was lucky enough to do so at a very early age. I had lots of lucky breaks in my life. I don't dwell on the bad things even though I've lived through and survived many tragedies. I am an optimist. I always forget the bad things. God gave me this ability to have only happy memories.

I lived through this war for a long time as a single woman and I know what it means to be a single woman and build a life on ones own. I also know what it is to be married to a man who understands that I am a professional woman, an independent person. When he writes me letters, when I travel, he asks the concierge to put them under my pillow and in those letters he always addresses

me as Mademoiselle Papou Lahoud, never Madame Saade. Everyone addresses me
by my maiden name. He is actually proud of that. My daughter and my son have
provided me with incredible experiences and emotions I didn't think possible.
Moving from being a single working woman to being a wife and mother, and continuing to work in my profession, is a big challenge. It's not easy because I always
want things to be done right. I always want to be with my husband and my children when they need me. How does one do it all? I can tell you I am very tired!

HOUDA AL-NAAMANI

POET, PAINTER AND PLAYWRIGHT

*Houda Al-Naamani is a petite, vivacious woman with laughing eyes
that promise to share a secret. Naamani has published numerous books of
poetry, held exhibitions of her paintings in Beirut, London, and Washington,
written critically acclaimed plays, and is a regular contributor to* Al-Nahar,
*Lebanon's leading newspaper. Mervyn Levy, critic at the Royal Academy in
London, describes Naamani's art as having "the power of Picasso, the madness of Dalí, and the innovation of Pollock." Her poetry, filled with mystical
illusions and startlingly vivid non sequitur imagery, can be described in similar terms. Like her art, Naamani's poetry is visual and vital. Strong, bold,
raw emotions leap out at you; yet, below the surface, a quiet, cerebral current flows.*

*The mother of two sons and the widow of a former dean of the Ameri-
can University of Cairo, Naamani comes from a family of politicians, scholars and Sufi mystics who trace their lineage to the Prophet Muhammad. In
1947, following family tradition, she attended law school at the Syrian University and upon graduation joined the law firm of her uncle, Said Al-Ghazzi,
a former Syrian prime minister. In 1952, she was awarded a scholarship to
pursue graduate studies in political science at Stanford University, but acqui-
escing to her family's wishes, chose marriage instead.*

*I interviewed Naamani in her cozy apartment decorated with paintings
and antiques from around the world. One of the first to return to her war-
ravaged neighborhood, which straddles the dividing line between East and
West Beirut, Naamani invited me to join her outside on a balcony. She was
editing a manuscript on this sunny, breezy morning and resorting to makeshift
paperweights. Although the sounds of the city intruded — car horns, heavy
construction, vegetable and fruit vendors pushing their carts and calling out
their contents — she was oblivious to them all. For Naamani, this was a typical morning in her beloved Beirut.*

*   *   *

What prompted you to write your first poem?

The reverence for poetry started in my childhood. The urge to write came later when our national dreams collapsed. I always wanted to be a poet. I remember when I was five or six years old, living in a large house in Damascus, how loneliness crept on me. The house was always filled with political and literary personalities. All through the years as I was growing up, they would visit and in their conversations they would quote poetry. We even had poetry readings in our house.

When I was about twelve, I used to write poems in my notebook and then erase them. My teacher, a nun at the Franciscaines School, came to me one day and said: "Houda, I want to speak to you after class." When the rest of the students left, she approached me and held my hand and said: "Houda, I notice from your writing that you are a poet. I will help you discover your talent by selecting books for you to read." I was so moved that I immediately started to cry. It was as though she had opened a whole new world for me.

When the French left Lebanon in 1945, I dreamed I would be the first female prime minister in the Arab world. I didn't know exactly what I wanted to be until I studied law and discovered that being a lawyer is restricting. As a lawyer, one serves a small group of people; as a politician, one serves, at most, one nation. But as a poet, one serves all of humanity. So, once again, I was determined to become a poet.

Can you tell me about your background?

I suffered duality from a young age. Syria, was my mother's homeland. There I was born. My mother comes from an old influential political family; my father, Fouad, from a Lebanese political family with strong business and commercial interests. [His uncle, Aref Al-Naamani, a man of great wealth, financed the revolution that led to Lebanon's independence.] My father traveled to Damascus and fell in love with my mother, a beautiful lady named Selwa, who was an artist and a poet. They were married in Beirut in a grandiose wedding. After eight happy years, they moved back to Damascus. My father didn't live long after the move. The Naamani family lost their wealth during the Crash of 1929. My father's health was affected. He died at the age of forty-two. I was eight years old. But life went on, my mother took charge.

I remember, as a child, political meetings being held at our home, and my parents lifting me up on a desk and asking me to recite poems written by prominent poets. In family discussions, invariably, we always talked about my great grandfather, Abdul Gani Nabulsi. He was born in 1640 and died in 1731. He was a scholar, a very important mystic thinker. He wrote poetry, philosophy, and biographies of important historical figures. He studied the Koran and wrote explanations of psalms. Most important of all, he wrote about his travels to Mecca, Palestine, and Lebanon — these books have been translated in many languages and are found in libraries around the world. His home in Damascus was turned into a mosque.

What are your most vivid memories of your childhood?

Mainly the house I was raised in, a honey-comb of tradition. All during my childhood, I was surrounded by wealth and interesting personalities, as well as music and art because of my mother's inter-ests. As a baby, I would open my eyes and there would be ribbons of all colors streaming down over my crib. We had several marble-inlaid fountains in the garden. At the beginning of the day the water would sound calm and serene. Then, gradually, the sound would change and pick up pace. It was like a continuous sym-phony that played day and night.

Houda Al-Naamani

There were birds on the trees and flowers everywhere. In the house, we kept cats and behind the house we had rabbits and gazelles. And there was always a sheep grazing ready to be slaughtered for visi-tors. Across from our house were the stables. This was life! Spinoza said it well, "Nature is God." Inside the house were many ornate salons with high ceilings, beautifully decorated with mosaics and murals. I remember during the summer, when certain rooms would be closed off and the furniture protected by dust covers, I would sneak into one of the rooms and close the door behind me. Then I would lie down and look up at the romantic murals on the ceiling and imag-ine wonderful stories. It was a place that let your imagination run free. I have always been inspired by beautiful things and visions. Thoughts, I believe, can be easier assimilated through dreams and beauty.

Do dreams influence your poetry?

Dreams are the world I move in. They are a mirror of my poetic vision. It is as though they lift and carry messages from God. My last book, *"Houda, I Am the Lord"* is based on one such wonderful experience.

Do you sleep well at night or do you anxiously await dreams?

[laughter] Yesterday, one of my poems was published in the newspaper, *Al-Nahar*, and in that poem I say, "If the dream does not appear, I just bang on the table and say: 'Tonight, you will come!'" In Islam, like the Greeks and the Romans, we believe that angels carry dreams to us from the skies!

What do you hope to communicate through your poetry?

Love changes the world! Islam is a world religion that uplifts from within. Unfortunately, Islam has been greatly misunderstood and even deliberately mis-interpreted by the West. Ignorance leads to hate. This misconception needs to be rectified because Islam offers a true foundation for world peace. In my life, knowledge of civilizations, human encounters, religion, literature, geography, history, law and art awakened in me a spirit of unity. I believe a new political vision is necessary to advance a world which has become one through the spread of technology. We all belong to one world and that is why we should learn to understand and love one another. There is a real need for intercultural truth, for exchange programs, travel and contact with other countries to eradicate igno-rance and teach that being different need not infer superiority or inferiority nor result in a galaxy of destruction.

I understand that you are a Sufist. Could you tell me about Sufism?

Sufism in Islam derives from a philosophical religious concept that is based on faith, love, and hope. It began in response to an urge to maintain a personal relation with God by seeking a return to simplicity, communing with nature, and going beyond ritual and formal religious doctrines. The ultimate objective of Sufism is the attainment of unity with the Deity through purifying ascetic practices and beliefs.

Why have you chosen Sufism?

In my estimation Sufism, with its uncommon inclination towards love and mystery, is the answer to humanity's pain. Sufism reaffirms the existence of rev-elations and resuscitates the individual's faith in the beyond. We come from the worship of one God. This knowledge should be our reality. The invariable mis-take, without proof, that we have no refuge, we are different from one another, must be expelled. It is in Sufism we find the sacrificial code of the world.

Is the emotion that inspires you to write poetry similar to the emotion that prompts you to paint?

For me, painting is a wonderland. It is like entering a forest or looking at the sea, a flower, children at play, the sky through the branches of a tree. Approaching poetry, on the other hand, is like coming close to a tornado of flames. The sublimation of the word, the philosophical symbolism of the word is, of course, different from the tangible symbolism of paint and this is why we Arabs feel that the word is God and God is the word. When I write, I always feel like I am getting ready to pray. My outlook is much more serious. There is a promise of bliss. Painting, for me, is relatively spontaneous, while writing is much more premeditated.

Do you feel the process of writing is a process of discovery?

Yes, discovery is creation. Only discovery is art. You just have to let things flow. I employ many different styles and approaches including mechanical writing. It all depends upon my mood and the subject matter because each subject has it's own mask. You cannot limit yourself.

In your poetry, you give words a three dimensional quality. They seem to fit together in such unexpected ways.

Yes, I have been told that often. In fact, one critic said that I build sculptures with my words. I sometimes feel that I hold my ideas in my hand and work with words as if I were molding clay. I am not trying to create a new reality, just a deeper reality...

What does art mean to you?

To me, art is trying to reach where nobody has reached before. It is an attempt to reach truth — to go inside things. I stop work when I feel I should not add one more word, one more line, or one more stroke.

Being an artist and a poet, how do you compare the two?

Art, like music, communicates to a larger audience because it has universal appeal, it goes beyond the barrier of language.

Do you believe that you are guided by a divine influence when you are writing poems or painting?

Yes, I always have a very warm and happy feeling when I am creating and able to communicate through words or paint what I feel. It is the most exciting and challenging experience to carry a halo above your head that no one sees...

What is the driving force in your life today?

The idea of love and reaching peace. I feel great pain hearing the shriek of the world: the wars, the destruction, the hate surrounding us. Sufism provides words for love and unity. I feel an obligation through my poetry to prepare humanity to meet God and live forever.

You view poetry as a springboard to the hereafter?

Any human being is afraid of death more than from anything else. Only faith saves him. Behind everything I write is the message: Don't be afraid to reach for one another, remember you are born to be eternal. I believe poetry is more effective than religion in reaching humanity. Poetry puts on a mask and then slowly penetrates the soul and the heart, without unleashing the dangerous destructive elements that religious institutions have imposed upon us through the centuries. Having one God, how can we differ? Creation is to survive death.

At what point did mysticism enter into your life?

The unknown opened its gates when I was only eight. My first memorable dream happened on the day my father died. I saw a bird on a tree outside my window. Then the dream ended and the bird became real and landed on my breast. I often allude to this dream in my poems because it opened the unknown to me. It was as though I had touched the beyond. This bird that flew out of my dream into reality proved to me that any vision can be real. This experience, I kept secret, and all my mystical dreams, even from my mother, until I started to write.

Is most of your poetry spiritual?

Yes and no. Any subject — an orange, a chair, a desk — can be given a spiritual dimension. Since I was very young anything I touched or felt or saw was a part of eternity. A childish fantasy, perhaps, but so rich and intense![laughter]

Were you an only child?

I was an only child for six years and then my sister was born. My parents lost a son six years earlier. Because of this long waiting period, my parents were extremely attached to me. So for years I was the unique love in their life. My mother, besides being a poet and an artist, was a social worker and had political interests, but she devoted herself to taking care of me. Her devotion and attention made my life very special.

What do you think is the essential component for creativity?

Creativity is being in a divine state. It is like an unexpected knocking at your door. It requires calmness, a certain transparency, readiness, and tranquility for you to open the door. Without peace of mind you cannot be receptive to creative impulses. You must become like a mirror ready to receive light and reflect it.

How did you manage to write poetry during the war with all the fighting and shelling around you?

The eleven years I spent in Lebanon, during the war, were the most important years of my life. I remained in this apartment, in the midst of the fighting, and underwent an incredibly rich spiritual experience that I would never have had were I sitting in a calm place on the Riviera or anywhere else in the world. The pain, the fear, the closeness of death intensified my prayers and brought me closer to God than during any other time. Yes, it was extremely stressful, but strangely enough, it made me grow as a human being.

My book, *I Remember I Was a Point, I Was a Circle*, was written right here on this desk. It is in essence a search for a new hope, a new beginning, amid the ruins. While writing it, I could hear and see armed young men below talking to each other as they took cigarette breaks from the fighting, their leaders meeting to discuss strategy. All this I wove into my poetry, realizing that even war must have an important human aim. God is not ignorant of what he is doing. War has the impetus to create not hate but love, when the last bullet is spent.

Weren't you ever afraid for your life during the fighting?

No, I was writing. I was inspired! I felt I was a tool in God's hand; therefore, I would be spared! God strengthened me through dreams. Sometimes, I would see buildings that were going to be hit. Once, I dreamt a black veiled woman looked out my window, shook her head, and then went up to the fourth floor. Five minutes later, the fourth floor was hit!

How do you identify with other Sufists?

We share a certain happiness. The highest level a Sufi can attain is happiness. I laugh a lot! This happiness comes from the security of knowing that I am like a child who is sure she is loved by her family. I have no worries about life. I don't fear death. I believe you cannot hold truth in your hand except after death when the spirit leaves its prison and you can look at reality from a higher perspective. I wrote about this theory in my play, "Vision Upon a Thrown," about Lebanon, using the four voices of those who were fighting: Sunni, Maronite, Druze, and Shiite. There is an echo at the beginning of the play. The echo— their conscience — is a parrot. It picks up a word and repeats it without thinking. At the beginning everyone kills everyone. Then they rise up, look down at the earth, analyze the war, and discuss why they killed each other. No one can come up with a worthy reason. As they talk, it slowly becomes clear to them that it was hate and ignorance that prevented them from living in harmony. Love and understanding would have conquered that. Having understood their failure, they meet God. Throughout the play, the parrot becomes more and more enlightened. Finally, in the end, he becomes light itself symbolizing, of course, the light of God, the universal being.

What was the most amazing dream you've experienced?

Seeing Christ and the Virgin Mary when I was in Cairo. One night, before I went to sleep, I said: "Virgin Mary, you have appeared in dreams to many people who denied you, why don't you appear to me?" And she did!

Why did you want to see the Virgin Mary?

My goodness! She is the most important woman of all ages! In Islam she is venerated. She is the mother of Jesus. This is why we must know more about each other to pave a new era of peace through knowledge and empathy. In my dream, the Virgin Mary said, "Make a wish." I said, "Humanity!" And she laughed.

I also saw Christ in my dream. He approached me looking as though He were in a picture. When He had almost reached me, He stepped out of the picture. I saw His eyes and He is different from all the paintings of Christ I have ever seen in all the museums of the world. He was so beautiful! So majestic and serene! As I saw Him walking towards me, I thought: I can touch His robe! In His hand He held a book and He was wearing two rings on His finger: a heart-shaped ruby ring encircled by diamonds and a gold wedding band. Taking my two hands into His, He stared deep into my eyes and urged me to read. At the time, I had earned a law degree and my husband was dean of the American University of Cairo. After this dream, I spent the next fifteen years as a student attending classes in a variety of subjects, including history, philosophy, literature, and art. I later learned of the symbolism of the two rings He wore: the gold ring stands for marriage and the ruby ring symbolizes a sacred relation with God. In Sufism, you cannot be a *Kotb* [leader] unless you are given "the ring." When He touched me, He gave me the ring.

Which writers have influenced you?

There are many I admire from different centuries. When I go to them it is with respect and, admittedly, a bit of curiosity. For instance, Victor Hugo used to complain of hearing voices and a knocking at his door when, in fact, there was no one. We know very little of the spiritual experiences of artists in literature and music. Michaelangelo saw an apparition of God up on the mountain and then painted the Sistine Chapel with that remarkable scene of God reaching for Adam. Many existentialists tried to create these experiences through drugs, but drugs have nothing to do with real spirituality. You cannot induce it artificially. It happens or it doesn't. It is God's will.

How do you feel about your country?

Our land in this part of the world is sacred. This is where all the prophets were born and where they lived. When I lived in the United States and in Europe, I searched for God but I never felt His presence — even in churches. But here, in the Middle East, I have always felt His presence. Whether in a stone or a tree, you notice here the age of humanity. In America, everything is new, unemotional. Here, you can go to Damascus, walk in the streets, look at the cobblestones and appreciate that they are thousands of years old. You feel a certain saintliness in people awaiting the end of the world or the return of Christ. Muslims, Christians and Jews believe that a cloud will come bearing the Messiah, who will come and unify all religions. This feeling of waiting, of readiness, is very beautiful and it is a very real and integral part of everyday life.

How did you start painting?

While working on *Vision on a Throne*, I asked a friend, a well-known calligrapher, to illustrate it. He kept postponing. One day, I told him: "If you don't do the drawings by the end of the day, I'll do them myself," and I did. After calligraphy, I moved on to watercolor, then to oil and mixed media. I paint as I write. I don't believe things should be too clear. I like to use symbols.

What type of symbols do you use?

First of all I use the path to God — all objects and dimensions revolve around it. It is a path between death and redemption. I have always painted abstract art in the belief that when you illustrate a message it is better not to be completely clear because the artist and the viewer each has his own vision. It is the artist's job to plant a seed and then it is up to the viewer to nourish the vision. Under the viewer's gaze, the vision on the canvas wilts or flourishes. Everyone has a different vision. The message is never interpreted the same way.

What are some of the themes you are currently working on?

I am still under the pressure of war, destruction, and pain. I am still painting the diaspora — people leaving Lebanon. I am using gold to simulate the light in my dreams, recalling the golden era of Islam.

So your paintings are like dreams?

They are dreams!

Do you visualize your paintings, as you do your poetry, in dreams?

Sometimes the subject of my painting is an answer to a question I thought about before I went to sleep. When I decided to do an exhibition in London, I had only completed six paintings. I needed sixty more. The answer came in my dream. I saw myself wearing bifocals and the lower magnified part of the eyeglasses were missing. The solution was obvious: "Make the art abstract and symbolic, don't make it clear." I poured wax and gold and the magic started!

It is said that Gertrude Stein on her deathbed was surrounded by friends and she looked at them and asked: "What is the answer?" No one said anything for a long while, so she said: "Okay then, what is the question?" You seem like someone who would know the answer, so I am going to ask you: what is the question?

[laughter] The question? Is love too great a price for the salvation of humanity? That is the question and the answer.

EMILY NASRALLAH

NOVELIST

In the introduction to her book of short stories, A House Not Her Own, *Emily Nasrallah writes: "And I must ask if there are still, in a world filled with the clamour of war machinery, ears that can hear the moans of the weak and the cries of the desperate." For the forgotten, Nasrallah confers a voice that is dignified, eloquent and timeless.*

Emily Nasrallah: novelist, journalist, teacher, lecturer, United Nations delegate, wife, mother of four, was born Emily Abi Rashed in the village of Kfeir, in the South of Lebanon, on July 6, 1931. She has published seven novels, five collections of short stories, and a book in three volumes on women pioneers. Although she writes in Arabic, her work has been translated into English, French, German, and Danish.

My meeting with Nasrallah was one that I savored because there was a time when I thought it would never take place. Several weeks earlier, her mother-in-law, also named Emily Nasrallah, passed away and the obituary notices confused the two women.

We met early in the afternoon on a sunny, winter day at her apartment in a Beirut high-rise. The first thing one notices about Nasrallah is her wonderful warmth and arresting tranquility. She appears at peace with herself. This demure appearance conceals, however, an iron will that enabled her to surmount age-old barriers and compose a life on her own terms.

* * *

Who is Emily Nasrallah?

I try to write short stories and novels to answer that question. Sometimes you see yourself as someone who is very simple; other times, you see yourself in so many words, so many people, so many selves. You ask yourself: Who is Emily Nasrallah — in the present, the past, the future? Who is this person who had to go through so many stages, endure so many struggles in her life? There are so many turning points in one's life and at each you become a different person. You can never be sure who you really are because life keeps changing you. Every experience changes you. As a novelist, I am always trying to grasp my reality. Although when I write, I don't only write about myself, I write about my community, about other people, but somehow the undercurrent of all that I write takes me on this trail of discovery that is an attempt to find myself.

If you want a simple response to your question, I come originally from a small village in southern Lebanon called Kfeir Al Zait [Village of Oil]. I was born in the village and I lived there through my childhood and part of my teen years. My family is related to a majority of the people in the village, most of

Emily Nasrallah

whom are small land owners. We have ancient olive groves and olive oil production is the traditional source of income of the village. We call the olive tree "the saintly tree," and we believe olive oil cures many illnesses. Oil plays an important role in the tradition of the village. It is used throughout one's life, beginning with a drop of oil at one's baptism and it is used to cleanse the dead.

Living in the village was not an easy life. As a young girl, I attended the only school in the village which consisted of one room for elementary classes. I was supposed to end my education at the third-grade level. There were no classes beyond that grade and my family, of course, was not thinking of sending a girl beyond the horizon of the village to pursue an education. For several years, I repeated the last class just to keep going to school. I worked in the field as did all small children: planting and harvesting the wheat, picking the grapes, and collecting the fruit of the olive trees. Plus, I helped my parents at home. The family in our society works together. No one is too young to work. Everybody lends a hand and because everyone is working, the work evolves into seasons of celebration. I am now trying to write some short stories capturing this experience as viewed through the eyes of a child revisiting the village in her memory.

Are most of your childhood memories happy ones?

What I am writing about are the happy memories. Somehow time wipes away the negative things, the pain, and what is left are the shining, happy faces and events. Why I am writing about those days, now, I still can't say. The village is the background of so many of my novels and short stories. I feel its essence deeply planted within me. My later works, which I wrote during the war, take place in Beirut, where I have been living since 1953. Yet, I often return to my village in my writings.

How did you go beyond the third grade?

That is when my struggle began. At home, I lived with not only my parents, brothers and sister, there was also my grandmother, on my mother's side, and her son, Ayub Abou Nasser, my uncle. In his early youth, he emigrated to the United States. He was a young man with a promising future. He wrote, drew cartoons, and belonged to the North American Union of Writers. He knew many of its members, including Kahlil Gibran. He was preparing to become a writer, when he suddenly fell ill and had to return to the village. I haven't touched on his story yet in my writings because he holds such a tremendous place in my background. In some of my works, he appears as a secondary character, but I feel someday I have to write about him as he deserves to be written.

My uncle was different from most of the inhabitants of the village. He had lived in New York and once had literary ambitions. He used to tell me stories about the big city, about girls going to university, and he always took the time to read the compositions I wrote for my third grade class. He encouraged me to write beyond classroom assignments. He would look at Mount Hermon, which is opposite our village, and ask me to describe the mountain and the color of the sky. He opened my eyes to the beauty of nature and the existence of a different life beyond the horizon of the village, where girls could walk freely with their hair falling loosely on their shoulders; not the way my grandmother used to tell me. She would say: "If you walk in the street, you should walk without moving your arms. You should walk stiffly." I can still hear the voice of my father telling me, "Wear long sleeves, cover your hair with a scarf."

I felt repressed by the strict conservatism of my parents and the limitations imposed upon a girl in a traditional society. All these contradictions worked on me and I started rebelling. I did not want to end my education at the age of nine or ten as did most of the girls in the village. I wanted to go beyond the third grade. But I was limited by my parents' sense of right and wrong, and by the fact that they didn't have the money to send me to a school outside of the village where I would have to live as a boarder. It was a very expensive proposition, and a girl living on her own outside of the village was just unheard of.

Consulting with my Uncle Ayub, he suggested I write a letter to his brother, my Uncle Toufic, a successful businessman in America, and tell him of my dilemma and my dream. I wrote him and I couldn't believe the quick response I received. Uncle Toufic immediately sent a telegram to my parents saying, "Send Emily to school." Later, when I met this uncle — he is now ninety-four and lives in Huntington, West Virginia — I asked him, "What made you respond so quickly to my letter?" He told me his story. As a young man living in the village, they would choose the brightest boys to attend high school in Nazareth [Palestine at the time] and his older brother, Ayub, was the first one in the family chosen to go. When his turn came and he was chosen, his father said: "It is enough that we are educating your older brother, you will stay here and help me tend the fields." Shortly thereafter circumstances required that he travel to the United States where he became a successful businessman. But he could never forget the missed opportunity of his youth. So when my letter arrived, it touched a very tender spot in him.

With my uncle's help, I was able to attend Shoueifat National School, where I completed four years of secondary education. After that my parents and most everybody else in the village thought that was more than enough education for a girl, because I now had the qualifications to become a teacher. They didn't know that once you taste knowledge, you cannot stop! I wanted to go on to university. Again, I had to fight with my parents to be allowed to leave the village and live on my own in Beirut. They finally agreed on one condition: I live in a boarding school.

I arrived in Beirut with no work and no connections. Immediately, I went looking for a job and a place to stay. I went to Ahlia School. A friend had given me the name of the president of that school and told me she was one of the country's pioneer educators. I went to see Wadad Kortas and explained my situation. She asked, "What can you teach?" I said, "Arabic." And she said, "Okay, you will have room and board for teaching two hours daily in the elementary school." Imagine my joy!

Securing room and board, I now had to secure fees for the university. As it turned out, one of the full-time teachers at Ahlia School had saved some money in the bank and offered to lend it to me for my tuition. To pay back this wonderful woman, I took all types of jobs. I started writing for a monthly magazine, translating, and giving private lessons. Even though I was doing so much, the money I earned was very little. To supplement my income, I was given an opportunity by another great lady, a pioneer in journalism, Edvic Shaiboub, to speak on her radio program once a month and to write for her magazine. With the money I earned, I was able to pay back my wonderful friend in small installments. At the end of the first year, I secured a job in one of our weeklies, *Al-Sayyad*. I was working at Ahlia School for room and board, attending lectures at Beirut University College and later at the American University of Beirut and, at night, I worked as a journalist. I worked like that for three years until I graduated with a Bachelor of Arts degree.

What did you major in?

My major was education and I minored in Arabic and English literature. There was no major in journalism at the time. Journalism was something I was practicing outside the classroom. Although I specialized in teaching and I liked my students, I started enjoying writing more than teaching and I began to feel that my interest in journalism was pulling me away from a teaching career. By the end of my third year in university, I met my husband, Philip Nasrallah. We became engaged and we married in 1957. I quit teaching at Ahlia School since I no longer needed to teach for room and board and continued with journalism. Philip and I moved in with his parents our first year of marriage! I graduated in 1958, but I could not sit for the exams with the other students because I was having my first child. It happened that 1958 was not a calm year in Lebanon.

There was a revolution, so I had to come back in October to sit for my exams. My son was already six-months-old. We did not plan a family. Family planning in our society is a very new concept. In my time, the natural progression of a relationship is: you meet, you fall in love, you agree on marriage, you marry, and then you have children! It was as natural as that. I was so crazy not to think: Wait you are still a student! Anyhow, I did not continue beyond my B.A. because it was not easy to cope with so many roles. But there was one thing I knew for sure: I did not want to quit writing.

How many brothers and sisters do you have?

I am the eldest of six children. I have four brothers and a sister. None continued their education beyond high school. A few quit at the elementary level. They emigrated early to Canada at different times, for different reasons. This really was the trauma of my life. It is because of their emigration that I wrote my first novel, *Birds of September*. In that book you will understand some of the pain and sorrow I endured as a young girl seeing my brothers and sister, who were all younger than myself, obliged to emigrate to seek educational and economic opportunities abroad. Their plight, sadly, was not the exception but the rule. Entire generations, not only from one village, but from all the rural areas in Lebanon left to seek a better life abroad.

In 1981, I published a second novel on the theme of emigration, *Flight Against Time*, but this time it was emigration from war, during the late 70s and early 80s. I still feel I am just discovering this theme because emigration is the big story of my life, my family, my village, my society, my people. Everybody suffered from this longing for loved ones who were obliged to leave.

Did you feel abandoned?

I left the village to come to Beirut before any of my brothers left. In a way, I was an emigrant, an alien in the city. I experienced the alienation one feels as a villager coming into the big city, where nobody knows you. It is especially numbing when you compare it with the familiarity of the village where everybody not only knows you, but cares about you. I poured all those feelings of alienation into my first novel.

Were there ever times when you were tempted to pack up and go back to your village?

Yes, I expressed this feeling in *Birds of September*. Mona, the main character, feels like going back because of this nostalgia, this point of fire, is eating her up. Although she has made a success of herself in the city, obtaining an education and a good job, she decides she must go back to her village. She goes back and discovers she is no longer accepted there. She has become a stranger. At least, that is the way she feels because the village has changed for her. It is no longer the same place she carries in her memory. The people have changed; she has changed. She discovers she can never go back. It's not easy to go back and continue as if nothing had happened. In the novel, Mona feels the neighbors are looking at her from their windows. They don't recognize her. So she runs to her car and as she drives away from the village, she thinks: "I am a question mark. Who am I? I don't belong to either place anymore." I think this is very true of many people who leave at an early stage in their life, go to another place, then try to return. It's not easy to go back.

What drew you to a career in writing? Was it to release those feelings of alienation you experienced?

I entered journalism by chance. It was a job that provided me with a paycheck at the end of the month to pay my university tuition without having to borrow from my friend. But the more I got involved in journalism, the more I liked it. It opened my eyes to so many different happenings in the city and introduced me to so many different people. It made me aware of current events. I was not assigned to just cover one area. I wrote about all types of events and people. I remember once, when I was still new on the job, my boss called me in and said: "Harlem is visiting Beirut. Go cover the story." Well, it turned out "Harlem" was the American basketball team — the Harlem Globe Trotters! The players had such a sense of humor and they made such fun of my questions. I felt like a tiny ball being dribbled by giants. Of course, at the time, I didn't know they were famous for their humor. I thought it was just me and my questions!

Sometimes, I found myself interviewing political figures and film stars. My experience that first year was quite memorable! There was a Hollywood actress by the name of Ann Miller who was visiting Beirut. I was asked by my boss to attend her press conference. I was still "the village girl": shy and very conservatively dressed. I went to the press conference and I was the only female journalist there. Ann Miller showed up an hour late wearing a very low neckline and these long gypsy earrings. After everyone had finished asking questions — I had been listening, I was too shy to ask any — she came and put her arm around my shoulder and said, "Let's take a photograph together. You are the only other girl here." The photographer took our picture. I was so afraid my father would see it in the newspaper that I pleaded with the photographer to destroy the picture. Even after I was married and had my own children, I could never tell my father that I took my children to the cinema — going to the movies was considered shameful.

The more knowledgeable I became about people, the more I wanted to become a writer rather than a journalist. I worked for *Al-Sayyad* magazine for fifteen years from 1955-1970, but I felt it was not my final job. I wanted to go into fictional writing. In 1962, I published my first novel, *Birds of September*, and it took me another eight years to make the decision to quit journalism. During that time, I was also raising a family and writing short stories.

Who has had the greatest influence on you?"

There are several people who played an important role in my life. My father did not read or write. He was a very traditional man but very intelligent. He encouraged me in his own way. He was so proud of me because he had been deprived of an education. Sometimes he didn't know how to help, but he had a strong will. My father used to carry me to school before I was old enough to attend. I would listen from outside the window and memorize the poems. Then he would take me home, put me up on the table and have me recite my little poems to his friends, who would be sitting around smoking and sipping coffee as is the pastime of village people. I would recite like a parrot and I could feel that he was so proud of me.

My mother lived in the village all her life, never traveled, and had only an elementary education. She had the traditional mentality of her time, that a woman's place is at home and that an elementary education for a girl is more than enough. She had a beautiful personality and I had good feelings for her. We were very good friends, but I felt my mother could never understand why I was tiring myself writing when I could relax, enjoy myself and my family. She used to say "Enough with the papers!"

I already told you about the great role my Uncle Ayub and my Uncle Toufic played in my life. The person closest to me on the spiritual and sentimental side was my grandmother who lived with us. She was my first "story inspirer," the first person to tell me stories. Even now, as I write, I feel she is telling her stories through me. Outside of the family, there were so many people who gave me their friendship and support, taught me, gave me opportunities and jobs. I remember a teacher of Arabic literature who used to send my articles to a newspaper to have them published when I was still in high school.

Then, of course, there is my husband, who really deserves the credit for encouraging and challenging me all these years. Sometimes a negative word can destroy you at an early stage when you are still tender. He understood that and he understood how important writing was for me. He did everything to make it possible for me to continue to write, including providing me with help at home. Housework can kill all your ambitions. In our traditional society a woman is expected to give so much of her time to caring for everyone in the family, making sure they are all happy, properly fed, clothed, and rested; yet, no one is there to care for her. The greatest gift one's family or society can give a woman is to allow her to keep growing; not to limit her to a certain role, or a certain area. Unfortunately, this freedom is given all too rarely. There are so many gifted women whose potential was killed through marriage.

In your writing you use the pronoun "I" a lot. Would you describe your writing style as intimate?

I use "I" sometimes even when I am not the hero. I enjoy feeling intimate with my words and my subject. For several months now I have been writing short stories with myself as the central figure. It is written from the point of view of this child remembering certain events that took place in her village. There are so many wonderful little bits of details. Writing these stories is like remembering the first bowl of ice cream you ever tasted! You keep eating it, hoping it will last forever. When I write, I feel the same way about my words. I like to savor each word.

Are you ever amazed by what you have written?

Sometimes. But I am more often angry and disappointed with myself. Sometimes, I destroy half of what I write. Other times, I set my writing aside hoping I might like it after a third reading! I have a lot of unfinished stories lying around. I am now convinced that once the mood is gone, it is better to destroy unfinished stories rather than to keep them. You sometimes think you can go back to a story with fresh eyes and pull the threads of an idea further, but I think, more often than not, a story that is completed after a lapse of time lacks a certain vitality.

Do you feel the seventeen years of war were wasted years?

Much of my work was destroyed during the Israeli invasion in 1982 when my house and my library were burned. I had a lot of work that was ready to be published. The entire house went up in flames. After rebuilding, we were again hit by rockets in 1984 and 1985. For more than two years, we covered the windows with plastic sheeting. You get tired of replacing shattered windowpanes. Other than the destruction caused by war, I think, for a writer, nothing is wasted. I used my suffering, my people's suffering, my country's trauma, as material for my stories. When I was young and living in the village, before going away to school, I used to go to the field and sit down and just gaze at nature. At the time, I remember thinking I was being lazy, wasting my time doing nothing. Now, when I look back, I realize how precious were those moments of meditation. Nature can only be studied and appreciated in such a way.

Could you actually think, let alone write, during periods of intense shelling?

I did most of my writing under shelling. There was nothing to do, nowhere to go. I was trying to survive by doing something that would take my mind off the fighting and keep me mentally alert. I wrote a short story once while we were hiding in the corridor. We don't have a shelter in this building and rockets were falling on us from all sides. I could hear voices screaming downstairs and a woman sobbing: "They killed me!"

To stay sane, I wrote everything that I heard and felt as I was hearing and feeling it. It was a test of nerves to see how long I could stay clear-headed and not panic in that situation. Artistically, it was not one of the greatest stories I've written, but it was accepted for publication and I wrote an introduction about how and under what circumstances the story had been written. In fact, many of the women who wrote during the war had never written before. Writing was an outlet for pent up feelings. You couldn't express rage and anxiety any other way. Writing allowed you to confront your fears and to scream — in silence.

Do you view those who left during the war to safer havens as unpatriotic?

During the first two years of the war only one class of people emigrated: the rich class. They could afford to leave Lebanon and live elsewhere. Those of us who remained were very angry. I described those feelings in *Those Memories*. I felt if you have money, you really don't have a country because you don't have this sense of loyalty to one place. You can afford to live anywhere — the whole world is your oyster. On the other hand, if you have no money even your own country has no place for you.

I was not angry as an individual. But as a writer, expressing the general sentiment of those of us remaining, there was this feeling that the rich, since their own lifestyle had been unaffected, could care less what was befalling their country. They continued to live lavishly, going from cabaret to cabaret, eating French bread in Beirut and *moujedra* in Paris. These people, of course, represent a class of society that you find everywhere. But because they were so showy, during a time when people were really suffering, they caused a lot of anger.

Those of us who could afford to leave but chose to remain, stayed because we felt it was our duty. We felt this is where we belonged; we would stay and endure no matter what. It was during this period that I observed how heroic our people are — even in the little deeds they were performing daily. I can't tell you how many times parents, taking their children to school, would drive with bombs falling in front of their car and behind. Some never made it. Or how often parents would arrive at the school, only to find a bomb had fallen in the playground, and teachers gathering the children to take them down to the shelter. Every morning, after a night of shelling, we would call our friends to make sure a "killing bomb" did not visit them, and ask: "Are you taking your children to school, today?" If the majority said "yes" we would take our children, too.

It was the nights that were especially awful. Bombardments often happened during the night. Sometimes, when dawn broke, I would peer out the window, sure I would not find a single stone remaining on top of another. To my continual amazement, I would see the silhouettes of buildings still looming. So, of course, there was a feeling of anger towards those who left. But later, emigration took on a new face. It wasn't just the rich who left but those threatened with kidnapping, those whose neighborhoods had become unsafe and unfriendly because they belonged to another party or confessional group, and then there were those who had no money or prospects to educate their children and put food on the table. Emigration had many faces.

What sort of discrimination offends you as a woman?

The way boys and girls are treated differently. For example, initially my younger brother was allowed to go to school and I was not. I felt then that boys were different from girls because he was given a right that I was not. Although I love my brother, at that moment, this anger started welling up within me. I thought: Why should I be treated differently? I never felt myself to be inferior to a boy, therefore why should I be treated as an inferior. I refused to be treated sub-human, as a person incapable of being responsible for myself. I have always believed that I am the mistress of my own destiny; nobody is my master. I worked too hard. Nothing was given to me per chance. During my days in the university, girls were not allowed to pursue many careers including, for example, engineering. Today, I have a daughter who is an architect and her friends are electronic, mechanical and civil engineers. And I have another daughter who is a medical doctor.

Was there a moment in your life which you consider a turning point?

Yes, there was such a moment! [laughter] I can never forget the day after I came to Ahlia School to board and work as a teacher. I carried my books and walked out of my room to go to the university and nobody asked, as I left: "Where are you going? When are you coming back? Who will you be seeing?" Nothing had changed about me from the outside, but that day I felt like a queen. Those simple, unnoticed steps were my first steps to freedom. It was the very first time I had ever felt I was an independent, free spirit.

How do you like to unwind after a long day of writing?

Nature is still my closest friend, my source of inspiration and relaxation. I like to work in the garden, to plant, and to take long walks. Sometimes I shut out the world through meditation and go into my own private, inside world.

What have you learned that has made a significant difference in your life?

Every moment that you are awake, provided that you are alert, you learn something new. The important thing is to be open to your surroundings and aware of what is happening around you. Otherwise, important things that could make a real difference in your life could pass you by. As a writer, every detail is important. Every detail counts. It is the little details that put life into a story and make it breathe.

∗   ∗   ∗

As the interview drew to an end, the doorbell rang. Startled, I became aware of our surroundings. The warm, sun-filled living room, where we had been sitting, was now cast in dark, evening shadows. Nasrallah turned on a few lights. As we parted, she said with an enigmatic smile, still alluding to my last question, "Nothing is wasted when you open your eyes." Outside her apartment door, I noticed for the first time, leaning against a corner wall, a glass windowpane shattered in the shape of a butterfly. Later, I learned, it was one of the few things saved from the house she had lost — a reminder that even from destruction beauty can emerge.

LEILA OSSEIRANE

NOVELIST

Leila Osseirane, author of ten books, including We Shall Not Die Tomorrow, Dumb Dialogue, The Empty City, *and* Dawn Birds, *is described as "a genuine person, possessing deep moral convictions." A political activist, Osseirane received her Bachelor of Arts degree in political science from the American University of Beirut and worked as a journalist for a number of years. Osseirane is married to Amin al-Hafez, chairman of the foreign affairs committee, economist and respected member of parliament, representing Tripoli.*

I met Osseirane at a book party, where she was autographing her latest novel. Despite hot, blinding television camera lights and a seemingly endless number of requests for personalized messages from the many political and literary dignitaries in attendance, Osseirane appeared relaxed and totally at ease.

Leila Osseirane

Several days later, we met at her apartment in Beirut in a building that was under tight security, reflecting modern political life in Lebanon.

* * *

Did you always want to be a novelist?

Yes, ever since I was very young. But it was always a struggle either to consecrate my urge in political activity or to literature. It was never easy! I used to build another world for myself. I still wonder what is real — what I feel and see —

or what appears to be real. I have what you may call a tormented nature. I am extremely sensitive; yet, at the same time, I am strong. There is always an anxiety inside of me that makes me continuously breathless. I am always searching for the truth. I can't just look at something from the outside. I have to experience it. This can be very painful. My husband always argues with me. He tells me: "Don't get too close to your subject, you will end up getting hurt." I tell him, if I don't get close, I cannot write. I write about what moves me: the tragedy of my people, my society, my country. When I see suffering, I can't look away.

What would you say are the general themes of your novels?

My writing is largely influenced by my surroundings and my current interests. I write about the experience of finding one's self. I believe you cannot just live your life, day after day, eating and sleeping without purpose. You have to have an aim in life. You have to achieve something. I wrote about a certain bourgeois society in this country, a very status-oriented group of people. I wrote two books about the Palestinians. I wrote a book, before the war began, about Beirut and how much freedom we had, but no cause. Our cause was either Arab-oriented or too oriented to the West.

Then I wrote about my son and I living in our house in East Beirut. My husband at the time was with his constituents in Tripoli. After the first two years of war, there was a kind of lull; we thought the war had ended. My husband and I believed Muslims could live among Christians. So we built our house in East Beirut. It was destroyed. Our cook was killed and what was not destroyed was stolen. We lost everything because of our religion. The novel I wrote, which was based on what had happened to us, was a success because so many felt I had told their story.

Was it therapeutic for you to write that novel?

No, it was not therapeutic. I relived the whole experience. The story was in my head, so I wrote it. I am a very anxious person and when I put all my feelings and perceptions down on paper, it exhausts me. I don't write in a cold-blooded manner. When I write, I am never detached.

What was the worst period for you during the war?

The worst was General Aoun's bombardment in 1989. The fighting was so intense, I wondered if there would still be a Lebanon when it was over. The tension during that time was horrible. I am not a person who is afraid of bombs, but I hated the sound — the terrible destruction and the loss of lives caused by those bombs. The fighting was so completely out of control. There was no purpose behind it. At the beginning of the war, I felt there was a reason for the fighting: Muslims were not given the same rights as Maronite Christians. Power was in the hands of the Maronites. I felt, politically, we had a right to be heard. So, at the time, when we were resisting and putting up with difficulties, I believed it was for a worthwhile cause. But when the war continued, year after year, I could no longer justify it.

Can you tell me about yourself, your background?

My mother was a Christian from the south of Lebanon. She married my father, who was Muslim, almost sixty years ago. I am almost sixty today! Because of my parents different backgrounds, their marriage was quite unusual at the time. My father died young. It was my mother who brought me up. She tried to make me an accomplished person. I always wished I could be like her. She was a remarkable woman. She used to paint, embroider, and read a lot. She was very interested in politics and, perhaps because of her, I became interested as well. I remember being fascinated by the national uprising in the fifties and sixties, which began as a very strong political and patriotic movement but, unfortunately, didn't lead to anything.

After I graduated from AUB, I worked as a journalist because I felt I wasn't quite ready to write a novel — I needed to experience a bit more of life. I attended high school in Cairo but it was later, when I returned to Egypt as a journalist, that I moved in a milieu of writers and associated with many of the leading political and social thinkers of the fifties and sixties. Egypt, at the time, was the center of the Arab world and that experience enriched my life. As a journalist, I reported on political events which, in those days, were not normally covered by a woman. I worked for a newspaper — it no longer exists — that belonged to a former prime minister who represented the Arab nationalist movement in this country. I also joined the Baath Political Party and became the first Lebanese woman to do so — I was still attending university at the time.

What did the Baath Party stand for?

The Baath Party was founded during World War II by Michel Aflaq, a French-educated Arab from a Christian family, and Salah Bitar, a Sunni Muslim from Damascus. Baathism stressed nationalism, unity, and socialism as the cornerstones of Arab society and the three forces necessary to rejuvenate and restore the Arab world to its former cultural and commercial prominence.

What type of activities were you involved in?

I was very much involved in the Palestinian struggle. I wrote two novels about the Palestinians and their plight. I didn't do any fighting though!

If you were asked, would you have?

It's not an easy question to answer. But I will say this: I believe in the justice of their cause. I believe in the liberation of Palestine.

What do you think of the peace agreement signed by Arafat and Rabin in Washington?

I don't know what type of peace agreement it is when more people are killed after the signing than before. It is very difficult for my generation who have been so actively involved in seeking justice for the Palestinians to accept peace with Israel. We have been threatened by this foreign force for so long. There was a time when we did not differentiate between Jews and Arabs. When the Arabs ruled Spain for eight hundred years, the Jewish people thrived. We have always lived peacefully together. We were friends. There were many Arab Jews all over the Arab world including Palestine. Of course, it is a complex subject. It is hard to understand both sides. You cannot stay neutral. Most people are on one side or the other. I think the whole situation is one of the miseries of history. I don't believe any one people has a right to take another people's land and claim it as their own. Land taken by force is no basis for peace. Jews can live with Palestinians on Arab land, but they shouldn't have left their countries all over Europe and the United States just to come and sit in Palestine.

Is it peace on Israeli terms that bothers you?

Yes! I am the wife of a politician. I know very well what the difference is between what is declared and what is actually executed. I have paid a high price for differentiating between what is moral and what is immoral. I know most people prefer taking the more pragmatic route. It is the younger generation who is usually more idealistic and concerned about morals. My generation has learned how difficult it is to live according to one's principles. But I have a very weak case because I can't say we've succeeded. There is a very deep sorrow inside most of us. I may smile on the outside, but on the inside I feel very different. I feel disillusioned and disappointed in the Arab world. I started writing about myself to run back to my childhood and my teenage years when I was so full of aspirations and wanted to leave traces of how my generation feels and thinks.

Did you have a happy childhood?

No, my childhood wasn't happy because there was always this feeling of incompleteness. I had no father. I had no sisters or brothers. Most of those who have read my latest book have described it as being very sad. I didn't realize it was sad. I suppose it comes from feeling spent and empty. My generation didn't know what we were up against. Everything that we thought stood for something, turned out not to stand for much. Many of us spent our energy pursuing principles that were unattainable. We were very naive. We didn't know what we were up against. As Lebanese, we should have believed in ourselves; not listened to outsiders. We should have made a single entity of East and West Beirut. It is a shame to quarrel on sectarian grounds.

Was the war in Lebanon strictly a religious war?

The fighting appeared along those lines. There is a tendency for those living in West Beirut to be pro–Arab and those in East Beirut to be pro–West. Many of us who graduated from foreign schools and universities are very open minded. We are not anti–West, only against imperialism. Don't forget, my generation in Syria, Jordan, Palestine, and Iraq, grew up at a time when we had just gained our independence from France and Britain. We had a good dialogue in the beginning with the United States until we started feeling the United States had become so unfairly pro–Israel. At first, we thought it was the result of a lack of information and knowledge about the Middle East but, over time, we realized we were making lame excuses for the decisionmakers of a country which knew exactly what it was doing. I always knew that if there were enough international forces prepared to agree to stop the fighting in Lebanon, the fighting would stop, as it finally did when the Taif Agreement was signed.

Do you socialize much when you are writing a novel?

No, very little. When I wrote my book about the south of Lebanon, I went and lived in villages along the Israeli-occupied zone. I saw houses that had been occupied by three, four generations of families, just blasted away by the Israelis. I saw how poor the people are and how difficult their lives are. They have nothing! Yet, they are decent and generous. I found so much richness of feeling and depth of character in those very calm-looking people. I could never comprehend how they could endure so much misery, yet remain so serene. As hard as I tried, I could not put myself in their shoes and stay calm.

Do you think their calmness stems from a belief in fatalism?

Yes, I believe the concept of fate — what God wants is what will be — plays an important role in their lives. There is so little else to comfort them. While I was writing about the South of Lebanon, I was totally absorbed in my novel. My heroine was a woman called Im Assim [the mother of Assim]. I would call a friend and tell her I was coming over for tea, then I would find myself in the midst of writing and unable to pull myself away. I would send flowers with a note of apology saying, "Sorry, I can't leave Im Assim, today."

I remember once, just after publishing my book, my husband and I were in Europe, watching the evening news, and the broadcaster announced that there had been heavy Israeli shelling in the South of Lebanon. I looked at my husband and said, "If I were back home, at least, I could go and visit Im Assim to see if she is okay." He looked at me with a curious expression and suddenly I realized I was talking about a character I had created. It was incredible! There, for a split second, Im Assim was real. It happened so spontaneously!

Do you believe in happy endings?

No. They are generally unrealistic. If you want to be truthful, happy endings in real life rarely happen. I don't paint the world black, but I don't deceive myself either.

As the wife of a well-known Lebanese politician, do you think literature and politics make good bedfellows?

No, they don't mix well even in Lebanon although it has a strong cultural milieu. Most politicians, especially the younger ones, are not interested in art or literature. My husband is different. He is very well read in art and literature and that is what brought us together. We enjoy visiting art exhibitions together, attending concerts, and spending quiet evenings at home reading or writing.

Did cultural and literary events persist during the war?

Yes, but of course not at the same level as before. For a country at war, we had an uncommon number of cultural activities. In some strange way, the war created many new writers, poets and artists. I never dared, for instance, have a book signing because we never knew what was going to happen that day. It was that tension that made one pick up a cigarette and light it. One couldn't control one's schedule. We would say, if nothing happens on such and such a day we will meet. It was very difficult to invite a group of friends over because everyone lived in a different area and fighting would erupt in some areas and not in others.

Did you ever think the war was going to last as long as it did?

No. A lot of us are feeling the consequences now. All of a sudden it seems everybody is tired. I even hear young people complain that they are tired. I think it is because we have put up with so much for so long. Now, that we no longer have this terrible need to struggle to survive, the tension is catching up with us. Sometimes, I don't know what is wrong with me. I know from experience, when there is a crisis, I react well. But soon afterwards I fall ill.

How did you write during the fighting?

It was difficult. Normally, I cannot concentrate if there is noise of any kind around me, not even music. I wrote a whole novel by candlelight at a time when we did not have a generator for electricity. Fortunately, I don't use a computer. I believe one thinks better when writing in longhand. I know it is old-fashioned but to me the printed word is so impersonal. When I see the first copy of my manuscript in print, I am always scared to death!

Have you lived outside of Lebanon?

I had a house in the South of France and I found the French to be very welcoming and warm. They say the south of any area is more friendly than the north. I believe that. I also spent several long sojourns in Madison, Wisconsin. Nobody there knew where Lebanon was located, but they would ask: "Is that the country where that war is going on?" I was never fond of speaking about the war, but the subject would come up quite often.

Has it been difficult being a writer and raising a family?

Everyone has difficulties in life. The world has gotten so much ahead of us. It is no longer such a big deal to have a career, be married, and be a mother. I had the help of my mother as well as help inside the house. As a result, I was given a chance to explore my interests: to pursue music, writing, and a social, literary, and political life. I was very lucky to have done all the things I did. I have one son, Ramzi, and he was brought up to be independent. He earned an MBA and a degree in industrial engineering from Madison, Wisconsin, where I often visited him.

Are you at peace with yourself?

I am very conscious of the price I have had to pay to remain a genuine human being. It is not easy to achieve peace with yourself when you want to do so much. Due to circumstances beyond your control, you find your options limited and your movements restricted. Now, I am tired and it's too early to be tired.

SABAH

SINGER AND ACTRESS

Singer, movie star, consummate entertainer, Sabah is a glamorous presence to behold. "Every day I see something new in her," says her daughter Houwaida. "When I was young, I resented her fame. Now, I am in awe of all that she has accomplished." Born Jeannette Feghali on October 10, 1927, Sabah is as famous for her blonde, glamorous looks as she is for her amazing vocal cords. A legend in her time, she is considered a superstar in the Arab world.

In addition to her native Lebanese citizenship, she is a citizen of Egypt, Jordan, and the United States. Among her many honors, she has received the National Order of Senegal and the Al-Kawkab Order of Jordan.

Sabah resides in the Beirut suburb of Hazmiyeh in the penthouse of the Sabah Building, located on Sabah Street. Ringing the doorbell to her apartment, I am greeted by Sabah's dapper brother. He leads me into the drawing room. There, looking radiant in a white designer pants suit, blond hair twisted to one side, brown eyes twinkling, is Sabah, wearing long, dangling pearl earrings and bright red lipstick. By her side, stands a tall, attractive brunette, her daughter, Houwaida, who is currently starring with her mother in a musical.

Sabah's latest song, "Khatwa, Khatwa" ("Step by Step"), is currently the number one hit song on the charts in Lebanon. As we chat, a delivery man arrives bearing a magnificent bouquet of flowers accompanied by a congratulatory message from Majida El Roumi, a popular, young Lebanese singer. Sabah's delight is contagious as she admires the bouquet and reads the note aloud. In spite of a career spanning fifty years, her obvious thrill at this "beau geste" explains, in part, her continued popularity.

When asked if she is accessible to young songwriters, Sabah replies: "They come knocking at the door!" Her brother, laughing, adds, "She doesn't have an open house, she has a house without doors!" As the interview progresses, the afternoon sky darkens dramatically and a raging thunderstorm ensues. In any other setting the storm would take center stage, in Sabah's presence, it is relegated to mere background noise.

* * *

How did you become such a superstar?

I am good with people. I am always laughing and that is why the public likes me. I always wanted to be as famous as my uncle, who was a great poet. When I was seven years old, I would sing his poetry. In school, I was always asked to sing for special occasions. One day, the manager of a great Egyptian singer heard me sing and I was invited to join the singer on her tour. I began my career in Egypt, which is considered the Hollywood of the Arab world. I started in films and my very first film was a big success. I was a film star first and then I became known as a singer. To date, I have made eighty-four films, sung three thousand songs, and participated in twelve festivals, eight of which were at Baalbek.

Where does the name "Sabah" come from?

In Cairo, the producer who gave me my first film role gave me the name Sabah, which means "Morning" in Arabic. My real name is Jeanette.

Do you ever feel like just being Jeanette again?

No, I prefer being Sabah! Of course, with my family I like being Jeanette but in public I prefer Sabah. I love to perform and to be noticed. I have been singing and acting now for a very long time. I lead a very busy life. I am always

Sabah

doing films, performing on stage or television, or giving interviews.

In 1974, I saw you perform in a play at the Picadilly Theater in Beirut. You wore a long white evening gown with tiny light bulbs that lit up. It was spectacular!

You remember! [laughter] I always enjoy going the extra distance to surprise my audience. I have a certain weakness for clothes. I like original dresses and I like to leave my audience with some-thing to remember — even at the risk of being elec-trocuted!

Do you come from a musical family?

No, I am the only singer in my family. But my daughter, Houwaida, is an actress and a singer. Her father, Anwar Mancy, is a violinist. My son has followed another path. He is a well known psychiatrist and has his practice in California. I don't give my children advice anymore, they now give me advice. [laughter]

You have quite a colorful reputation when it comes to marriage. I understand you've been married ... seven times?

There are many artists who have married many more times than I, but for some reason people always dwell upon my marriages. I don't know why. I don't seem to have much luck with husbands. They become jealous and then they acquire a complex. I get tired of dealing with that and I move on. It is unbe-lievable! My family is always proud of me but my husbands are always jealous.

What attracts you to a man?

Not much these days! [laughter] I like men who encourage and support me in my work and who are frank and generous. Unfortunately, when I am mar-ried, my husband tells me: "Don't work. Don't go out. Don't do this. Don't do that." I then do just what I please and the marriage is over! I don't like to feel that I am in jail. I like my freedom and I have worked very hard for it. I have broad shoulders and a big heart, I can take a lot up to a point, then it is over. I am, what you call in your last book, "a working woman with a double shift."

How old were you when you married for the first time?

I was nineteen. My husband was older than I by twenty years. Now, I have reversed that. I married someone much younger than myself and now it is I who provide the experience! [laughter] Age really has nothing to do with how you feel. It depends entirely upon each individual.

What is your secret for always looking so fit and radiant?

I look after myself and God looks after me. I walk a lot on my treadmill, I eat carefully, and I try to get eight hours of sleep. Off stage, I am the same person you see on stage. I never change. It is something from God, believe me. I don't smoke and I rarely drink alcohol. In life you have a lot of worries, especially in my business, but I have learned to push worries aside.

How do you manage to do that?

I forget yesterday's worries, and tomorrow is very far away. I live for the moment and I live each moment to the fullest.

Do you remember the first time you were paid to perform?

Yes, I sang at the Grande Theater in the very elegant Borge area, which has now all been destroyed by the war. Before the war, it was the grandest place in Beirut. My first paid performance was for the Syndicate of Journalists. I was accompanied by one musician. I remember being a little afraid but it wasn't a problem because my desire to be a big star outweighed my fear of performing! [laughter] Everyone was very nice to me because they knew my uncle, the poet. He was called Chahrour, which is the name of a bird as well as the name of our village, Wadi Chahrour. It is the only place in Lebanon where the Chahrour bird is found. After my performance, they all called me "Chahroura." I am very proud that the people of my village have named a street in my honor. This year, I participated in two festivals to raise funds to help rebuild parts of the village that were damaged by the war. More than 60,000 people attended.

Were you in Lebanon during most of the war?

I traveled between Lebanon and Egypt, where I also have a home. I did two plays in Lebanon during the war: one with the Rahbani brothers and the other at the Casino of Lebanon. I felt very sad and insignificant during this terrible period. There is nothing more important than one's home and one's country. Without a country you are nothing. Every time this building was shelled, we would rebuild. I tried to unite the country by singing songs about Lebanon. War is so terrible. It is sad what has happened to us.

What type of childhood did you have?

I had a happy childhood. I left my village for Beirut when I was young. But it was difficult for me to sing and be an artist because my family was very strict and religious. My grandfather was a priest in our village and my father was not at all happy about my desire to become a singer, but my mother fortunately was very supportive.

So many people enjoy waking up listening to your voice on the radio, who do you enjoy listening to in the morning?

I like silence in the morning. When I don't have anything scheduled, I get up late. I like to have my cup of coffee when everything is nice and quiet.

I interviewed Fayrouz, but I avoided asking her such a question because she had a plaque on the wall that said: "I hate people who sing in the morning!"

[laughter] I like Fayrouz, she is a very good classical singer. My songs are more on the folkloric and popular side. But we both share the same astrological sign: We are both scorpions, would you believe?

There has been so much written and said about your voice, is there any one description that appeals to you most?

I like it best when the critics compare my voice to the strong, pure sound of the Chahrour bird, whose song is composed of long notes. I am especially known for singing folkloric songs and singing OHHHHHHHF in one long breath, which can last longer than a minute. No one can hold a note longer than I. It is my trademark. One man from Tripoli, Lebanon, received his Ph.D. from France by studying my voice. In Paris, they did not believe his findings because they did not think it was possible to hold a note for so long. They were not convinced until he let them hear a recording of my voice. Then, they believed him! [laughter]

How do you protect your voice?

I don't smoke and I don't drink anything cold or with ice. When I go out and it is windy, I wrap a scarf around my head.

Do you ever wear disguises so people won't recognize you?

No, never! I don't go shopping. My daughter does that for me. If I go out to buy something, I attract a crowd and my daughter says I never get my errands done! I do most of my shopping in Europe. But even, there, people are always looking at me. Sometimes they come up to me and say: "You look famous. Who are you?"

Are you happiest on stage or off stage?

I am always happy. I love life! I have learned that "when you laugh the world laughs with you and when you cry you cry alone." When I perform I am happy to perform whether I am paid or not. Making people happy makes me happy.

You have performed on so many stages, do you have a favorite?

I have many favorites: Baalbek, for one. When you look out and see the majestic ruins and the thousands of people in the audience, you feel like a queen. I also like the Olympia in Paris and the Taj Mahal Casino in Atlantic City, where once one thousand people were invited to hear me sing and six thousand showed up.

When you sing, do you look at the audience or do you look past the audience?

I look at everyone in the audience. If someone I know gets up during my performance, I will ask them later: "Where did you go?" [laughter] I have a lot of self-confidence. I am a strong woman and I like to take control of the stage.

What are some examples of the devotion shown to you by your fans?

Some fans are so overcome when I sing that they faint. One fan, when I remarried, committed suicide; another, would regularly wait twenty-four hours at a time outside my building to catch a glimpse of me.

Isn't it exhausting being glamorous all the time?

No, that's me! I always like to have my hair done and look my best. Once, I was walking in Beverly Hills, California, wearing a cape and my hair was flowing free; the drivers of several cars were looking at me instead of at the road, and they crashed into each other! The same thing happens here in Beirut!

What is it like to be Sabah all day?

[laughter] A lot of fun! I work hard at being Sabah. I am a very correct woman and I love life. I love people and every year I try to give my public something new: a song, a film or a play. I always pray before I sleep and before I sing. I have learned to be patient, to be kind to people, and to have a lot of faith in God. I am a survivor: I am Lebanese.

JULIANA SERAPHIM

PAINTER

With pigments of paint and boundless imagination, artist Juliana Seraphim has singlehandedly created a fantastic universe abounding with ethereal creatures: exotic birds; flying horses; alluring women sprouting from ripening flower blossoms — floating, prancing, cavorting, enigmatic creatures all. Art critic Helen Khal has said: "Her paintings are a gossamer world of dreams. When she took up pen and began to draw, it became almost like another kind of writing, a poetry not of words but of lines."

Seraphim's paintings are found in museums in Florence, Paris, Amman and Beirut. She has illustrated books, designed jewelry and held one-woman exhibitions of her paintings in Italy, France, Spain, England, Egypt, Kuwait, Jordan, Qatar, Syria and Lebanon.

In 1948, at age fourteen, Seraphim fled with her family from their home in Jaffa, Palestine, and took refuge in Lebanon. The eldest of four children, she attended a Catholic boarding school in Sidon, Lebanon, took business administration courses at night school, and then worked as a secretary to help support her family. She did not begin to paint until the age of twenty-four. With the aid of scholarships, she traveled to Europe and studied art in Florence, Madrid, and Paris. Her big break occurred when her drawings appeared in a French art magazine and were noticed by a New York publisher, who promptly commissioned her to execute a series of engravings to illustrate an anthology featuring the works of nine Nobel Prize winners in literature, including T.S. Eliot, Samuel Beckett, and Thomas Mann.

I met Juliana Seraphim at her apartment/atelier located on a quaint, boutique-lined street in Jounieh, Lebanon, a seaport on the Mediterranean. It was a sunny, breezy day and windows were thrown open, showcasing a medley of bright Mediterranean colors: orange-tiled roofs, azure blue sea, and vibrant green cypresses. And in the near distance, if one stopped to listen, the rhythmic sound of the surf could be heard teasing the shore. The apartment, like its owner, was intriguing. The sitting room was light and airy, accented by colorfully patterned tablecloths, well-worn oriental carpets, mother-of-pearl inlaid antique furniture and an assortment of modern sculptures. An easel set up by an open window and whitewashed walls adorned with the artist's paintings completed the room. In this setting, Seraphim, speaking in a resonant voice and wearing a flowing abaya, was very much the "sovereign woman" depicted in her paintings.

*   *   *

Who is Juliana Seraphim?

I am a woman who happens to be an artist. Being an artist gives you a certain aura. In the Orient, women artists are looked upon as eccentric. In the Occident, we are perceived the same way but to a lesser degree. [laughter] As I look at my life, how it developed, I am happy to be an artist and to have chosen art. Art for me has been all consuming. I did not come by art easily. I had to struggle within my family and then within society to be accepted as an artist. My family would have preferred a more traditional route. They would have preferred that I marry, have children, and become a housewife. But in spite of their traditional values, I am lucky I had the parents I did because they made it possible for me to become an artist.

I needed to go to Europe to study art. I went first to Florence. What an adventure! I was twenty-four. I was not a child, but it was the first time I was on my own. I started to draw by studying the great masters, visiting museums and attending art classes. I breathed art all day and, at night, I dreamed about the paintings I would paint. Bit by bit, I started to grow more confident and draw the human anatomy without following the lines of the great masters. Before I left Florence, I had an exhibition of my paintings and it was at that point that I considered myself a bona fide artist.

From the start, I was stubborn. I felt if I don't do art, what would I do with my life? I wasn't interested in marrying and raising a family. I had seen too many women suffer from marriage. I was from the world of the Orient but I came of age at a time when Occidental women were getting their liberty and freedom. I always felt this tug between myself, my art, my parents, and my surroundings. I had been exposed to a certain freedom and liberty in Europe, to a life quite different from that of a woman living in the Orient. It was always a struggle. Living in Europe, I had the values of the Orient; and in the Orient, I had the values of Europe. I finally decided to make a choice. I opted to stay in Europe and it was there that my reputation as an artist grew.

I have achieved an interesting life as an artist. After spending some twenty

Juliana Seraphim

years in Europe, I decided to return to Lebanon where once more I feel the tug of two worlds. I find women here don't enjoy the same status as women in the Occident. A woman is considered *moitie* [half], no matter what her achievements. She is still identified as the wife, daughter, sister, or mother of so and so. Bit by bit, I think, Lebanese society is beginning to recognize that a woman can have her own identity. I still feel there is a question mark regarding the status of a single woman. Everybody wants to know: "Why isn't she married? Why this? Why that?" The famous French writer, Simone de Beauvoir, one of this century's most independent women and considered by many as the first feminist, said at the end of her life: "*Le monde est male*" [the world is male]. I think that is true.

What attracted you to art?

I have always felt that I needed to communicate something deep within me; something beyond the "everyday". I tried poetry and sculpture, but neither fulfilled me. Finally, I realized I was attracted to colors. Painting satisfied my soul. It expressed all the things in me that I wanted to say about happiness, sorrow, beauty, love. It enabled me to fantasize. Art has been for me a medium of happiness and self-expression. What I have to communicate is neither social nor political. It has to do with metaphysics, the subconscious, as well as *l'inconscient collectif*. It has to do with sentimental problems and happiness. In my art, I try to reflect the feelings of the soul. With art, I don't believe that there is death. Art gives you the feeling that you are eternal on earth.

Do you fear death?

No, but I feel a need to know that something of me will endure when I am gone.

Where does your inspiration come from?

I like to be bewildered and amazed by things that I see. I like to have beautiful things around me. I am inspired by love, the sea, the sun, architecture, latticework, and anything that lives…flowers, trees, plants, vegetables. In school, the first time I heard about the Italian Renaissance, I knew I had to go and visit Florence. Subconsciously, I have been influenced by so many artists including Hieronymus Bosch and Max Ernst. For example, when I start with an empty canvas, I know what I want to do as far as the architecture is concerned; the rest comes as I work. You have to mature your idea and technique. Painting, in a way, is spontaneous but it is also studied. It's like a writer working on a book. He begins with an idea, followed by an outline and then gradually he fills in the words, sentences, paragraphs, pages, chapters and *voila*—you have a book! I never know how I am going to finish my canvas. That is why I say: When you paint, you enter a world of mystery. Every time a canvas is completed the end result is a miracle. I have never felt I have completely finished a painting because if you are striving for perfection, it is very hard to pull yourself away from the canvas. I am always very nervous when I put the final touches.

What is challenging about art?

Imposing ideas on others is challenging. Sometimes your ideas are accepted and sometimes they are not. With each painting you are introducing a unique vision to the world. A spectator viewing your canvas either loves it or hates it;

either way you affect him or her because he or she is seeing something for the first time. It is an image that doesn't change. It is there.

When you paint, are you concerned about how people will react to your art?

No. I wouldn't be able to create anything if I thought that way. When I work, my only concern is my vision and my freedom of expression. For example, I can't copy. Copying for me means I am no longer free. When I am painting, I want to be at liberty to express myself in front of my art. It is a *parcours* [a trip], as they say in French. And I don't take hash! When I paint, I take trips with my imagination into my soul. After looking at my art, an art critic once asked me: "Are you sure you don't take hash?" I told him I have never taken drugs or needed drugs because I was born "tripping"! [laughter] There is a kind of imagination that spawns an entire family of imagination.

Are you talking about "fantastic" art?

Yes. I am thinking about the school of art that gives you this liberty of imagination. The creative arts! The great master of this school was Bosch. Perhaps the first one to introduce this school was the person who created a god. He was an imaginative artist. He created a figure, a form, and adored it.

What is the motivation behind your art?

My motivation is to find God, beauty, serenity — everything that you usually don't find in life. When you live in society, it's a struggle — not only a struggle — it's a battle all day long! On the other hand, when you are with your easel, you have peace, silence, and an unfolding, exploding vision before you. I pray the 21st century will bring an end to war and that we will see another world with much more happiness and justice; a world which honors art and peace.

Having endured war, does art still hold the same importance to you?

Yes, if anything, more so! People need art. Without art, there is no civilization. What makes Italy special? What distinguishes the Renaissance? It is art! Imagine France without art! Why do people go to the Vatican? To see art. We are mesmerized by art. It gives mankind a look at another dimension and provides escape from the humdrum of existence.

How did the war affect your work?

I did a series of paintings that were inspired by the war but then I found it too hard to continue. The subject was just too emotionally draining. At the time, it was important for me to paint the war because I was preoccupied by it. It gave me a medium to vent my emotions.

How did you cope during the war years?

I spent most of the war years in Paris. But when I returned to Lebanon, I experienced two devastating years. The first time I heard shelling, I said to myself: I am going to continue working and ignore the shells. I was doing fine until several of my neighbors came banging on my door and said, "Are you foolish! Do you want to be killed?" I said, "No, I want to prove to myself that I am not afraid." It was my first war experience. Shortly, thereafter, my hands started shaking and it was impossible for me to paint.

War is frightening. As courageous as you might think you are, it is not easy to face. War is something that destroys. It destroys your mind, your nerves, your heart. It unbalances you. It is the most horrible experience I have ever had to endure. When the shelling starts, the fear of being killed combined with the fear of not knowing what is going to happen next and having nowhere to escape, is terrifying. We had so many days of intensive shelling. Sometimes you did not know whether to stand up, lay down, protect your head or protect your feet; where to hide, what to do. There was no one to raise a white flag to. There was no one in control to shout: "STOP IT!" At those moments, your heart beats fast and your pulse starts racing. The noise of the shells exploding was the most terrible thing. I became an armament expert. I could tell by the sound what kind of armament they were killing us with, and depending on which direction it was coming from, whether it was American, French or Russian-made.

You create a whole new world in your art. Is it an attempt to escape reality?

Yes, of course. The world I have created in my art is my refuge against loneliness. When I am painting, I am never lonely.

Do you find it difficult to part with your paintings?

Yes, I am very attached to my work but when I became a professional artist I understood that I had to sell my art to live. During the war, many of my paintings, photographs and much of the bibliography was destroyed. My atelier was also robbed. You might say I have lived through two wars: an internal war and an external one.

Since you live on the income generated from your art, do you feel pressured to paint what you think will sell?

I am not an amateur. There is a big difference between an amateur and a professional artist. An amateur would say, "I don't have to paint because I can rely on my spouse, my parents, et cetera." But when you become a professional artist, you rely on your art to survive, and in doing so, you develop your art. If you depend upon another source of income, you will not be forced to grow as an artist. I told that to one of my apprentices, who was thinking of becoming an art professor. I advised him against it. With art, you have to give your life over completely. Art requires a total commitment of all your time.

Do you feel that you have sacrificed, perhaps, too much for your art?

No! When people ask me that question, I feel they really don't understand what art is or the importance of art. When you love what you do, it is not a sacrifice. I would have had to make a huge sacrifice if I had to do something other than art. Art is my joy! Had it not been my joy, I certainly would have done something else. Perhaps, I would have married, had children, and so on. But that is not what I wanted. I was engaged many times, but I learned that you cannot serve God and the Devil at the same time!

Do you have any regrets?

None at all! Every day I tell myself, "God loves me!" I can devote all my time, all my thoughts, all my energy to my work. I am blessed. A woman's freedom has always been freedom from — never freedom for — work. I have freedom for work.

I've always imagined what fun it would be to be an artist and to walk incognito through an exhibition of my work! Do you do that?

Sometimes! I am very happy when I am not recognized. Sometimes, I hear them say wonderful things about my work; sometimes, they hate it. The important thing is that they are not indifferent. It is at such times that you feel you need society and society needs you. In general, society is very forgiving towards artists because we are considered outside of its sphere of influence, since we do not cling to the same value system. For example, for me, the most important value is not money but beauty. The majority of artists are poor. The values we build our life on are different from the values of most people. Sometimes, I wonder why people struggle so much to have so little. Even the very rich, by collecting our work and hanging our paintings on their walls, need us to show their wealth and affirm their position in society. Art, whether you like it or not, gives people a touch of class and it is through one's choice of art that you can judge a person's taste.

What type of mood do you prefer to be in when you paint?"

I need serenity. I need to have a certain equilibrium and peace of mind. If my hand shakes, I didn't sleep well, or I have problems — I can't paint. I used to listen to music when I worked but, now, I have the sound of the sea. When I returned to Lebanon, I realized I needed to have contact with nature. In Paris, that was not necessary because Paris is a very beautiful city and I was surrounded by beauty. Here, in Jounieh, I look out my window and I see the sea and, at night, I hear the surf pounding. I love to watch sunrises and sunsets by the sea. I have always wanted to live by the seashore and gaze at emerald mountains. Now, I have both.

How many different expressions have you gone through in your art?

I went through quite a few. I was an abstract artist, surrealist, materialist, realist, and I did calligraphy and sand technique. My current expression, fantastic art, is the result of all of my searching. This form gives me the most satisfaction. Through it, I can express myself: I can dream, I can develop, I can speak.

The women in your paintings appear to have a superior attitude. If they could talk, what language would they speak and what would they say?

(laughter) The woman I paint, today, is sophisticated and cosmopolitan. She speaks many languages and is comfortable in different cultures. By nationality, she could well be Lebanese. If she were to speak, she would probably speak in French and she would say: "I am a woman and I am complete!" I have not always painted her as a superior being. After all, she has had to struggle against men. But, I believe, women of the Arab world, even though they are still under the submission of men, are the last princesses. They are "*la femme souveraine.*"

Why do most of the women in your paintings wear masks?

Our society is very puritanical and women are not free to be what they want to be or what they are. The mask is a symbol of that. Also, it is very hard for an unmarried woman to live in the Arab world without being looked upon as an aberration.

Have you experienced discrimination as an artist?

Ironically, I find discrimination against women in the Arab world comes from women as compared to Europe where the discrimination comes mostly from men. When I was in Paris, there was a French collector who once told me that he loved my art but he was very reluctant to buy my paintings. Why? Because I was a woman!

How did you respond to that?

I told him, "I suspect you must have a very dull collection!"

What do you tell people who say your art is "too feminine"?

I tell them, "I consider that to be a compliment." I don't see why I should paint like a man. I would hate the idea of my art being described as "masculine"! In this expression [she says pointing towards a very dark, heavy-looking abstract painting hanging on the wall], that looks "very masculine". I wanted to prove that we have muscles in our mind too! But, in truth, that kind of art form is not my real sensitivity. There is a great difference between the sensitivity of a man and the sensitivity of a woman. I don't see why I should paint like a man if I am a woman.

EDUCATION

RAYMONDE ABOU

EDUCATOR

In Beirut, anyone who attended or knows someone who attended Louise Wegman College, has something positive to say about Raymonde Abou, the school's head-mistress for the past twenty-five years. All agree that she is an inspiring individual, devoted to her students, and committed to upholding the rigorous academic standards of the school. Abou is especially admired for her courage in keeping Louise Wegman open throughout the Lebanese Civil War.

The majority of Louise Wegman students attend the school from the first to the twelfth grade. As testimony to the school's excellence, many parents chose to remain in Lebanon, during the war years, rather than interrupt their children's education.

Abou's tact in dealing with errant youth is legendary. A former student (now a prominent businessman), recalled how at the age of fourteen he was caught red-handed with pages from Playboy *magazine. He was sent directly to "Miss Abou's" office where he was engaged in a discussion on the difference between sex and love. He left the head-mistress's office "a wiser, more mature person," feeling she had cared enough about him to discuss a subject his own parents had not dared delve into.*

Ringing the doorbell to Abou's apartment in Beirut, late one evening, I had a vision of being greeted by a stern, rather stout, gray-haired matron; instead, the door was opened by a slender, attractive brunette with a gentle demeanor. After refreshments were served, the interview began.

* * *

Could you tell me about yourself?

I am the youngest of four children. I was born into a Lebanese Francophile family. I have three brothers: one is a banker, another is a Jesuit educator, and the third was a musician. He was killed in a bomb explosion in Beirut in 1980. I have always loved books. I attended a French nun's school and I was often asked to teach or monitor classes when an instructor was absent. Based on that experience I decided to pursue a career in education.

You always knew you wanted to be a teacher?

Actually, I wanted to be a doctor, but the year was 1952 and my father felt it would take too long to study to become a doctor. He said, "You want to spend seven more years studying!" It was the custom in Lebanon for parents to marry their daughters young. As it turned out, it would not have made any difference. I never married. I really had a passion for both education and medicine.

I taught French for fifteen years, obtained a degree in children's education, and became head-mistress at another school. When I received an offer to work at Louise Wegman, my first reaction was: "No, I am not interested. I am content where I am and there is no reason for me to change schools." A friend, who was on the Louise Wegman school board, called and said, "I made an appointment with the president of the college. You have to come and meet with him." I said, "I don't have the time!" She insisted it would only take half-an-hour so I went. Right from the beginning, I was fascinated by the concept behind Louise Wegman. The school was newly established and they were planning to begin with a few small classes. Then every year add a class so the school would literally grow with the students. I liked the idea of seeing both the school and students grow and develop together. I am now in my twenty-fifth year at Louise Wegman! All during the war we worked very hard not to compromise the standards of the school or to fall behind. I think we succeeded. When the fighting was intense and the children couldn't come to school, we would make-up school days during vacation periods.

I understand as head-mistress, you review all the students' homework. Is that true?

Until last year, I used to do it by myself but, now, with almost fifteen hundred students, we have become too numerous. I have an assistant and we share reviewing the homework. Of course, the teachers correct the homework, but I like to review the notebooks to keep informed on the progress each student is making. Only two students this year from our graduating class didn't continue on to university: both girls married after graduating. But I was assured by the husband of one of the students that she would continue her education.

Having visited schools in the United States, how would you compare the level of education with that in Lebanon?

In 1976, I found the academic level very low in the United States as compared with our academic level. I was astonished by the lack of discipline in many of the schools. In one junior high school we visited in New York, they had smoking and nonsmoking classes! I asked the principal: "How do you decide at the age of twelve if you are a smoker or nonsmoker?" He said, "We ask the parents and they tell us." Imagine! On a more recent trip to the United States, I visited several private schools in Boston, including Milton Academy and Philips Exeter, as well as a few schools in Washington, D.C. and New York. After so many years of war, I wanted to see if Louise Wegman was on the same academic level as these fine schools. I was very pleased with the results. The only area I felt we could make improvements was in the area of extracurricular activities. I was especially impressed with the concept of debating teams.

Are you taking any special measures to prepare students for postwar Lebanon?

Yes. We are now placing more emphasis on civic duty. One of the found-

Raymonde Abou

ing principles of the college is to be national and multiconfessional. Before the war, students of mixed backgrounds attended classes together and we never had problems. During the war, we were sometimes obliged to work in small groups at various locations. When the situation improved, we returned to the old school and students from all sides attended. In 1982, when the Israelis invaded Lebanon, we rented a school which was located in the middle between both sides. We were able to stay together as one student body until 1984 at which time there was a huge battle between the militias and that was the final straw. After 1984, we were obliged to rent space from an English school in the East, in Broummana, as well as space, in Beirut, from the American Community School. As a result, we unfortunately are not as well integrated as we were once. The student body used to be fifty/fifty as far as being multiconfessional. Now, in one school, only twelve percent of the student body is Christian, and in the other school only four percent are Muslim. To counter this imbalance, we have courses open to students from both schools so they can have an opportunity to know one another better. We also attend theater and cultural events together, compete in sports, have joint field trips, week-long ski trips, and a yearly outing.

What type of contingency plan did you have for opening or closing the school during the war?

I had an understanding with the parents that if they felt the situation in their neighborhood was dangerous, they should not send their children to school. Also, we agreed that if the situation degenerated while the students were in school, the parents were not to pick up their children. I would look after them and they would sleep at school — that happened quite a few times. Once, we had to keep sixty students at school for three days.

Experiencing such situations together must have created incredible bonds between students and teachers.

Yes, very much so. We have shared a great deal together and we have learned to survive together. We often receive visits from our graduates and former students when they are in town. I have always tried to create a family atmosphere at school. I believe I have succeeded. We are all like one big family. In fact, there are many members of the same family enrolled and we now have second generations of family members as well.

Do you draw comparisons between students and their parents?

No, I make it a rule never to compare students, unless, of course, it is a positive comparison! [laughter]

How do you relax?

I go to the cinema and when I have a free week-end, I like to spend it in the mountains.

What was the worst time for you during the war?

An event that deeply marked me was an accident with a school bus full of our students. Fortunately, no one died, but there were injuries. It was the worst month of my life. We had kept the students over for two nights because of fighting between the Lebanese Army and a militia. There was a cease-fire and we decided it was okay to let the children go home. I remained at the school because there were students whose neighborhoods were still unsafe to risk a ride home. I sent out four school buses that day. One of them went over a mine planted on the road and a row of students sitting in the back of the bus were injured. Thank God, no one died. I never suffered more than when I heard one of our school buses had been hit. There were many other bad moments, but that one stands out because the children were my responsibility.

You must have been under tremendous stress. I was talking to a teacher, who was in a similar situation, and she said she took up smoking. How did you counter the stress?

By smoking. It must be an occupational hazard. I had never touched a cigarette before 1975. Every time there was an escalation in the fighting, I would think of the danger to students and teachers coming to school, and I would need a cigarette. Every time violence broke out, I would say to myself: "I am going to close the school. I am not going to go through this again!" But as soon as there was a lull in the fighting, I would think: "What is going to happen to the children? They are going to lose a year and they are going to fall behind!" I don't know where the strength would come from, but we would reopen time and time again.

How were you able to teach students who had spent the night under bombs in a shelter?

We paid close attention to the mental and physical health of the children. When we were aware that a certain neighborhood had been bombarded, the night before, we would be less demanding on the children from that area. There were a few years when the senior class could not complete their academic program. In Lebanon, seniors are required to take the government sponsored Baccalaureate Examination on a set date. Even during the worst of times, the government never changed the date of the examination. To meet that deadline, I took all the seniors along with their teachers to the mountains, where we rented a building. We were able to complete the program for the scholastic year, just in time for the seniors to take the examination. Another time, in 1989, the senior class stayed on as boarders to finish their program. The school was bombarded, so we packed and went to a hotel in Ehden, in the mountains. How we got to Ehden was amusing in hindsight but, at the time, I would not have described it in those terms!

How did you get to Ehden?

There were two ways to get there: by road, which would require passing through several road blocks and risk being shelled; or via the airport and boarding a small airplane. Ehden was an hour away by car; ten minutes by airplane. But to take the plane, we had to go to the airport, wait for the plane, and then we had to land at an airport which was a one-hour-and-a-half drive from our destination. We spent two months in Ehden. Parents would come and visit on weekends. The day before the Baccalaureate Examination, we went down to Beirut and made arrangements for the students to stay together in a hotel during the three days of the examination. We wanted to make sure they made it safely to the examination site after all their hard work. Every one of the students passed!

Traveling regularly between both your campuses, must have resulted in some perilous experiences for you.

I had two bad experiences. The first was in 1976 when all the roads and schools were closed for a month. To compensate for that lost month, we held classes in August. It was the end of the month and school personnel, who lived in Beirut, could not cross over to the East side to collect their salaries because of the fighting. Many of them desperately needed money. I decided to deliver their salaries to them. At the crossing, on the East side, I was told by the soldiers: "The fighting is very bad today, don't pass." But I insisted, and they let me go. When I reached the other side of the crossing, I was asked: "What are you coming to do?" I said, "I am going to my school," and they let me pass.

I didn't realize I was being followed. I stopped at a gas station to make a phone call to one of the teachers to ask her to gather everyone at her home so I could pay them. When I hung up the telephone, two militiamen came up and asked me: "Do you want gas?" (At the time we did not have gas in the East.) I said, "No," and I walked back to my Renault. Three other militiamen then came up to me and asked: "Who does this car belong to?" I said, "It is mine." They said, "You will come with us to our headquarters so we can confirm why you are in this area." I was calm. I thought, no problem. I was about to get into my car to follow them, when one of the militiamen said, "No, I will drive." I sat in the back seat and the other two militiamen followed in another car. We drove through neighborhoods that were unfamiliar to me. I asked the driver, "Where is your headquarters?" He said: "It is nearby. If you haven't done anything wrong, you have nothing to fear."

He stopped in a vacant lot and told me to get out of the car. I stepped out, still thinking they were taking me to their headquarters. Both cars then made a U-turn, zoomed off, and left me stranded, holding my handbag full of cash! I walked for about an hour. I didn't dare ask anyone for directions because I didn't want to arouse suspicion. Finally, I saw a taxi and I instructed the driver to take me to a friend's house. I have to tell you, the moment I entered her house and felt safe, I fainted away!

Did you ever get your car back?

My friend knew a lot of influential people in the area. She called a neighbor, who was familiar with the political situation, and he was outraged that this had happened in the neighborhood. He contacted a few people. That same afternoon, several militiamen came and asked me to take them to where I had been abandoned. Having had enough excitement for one day, I politely refused. A week later, the car was miraculously found and a finder's fee of $1,500 dollars was demanded. Initially, on principle, I refused to buy back my car. Once I had time to get used to the idea, I decided it was less expensive than buying a new car.

My second really bad experience was in 1986 when things were relatively stable except for a few occasional bombardments. The road to the museum, which was the crossing point between both sides, was open but supervised by soldiers. A friend, who was a member of the school board and who wanted to visit his mother in West Beirut, asked me if I would give him a ride when I crossed from the East to the West side. I was planning to attend a board meeting at noon in West Beirut the following day, and he joined me.

We left at eight in the morning and I dropped him off at his mother's house. Later, I picked him up at noon so we could both attend the meeting together. There was hardly any shelling that day. On the way back, we reached the museum area where the barriers were set up between both sides. There was an unusually large number of cars waiting to cross over to the East side. I had a permit to cross, so I told my friend: "I am going to see what is holding up the passage." Just as I was stepping out of the car, bombs started falling all around us. The first shell hit the car next to us and burst into flames. I yelled for my friend to get out of the car. Once out, there was no place to hide. We were in an open space. The second shell hit another car and a passerby was totally engulfed in flames. There was nowhere to go! We laid down flat against the little indentation between the road and the sidewalk. At that moment, another shell hit and a piece of shrapnel entered my back. It was not a grave injury, but it felt like a red-hot knife had penetrated my body.

When there was a break in the shelling, I was helped into a little, dilapidated room. Eventually, we made our way down some alleys to the house of the same friend I had gone to earlier when my car had been stolen. We rested at her place, for a couple of hours, and then we returned to the car and found two Syrian soldiers trying to get the engine started. I said, "What are you doing in my car?" They got out and demanded, "Why didn't you leave your keys? Your car is blocking the road and we were trying to drive it to the side." I said, "Who is it blocking?" We were the only ones there! They shrugged and I noticed items I had left in the back seat were missing, but I didn't feel like arguing. I just wanted to get into the car and drive home.

After all you have been through, do you wish to live elsewhere?

Absolutely not! In Lebanon we are allowed to have dual citizenship. Before I was given my French citizenship, the French official asked me: "If you had to give up one of your nationalities, which one would you give up?" I said, "The French, of course!" In spite of that response, they gave me French citizenship! I think that answers your question.

LEILA BADRE

ARCHAEOLOGIST AND MUSEUM CURATOR

"Moving along from one unexpected project to another is what makes life interesting," says Leila Badre, archaeologist, professor of ancient history, excavation leader, and curator of the American University of Beirut Archaeological Museum.

A noted expert in terra cotta figurines, Badre received her B.A. in ancient history from the American University of Beirut (AUB) and her M.A. in archaeology. In 1976, she earned a Ph.D. in archaeology from the Sorbonne. As curator of the AUB Museum, since 1979, Badre has made the museum an integral part of the community by creating the Society of the Friends of the Museum, which sponsors educational activities for adults and children.

Badre, author of Terra Cotta Human Figurines of the Bronze Age in Syria, *has led excavations in Lebanon, Syria, Dubai, and Yemen. She is a frequent participant in international conferences and has organized archaeological exhibitions in Beirut and joined international ones in Brussels, Luxembourg, and Venice. In 1988, she addressed a symposium on the Heritage of Tyre, held at the Smithsonian Institution in Washington, D.C.*

I met Leila Badre, a crisp, athletic woman, with the alert demeanor of one accustomed to sifting through cryptic clues — and finding answers — at her museum office brimming with books, maps, and artifacts. She had just returned from an afternoon spent supervising an excavation in downtown Beirut.

*   *   *

How is your excavation progressing?

It's pure excitement! We are, now, searching for Phoenician Beirut and the famous law school in downtown Beirut. The site, where we work, is in a part of town we would never have dreamed of having the chance to excavate before the war. It is now uninhabited: buildings lie in ruins and vegetation grows wild in the streets. The irony is, without the war, we wouldn't have had this unique opportunity to dig in the center of the city.

In your wildest fantasies, what would you like to uncover in this dig?

[laughter] Phoenician Beirut! We shall dig in the central part of the city as deep as bedrock, which is about fifteen meters below the surface. As yet, we don't know how deep the Phoenician level is. I am looking for the Phoenician stratum of Beirut that has never been reached. The goal of every dig, of course, is to seek answers through hard evidence. Beirut, until our discovery, was totally unknown in Phoenician history. It was never mentioned with the other Phoenician cities in the ancient texts.

How does delving into the past affect your outlook and feelings towards your country?

It is good to know that the people who have occupied this land have always been clever, enterprising people, with a great deal of initiative. They revered, not only wealth, but learning and enjoyed acquiring and spreading knowledge. I am proud of all civilizations which possess a rich heritage. A people anchored to a past, I believe, have a great deal more depth by way of culture and tradition. It is true that in Lebanon, wars have come and gone, but the culture has always survived. I feel badly for those who don't have a heritage to claim. I often tease my American friends about their young history and lack of traditions compared to us.

What was your rationale for keeping the museum open during the war?

We kept it open out of a sense of duty and a refusal to stop living. I thought it was important to keep it operating because people needed to visit the museum more than ever before. More than ever, Lebanese needed to feel close and related to their roots. It was the only museum that was open in the entire country — the only place where cultural activities were ongoing.

You must have experienced Kafkaesque thoughts protecting ancient artifacts when everything around you was being transformed into modern-day artifacts. How did you deal with that?

You will be surprised! People never had a greater desire to know more about their past than during the war. The war sparked a need for people to know about

Leila Badre

their heritage and roots. Each confession, because it was a confessional war, went deep into their origins wanting to know more about their history. The museum played a vital role in establishing a link with the past and provided hope for the future. Admittedly, I felt a certain irony coming to work during the middle of the war when we did not know whether we would survive until the next day or not. It so happened that at about that time, I received an invitation to travel to Venice to join a Phoenician exhibition. They wanted me to bring along some valuable Phoenician artifacts from our museum. As I catalogued and prepared the objects to accompany me to the exhibition in Venice, I became very concerned about the risk of transporting the objects out of Lebanon. I had sleepless nights thinking I could be stopped and robbed on the way to the airport. I did not take the artifacts out of the museum until I was assured I would be given both military and militia escorts all the way to the plane and that I would be allowed to personally supervise the loading of the artifacts.

From the moment the pieces left the museum, to the moment the last one was loaded into the plane's cargo hold, they never left my sight. I even checked my luggage in, the day before, so I wouldn't be distracted. I couldn't relax until we reached the first leg of the journey, Brussels, where they had special security in place to insure the safe transportation of cultural artifacts. It was at that moment that it occurred to me that if I was so tense and concerned for the safety of artifacts, how did my friends feel when they sent their children to school and heard shells exploding in the streets!

When you graduated from AUB with a B.A. in ancient history, did you think that you would one day become a museum curator?

Not in my wildest dreams! I had no thoughts about a career. As a matter of fact, I enjoyed archaeology, but I had no idea what I was going to be. There were no Lebanese women archaeologists to serve as role models. I had a B.A. and I felt that I hadn't really mastered anything at that level so I continued and earned an M.A. I started work on my Master's with no idea what I was going to do with it. I thought I would marry and raise a family as was expected of an Oriental woman of my generation. I wasn't raised to think about a career. In fact, I am the first career woman in my family.

Tell me about your background.

I am a third daughter in a family of four children. My brother is the youngest. I was not a very wanted child being a third daughter! [laughter] To make matters worse, I am the middle child between a brother and sister with very high IQs. I always felt I had to work very hard to keep up with them. My brother is a brilliant computer expert. He is one of the rare foreign polytechnicians of his generation graduated from France. My sister was an economist but she abandoned her career when she married.

When I attended school, I studied to be an educated person; not to prepare myself for a career. When I decided to major in archaeology, I discussed it with my father and he thought it wasn't a "woman's field". So I went into political science, which I figured would provide me with the broadest general culture. I soon discovered I hated politics and that the first semester of political science consists of philosophy and economic courses — neither of which I was particularly partial to! It just so happened a French princess, Isabelle de France, came to visit Lebanon. My uncle, Gabriel Saade, a historian and amature archaeologist, was asked to accompany her to some archaeological sites in Syria and he invited me to join them. The experience was an eye-opener. During four days, we had an excellent guided-tour of coastal and north-west Syrian sites. It made me realize how much more I enjoyed archaeology in comparison to what I was studying. When we returned, I discussed it with my father and he said, "Okay, do what you want." So I switched my major to ancient history.

Did you ever feel that you were passed over or discriminated against because you are a woman?

No. Personally, I've never felt that. I do realize that when there is a job opening and a man and a woman are competing for the same job, the preference usually goes to the man. Recently, I was at a university board of trustees meeting and out of forty people in the room, I was the only woman. I hadn't even noticed that until the president of the university made that observation. I guess I am gender blind or I have thick skin! On the other hand, I believe the field of archaeology is being taken over by women. If you visit our excavation site in downtown Beirut, you will find that at least ninety percent of the staff is composed of women. I feel women play a very important role in our society behind the scenes. Women are the real leaders. Ours is a matriarchal society whether men like it or not. Some women don't realize this, but the smart ones do! [laughter]

How did you select the topic of your M.A. thesis?

I chose my subject as a result of finding a terra cotta figurine as I was walking and prospecting a site with my uncle, Gabriel Saade. I was intrigued by it and I asked him, "How do you date such a figurine?" He said, "I don't know. Why don't you find out?" I went to the library and there was nothing on the subject. I informed my advisor I was going to do research on figurines and I became so involved I made it the subject of my M.A. thesis. It was my good fortune, just when I finished writing my thesis, in 1980, excavation sites in northern Syria (in the Euphrates), yielded thousands of figurines. I decided to develop this subject for a Ph.D. thesis, which I presented at the Sorbonne. I became "the expert" in a field no one had done any research in. My thesis was published in France and it became a reference book.

What motivated you to spend five years at the Sorbonne pursuing a Ph.D. in archaeology?

I am French educated. It was a matter of *joie d'utile à l'agréable*. I enjoyed doing research and traveling to museums and excavation sites around the world. In my quest to study figurines, the more I traveled, the more interesting my subject became. I didn't spend five straight years at the Sorbonne! While working on my Ph.D., I also had a job at AUB as a research assistant. I was enjoying life tremendously. I was based in Beirut, traveling constantly, and just beginning to excavate.

My first excavation was in 1970, and I have been digging ever since! Typically, I would be involved in several campaigns a year. I would finish a dig on the coast of Lebanon, go to the Bekaa Valley, and then later fly off to a third destination, Dubai. I was in demand! There were not many archaeologists around. For example, when Dr. J. B. Pritchard came from Pennsylvania as a visiting professor to AUB and decided to do an excavation at Sarafand, a Phoenician site, he asked me to join his team. It was a real honor! After I excavated with Pritchard, I joined my predecessor, Dr. Dimitri Baramki, the former curator of this museum, and one of the rare archaeologists in the Middle East to excavate a site in the Emirates. Out of the blue, he had received a telex from Dubai stating they had just discovered ruins; could he come. It is these unexpected discoveries that make life interesting as an archaeologist.

As the curator of the American University of Beirut Archaeological Museum, what is your goal for the museum?

My goal is to have the museum play a more active role in the community. I founded The Society of the Friends of the Museum for that purpose. It has served to bring together all the people who are interested in archaeology. Some of our more popular activities, include lectures, excavations and trips to historical sites, as well as organizing activities for children such as: showing them how papyrus was made, how to write their names in Phoenician alphabet on clay tablets, and how to make mosaics. I am very proud of creating a special museum program for the visually handicapped, where we explain and describe the artifacts and let them touch them. It is a wonderfully moving experience to awaken an excitement in archaeology in those who can't see.

In your archeological digs, what have you uncovered that has really excited you?

Each excavation has its own excitement. Once, while excavating in Sarafand with Pritchard, I found a seal. It bore the name of the site: Sarepta, which is the Phoenician translation of Sarafand. The seal provided undisputable evidence that Sarafand was a Phoenician site! Thank God, the importance of my find did not hit me right away. First, we had to clean the seal and then work on deciphering it. Its significance came in stages; otherwise, I would have had a heart attack on the spot! Recently, the most exciting and rewarding experience was discovering Canaanite and Phoenician Beirut, adding new pages to the history of the city.

MARIAM GHANDOUR

UNIVERSITY COUNSELOR

Mariam Ghandour heads up the Counseling Department at the American University of Beirut (AUB). As she strolls across campus, Ghandour is clearly at home, having spent years at AUB as a student and faculty member. Ghandour received Bachelor and Master's degrees in psychology, from AUB, and a Ph.D. in counseling psychology from Columbia University.

A faculty instructor in psychology, she was appointed to the Education Department where she is currently conducting research on the effects of the civil war on Lebanese society. When not counseling students, Ghandour can be found in her office with a coterie of graduate students, reviewing student questionnaires and assimilating data for her many research projects.

The mother of three children, she exudes a certain largesse and the relaxed, easy rapport of a good listener. Ghandour is married to Judge Abdel Basset Ghandour, president of Lebanon's Judiciary Inspection Council. She enjoys swimming, skiing and horseback riding.

*   *   *

Mariam Ghandour

Could you tell me about yourself?

I married when I was a sophomore in college and I had my children when I was still in school. I was a pre-med student. I loved biology and chemistry, but my husband thought it would not be practical to raise a family and pursue medical studies so I shifted my major to psychology. I worked hard to stay on top of my studies and, at the same time, be an involved mother. In raising children, I believe there is no substitute for a mother's love and attention. My afternoons were reserved for the children. We would play, go out together, and I would supervise their homework. My husband was fully occupied in his job and I felt managing the children's activities was a mother's responsibility. We cannot change that role no matter how much we insist on equality! Along the way, I earned two bachelor degrees, a teaching diploma in elementary education as well as a diploma to teach English as a foreign language, and a Master's in counseling psychology. Later, when my three children were older, I had the unique opportunity to pursue a Ph.D. at Columbia University.

Did your husband support your decision to continue your studies?

Yes, he realized it was a golden opportunity and he and the children encouraged me to go. AUB had offered to pay for everything: books, tuition, travel, room and board. But even though I knew my husband and my sister would take very good care of the children, and I had a nanny who had been with us since the children were born — I was, still, very reluctant to leave. When I left, in 1987, the situation was calm but shortly thereafter, from 1987 to 1990, the cruelest fighting of the civil war began. My daughter was thirteen-years-old and my boys were sixteen and nineteen. I went to the States for one semester and then returned to Beirut and brought the children back with me to New York. My husband and I decided it was best to take the children out of Lebanon. My daughter stayed with me at Columbia University and my two sons went on to Canada to attend college.

What was it like for you to be on your own in the States as a full-time student?

I had married young and I had never lived alone before. It gave me a chance to evaluate what I had achieved in life. To ask myself: Is this what I really want to do? Am I going in the right direction? I really enjoyed learning. I jumped at the opportunity to attend conferences in my field all over the United States. It gave me enormous satisfaction. I was honored to be among the first to be selected among the AUB faculty to be sent to the States. But leaving my husband and children to pursue my education was something that was just not done. I was torn. I was encouraged by some and criticized by others. They would say: "At her age she wants to go and pursue her education!" I was thirty-nine then. I am now forty-five. To be divorced and pursue your education was fine, but to be in your late thirties, married with children, and still want to continue your education — that was another story! Everyone was stunned and surprised. They would say: "How could Judge Ghandour accept this?" We were a great source of interest for the gossip mill!

Beside worrying about leaving my family, I wondered: "How am I going to fit in as a student? Will I be able to follow class discussions? Can I get high enough marks to continue in the Ph.D. program? Will I be the oldest in the class?" The first night I arrived in New York, I couldn't sleep. The next day was the first day of the academic year and I was so eager to go to class and meet the other students. Much to my surprise, I discovered I was not the oldest! There were students in their fifties, sixties and even seventies attending my class! I later learned that the average age for a Ph.D. student at Columbia was forty-three and at Harvard, it was forty-seven.

What have you learned that has made a difference in your life?

I live my life according to the belief that there is no problem love cannot surmount. I have learned that there is nothing in life worth being anxious or stressed out about. Conflicts are a two-way street and should be quickly resolved. I always give people the benefit of the doubt. If someone is rude, I generally attribute it to stress. I try not to perceive it as being directed towards me personally. I often approach the person and try to discover what is bothering him or her and inquire how I can help. My hunch is that culture has a lot to do with the way people behave. In Lebanon, people tend to be a bit more impulsive.

What drew you to the field of counseling psychology?

I enjoy counseling psychology because it is clinically-oriented and reminds me of my first love: medicine. It combines theory and practice and gives you the opportunity to teach at the same time. My focus is children and adolescents because adolescence is a very stressful period. I also had the advantage of having children of my own. My house was my laboratory all through my studies. Everything that I read or learned, I would apply at home: whether it was classical conditioning, social learning theory or dream analysis.

Who has had the greatest influence on you?

My parents. They brought me up to be very sure of myself and instilled in me a lot of confidence. They had five children. I was the youngest and they had high expectations for me. I was on the honor roll and always aspired to be the first in my class. If I wasn't, I would get very upset. My father, in fact, would placate me by saying: "If you don't get the highest grade, I will give you money!" [laughter] I always had this desire to be a high achiever.

As head of the Counseling Department at AUB, what are the most common complaints among AUB students?

When I was sent to the United States to get a Ph.D., my mission was to return and establish a counseling center that would deal with the academic and psychological problems of students. In many instances, academic problems are related to emotional problems and lack of self-esteem. We deal with a range of issues including, study habits, school absences, time management, test anxiety, phobias, lack of assertiveness and depression. I teach students relaxation techniques such as cognitive reinstruction, whereby you tell yourself: "Today, I feel strong and energetic. I feel invincible!" And things as simple as inhaling and exhaling.

When we started the center, we sent flyers to all 5000 students at the Faculty of Arts and Sciences, informing them that we are here with peer counselors to talk to students about anything that is bothering them. We advise students who are on academic probation, which represents about ten percent of the students. I believe academic achievement and self-esteem are highly correlated. Stress is the main problem that we deal with. Before, stress was academic related, now, it is more related to finances. For the men, especially, money is a tough issue. As a result of the devaluation of the Lebanese pound, students don't know how they are going to pay for their tuition and books. I also deal with substance abuse. With women the overall problem is largely a lack of assertiveness. I thought I would be seeing a lot more female students than male students; instead, it's just the opposite.

Has it been difficult being a female academician in Lebanon?

Oh yes! After returning with my Ph.D., I remember a prominent faculty member telling me and a few other women present: "You are very well known in society, you belong to committees and social organizations, why don't you just work part-time? Why the hell do you want to go into research and do all that hard work? Why do you want to attend seminars? Why don't you go and have fun and enjoy yourselves?"

I would never think of saying something like that to a man, yet some men have no problem talking that way to a woman. I feel I have to prove myself every time I am selected to be on a committee as the only woman. I always have the feeling that the other members on the committee are wondering: "Who is this woman? Why is she here?" I was recently asked to be a member of the selection committee to select candidates for our diplomatic corps. There were fifteen of us and I was the only woman on the committee; yet, there were an almost equal amount of male and female candidates to be interviewed!

What changes would you like to see occur in Lebanese society?

I would like to see more women given the opportunity to fulfill their dreams. Unfortunately many of my friends who received their B.A. and B.S. degrees are now sitting at home having morning coffee, afternoon tea, complaining of psychosomatic problems, ulcers and migraines. They are not fulfilling themselves as human beings and as a result many feel lonely and depressed. I believe a woman should be free to choose whether she wants to be a mother, wife, career woman, or all three. I want women to have control over their lives. Being tough and feminine should not be considered contradictory. I also believe, if a woman chooses to have a family, she should not sacrifice her family for a career. What is the use of being a prominent career woman if one is a failure as a mother?

How did you manage to do both?

It had everything to do with timing. If the opportunity to earn a Ph.D. presented itself when my children were young, I would never have pursued it.

What was your worst experience during the war?

One of my worst experiences happened one day as I was picking my children from school. The shelling started and we had to jump out of the car and run into a nearby building. As we waited, the shelling progressively became more intense. We were stuck there for three days. Buildings were being hit all around us and there were many casualties. I couldn't get a message to my husband. Finally, a militiaman, who knew my husband, was passing by and I stopped him and asked if he could take us home. He said, "Pray and we will see." I gathered the children in my arms and prayed if anything were to happen it would happen to me alone.

What is the driving force in your life today?

For me, it is a luxury to teach and to continue to learn. The more I learn, the more I feel I don't know. Now, I am into research and I have become a research addict. Every day we have a new topic we want to research. It is a continuous challenge. If I have the chance to travel and pursue another Ph.D., I would do it again.

When you travel outside of Lebanon and people learn you are Lebanese, what is their general reaction?

When I arrived in New York, I was met by a welcoming committee from Columbia University. The first question I was asked (I suppose because of my blond hair and blue eyes) was: "Are you sure you are Lebanese and not German or Swedish?" Then they asked, "How come you speak English?" I told them,

"Almost everyone in Lebanon speaks English and many of us are trilingual: We speak Arabic, French and English." They touched my suit jacket and inquired, "Where did you buy your suit?" I said, "I bought it in Lebanon and it is made in Lebanon." They said, "You have clothes like this in Lebanon?" They showered me with questions. "Are you divorced? How did your husband let you come by yourself?" They were simply astonished that I was Lebanese. I don't know what they had expected!

NAJLA HAMADEH

PROFESSOR OF PHILOSOPHY

Najla Hamadeh, descendant of distinguished Lebanese family, is professor of philosophy at the American University of Beirut (AUB). Her grandfather, Ahmad el Asaad; her uncle, Kamal el Asaad; and her father, Sabri Hamadeh, were all prominent Shiite Muslim leaders.

Hamadeh received her Bachelor and Master of Arts degrees in philosophy, from AUB, and her Ph.D., from Georgetown University. She teaches a wide variety of courses at AUB, including ancient culture, Medieval and Renaissance works, modern philosophical texts, and contemporary works of fiction with a special focus on the rights of women. She began her teaching career at Ahlia College for Girls, where she taught logic and ethic courses.

Hamadeh, has published numerous articles; lectured on Socrates, Descartes, Kant, Marx, Hegel and Freud; and conducted graduate seminars on Existentialism and the Philosophy of Psychoanalysis. She has also worked as a translator, journalist, and an art critic (writing under the pen name, "Salwa Baaklini").

The mother of three grown children, Hamadeh, a winsome green-eyed brunette, married to the scion of a prominent Lebanese family, can still easily be mistaken for a graduate student. We met in her sunny duplex apartment in Beirut, with its open view of the Mediterranean Sea.

*   *   *

Can you tell me about yourself?
I come from a conservative family. My father was in politics, which made us quite conspicuous in public. Consequently, we had to observe traditions even more than usual. My childhood and teenage years were very restricted in many ways. My parents were traditional, not highly educated, but very rational people.

Najla Hamadeh (left) with the author.

My father had been married before and he had two children from a previous marriage but, for my mother, I was her first born. As a child, I began talking very early. My parents, it seemed, expected a lot from me. I was the center of a lot of attention. They thought I was very intelligent. At the age of one-and-a-half, I was memorizing and reciting verses. As I grew older, I started thinking about my future prospects. I thought I was probably never going to get married because my family did not allow women to marry outside the family. (As it happened, I was the first to do so.) I thought very possibly, I was not going to be allowed to work because of my family's conservatism. Moreover, although my father was not a rich man, girls, according to our tradition, do not inherit. So I had a bleak future to look forward to. I realized the only thing that could help me was a good education.

I was always fond of literature, languages, and nice expressions. I read all the time because, besides being traditional, my mother was very protective and did not allow us to go outside and play with other children. Fortunately, there were five of us and we were all born within a period of seven years. So we had each other as playmates. I couldn't swim, ski, or play tennis — those sports were considered modern activities that a traditional girl should not indulge in, but my parents did allow me to go riding. I took ballet and piano lessons and did what I could within the limitations set for me. My main activity was reading. I read all the time. From a very tender age, my dream was to become a writer. I always got goose pimples whenever I read something beautiful. In school, I did well in the basic subjects, but I was not a very conventional student. With the exception of math and language courses, which I enjoyed, I often skipped classes.

The school I attended provided instruction in Arabic and French, the first two years, and thereafter English was added as a third language to the curriculum. The school's educational philosophy was wonderful because there wasn't much emphasis on grades. It wasn't a traditional girls education at all. The school was called Ahlia. Most of the girls in our society, who later achieved in life, were Ahlia graduates. Our teachers encouraged us and did a lot to make us feel that, even as girls, we were human beings with something important to contribute to society.

Was that different from the way you were brought up to feel at home?

No, not really. At home, there were a lot of restrictions placed on us concerning things with sexual overtones, such as: the clothes we wore, who we spoke with, who we went out with. But, at the same time, my parents were very open-minded. They believed a girl who gets married early is one who has no other prospects. But, at times, I felt their attitude wasn't realistic because if you don't marry, are not allowed to work, and can't go out, what can you do? Nothing! There was a discrepancy between what they believed and what they thought their traditional milieu would accept. Fortunately, more often than not, I could convince my father to see things my way. Unlike most traditional families, my parents were willing to listen to what we had to say. My mother was very young when she married. She had five children by the age of twenty-three and thereafter she had three boys — one every five years. All together we are eight: five boys and three girls. Next to me in age is my brother, Nadi, a former minister of education.

Was there a discrepancy between the way girls and boys were treated in your family?

Yes and no. My upbringing wasn't a conventional one in a traditional sense. I was given a lot of attention and respect because I was considered very smart. Moreover, my grandparents doted on me. I had, for example, much more pocket money than did my brother! My parents raised their girls to feel protective towards our brothers. As the eldest, I still feel very protective towards all my siblings, but especially my brothers. I think in our society, sisters, in general, are brought up that way. We have the same feelings for our brothers as we have for our own children. We want to help them succeed. The source of this identification is due to the Arab way of identifying with one's family. The boy is the one who carries the family name and therefore the continuity of your family is dependent on your brother and his children. That is why we feel very protective about the men in the family. I think, as a result, we suffer in our society from the lack of male responsibility because they have it too easy! Very often, women in the family are much more responsible. They carry the heavier burden in many ways. This was especially noticeable during the war years.

How old were you when you married?

I was twenty-one; by twenty-three I had two small children. I didn't waste time! I made one of those decisions, one makes in childhood, that were I to have children, I was going to have them when I was young or not at all. My father was very old to be our father. He was eight years older than my maternal grandfather. I felt this was unfair to us as children. I thought it would have been much nicer if my father were younger. Consequently, I didn't want to have a big age difference between myself and my children. Another decision I made when I was about six or seven years old was not to ever be in my mother's situation. Every morning, my father would go to work, we would go to school, and my mother would be left alone to take care of a messy house, still wearing her robe. I used to feel so sorry for her. We were going out to explore the world, meet new people, have new experiences and she was left behind to fix a messy house. I always told myself never ever get caught in that situation.

There must be days, now, when you wish you could stay at home in your robe!

No, not really! [laughter] I experienced that lifestyle the first three years of my marriage. I wasn't doing anything except a few movie script translations which I worked on at home to earn some money. I felt dead. I was so unhappy, I lost a lot of weight. I didn't even have the desire to enjoy music or nature. I felt life had passed me by. When I started working and using my mind again everything changed. I was in seventh heaven!

Who were your role models?

I very much admired my grandmother. She was a very special person. She came from a traditional family, yet indulged in politics. She was a political leader and was known as the "man" behind my grandfather and my uncle. My grandfather, Ahmad el Asaad, was a very popular political leader. He was speaker of parliament and minister of public affairs for many years. My uncle, Kamal el Asaad, followed his father as speaker of parliament. My family is very much a political family and my grandmother, in many ways, was the one running the show. She is known as Im Kamal; much has been written about her. Although she wasn't educated, she was very intelligent and had a magnetic personality. When I was growing up, my grandmother could convince me about almost anything. It was only after I would leave her presence that I would stop and wonder: "Is that the way I really think?" [laughter]

From her I learned that a person's worth is not determined by wealth, rank or family. What is important is the individual. She would often say: "No one but yourself can take away your honor." Also, she wasn't conventional in the least. She rarely visited anyone! Nevertheless, people constantly came to seek her out. She would hold animated political discussions and converse about world figures, literature, poetry (which she wrote) and religion. She very much had her own point of view and was very avant-garde. For example, she wouldn't wear a veil; instead, she would ask the men to lower their eyes and look at the ground when they spoke to her!

I also had a wonderful teacher, Hoda Baroody, who died young. I was deeply affected by her death. She was my English teacher, a fantastic woman with a very refined taste in literature. While teaching us English, she also taught us how to think, how to express ourselves, and tidied up our minds for calculus and physics. When I reminisce with my classmates, she is the one who clearly stands out among our teachers as having had the greatest impact on us.

I understand you are writing a novel?

Yes, I have a French publisher but the novel is being written in English. When it is completed, it will be translated into French. It is about the relationship, in this past century, between peasants and feudal lords in Lebanon. I have access to a lot of material on this subject because my family, on both sides, were feudal lords as were my husband's. I am trying to capture how things were and weave it into a story.

Why did you choose philosophy as a course of study?

Because I had so many questions! I was hoping the study of philosophy would answer, at least, some of them. But, in studying philosophy, I discovered it only multiplies the questions you have. At one point, I was planning to change my major, but an American philosopher, Henry Johnston, whom I admire very much, came as a visiting professor to AUB and his outlook regarding philosophy convinced me to continue working on my Master's. He viewed philosophy as simply being a skill in argumentation. I liked that. I thought that people who thought philosophy had an impact on life and on the comprehension of issues were stretching it.

Which of the philosophers do you particularly identify with?

I have great admiration for Hegel whom I teach. I like the Existentialists. At one point, Kierkegaard, had a great impact on me. I was enchanted by him. I skipped a lot of classes in my junior year sitting in the library reading Kierkegaard and it was through him that I regained my faith. I like Nietzsche, too. I teach Nietzsche and I became interested in philosophers who deal with psychoanalysis. The philosophy of the mind: what motivates man, what is behind our actions — fascinates me. I did my Masters in analytic logic. When I was studying for my Ph.D., I became more interested in things that have to do with life and less interested in abstract subjects. My Ph.D. was on Freud's theory and Lacan's interpretation of the death instinct.

Circumstances took me to Washington, D.C. where I pursued my Ph.D. at Georgetown University. The war was in full swing in 1976 and my father had just passed away. I was very depressed. My husband, whose work often took him abroad, wanted us to leave Beirut, but I didn't want to go. He played a trick on me. One day, he said: "Why don't you go and visit your friend in Washington, D.C., for just a couple of weeks." I said, "Okay, if you stay with the children." I left and shortly thereafter he packed and followed me with the children. Since I was in Washington, even though my first priority was to be a writer, I thought, why not continue my education. (Some people have an affinity for following the tougher path rather than the more natural one. I think I am one of those people!) At first, I wasn't very enthusiastic about devoting so many years of my life to academia. Looking back, it seems that circumstances always pushed me in the direction of academia in spite of myself. I wasn't lucky when I went

in the direction of my first choice: writing. For example, I worked as a journalist and as an art critic in 1973 and 1974. I loved my job but, unfortunately, the
magazine I worked for folded up and then the war broke out. I really do believe
that we are not the engineers of our destiny. Circumstances push you in directions you have no control over, especially if you are tied to a family and have
the responsibility of raising children.

*When you were living in the United States, what was the general reaction of
people when you told them you came from Lebanon?*

Some people reacted in a way that wasn't complimentary to themselves.
For example, they would ask: "Are your children experiencing culture-shock
seeing women unveiled in the streets?" They really had no idea what Lebanon is
like! This was asked of me by some seemingly well-educated people. The first
time I went to see a professor, who eventually was to become my mentor, he
asked me: "Where do you come from?" I said, "I am Lebanese." His next set of
questions were quite baffling. He asked: "Why aren't you short?" I told him,
"Who told you Lebanese are midgets?" He said: "Well, maybe your complexion
is different." I said, "What do you mean?" He replied, "You are not dark." I said,
"I happen to be one of the darker Lebanese!" It was a rather extraordinary
exchange!

Living in the States, in many ways, was very broadening. The other day, I
was analyzing that experience with my daughter. The America I knew, before
living there, was the one I saw in movies. I went there expecting reality to be
different but, strangely enough, I found it to be very much like the movies!

NINA JIDEJIAN

HISTORIAN AND AUTHOR

*In a quest to preserve history, historian Nina Jidejian has written four-
teen books on Lebanon, including six books in the series,* Through the Ages,
covering: Byblos, Tyre, Sidon, Beirut, Tripoli, *and* Baalbek-Hiliopolis. *Other
books include:* The Story of Lebanon in Pictures, Lebanon: Its Gods, Leg-
ends & Myths, Lebanon and the Greek World, *and four volumes in the
series* I Love Lebanon. *Her books have been translated in French and can be
found in libraries and bookstores around the world.*

*Jidejian has lectured on Lebanon, far and wide, including at Amherst
College in Massachusetts and the Cosmopolitan Club in New York. She is a
founding member of the Baalbek International Festival, a former president
of the Festival of Anjar, and an active member of the Association of Friends
of the National Museum of Beirut, where she is engaged in restoring the
museum back to its prewar condition.*

Married to the late Dr. Yervant Jidejian, a prominent Lebanese surgeon who died in 1989, Jidejian has a grown daughter and lives in a lovely villa surrounded by pine trees, overlooking Beirut. The interview took place on a patio flanked by arabesque arches at her home in the Beirut suburb of Yarze. Her German shepherd, Major, lying protectively nearby, kept a watchful eye.

* * *

What is it about Lebanon that inspired you to become a historian?

Seven thousand years of history in one very small area makes this country quite unique. I wanted to write about this area because it is so very rich in history and archaeology. You have the coastal strip, a commercial route, where ancient people crossed from East to West and armies passed by on their way to conquests from Egypt up towards the Hittites. There was constant activity. Lebanon was situated on the central highway of the ancient world. So much happened here! Conquerors came and conquerors went. What was amazing to me was that the ancient Lebanese always survived. Despite the fact that they were attacked and their cities burned, new cities would always spring up again. The people were extraordinarily resilient and it was this indomitable spirit that so fascinated me. Moreover, the ancient Phoenicians were not only resilient but courageous as well. They sailed at night navigating by the stars. They would come into a port, display their wares on the beach, and then alert the town to their arrival by lighting a bonfire and setting off smoke signals. When the town's folks arrived, the merchants would retire to their vessels and give the people a chance to view the merchandise at their leisure. Consequently, they were liked and trusted wherever they went.

The first book you published was in 1968 and it was on the city of Byblos. What sparked your interest in Byblos?

Byblos was the topic of my M.A. thesis. I had a wonderful advisor, Dr. John Pairman Brown, and he told me: "Byblos has been escavated by the French but there is nothing that the public can read on Byblos except the escavation reports which are too technical. Why don't you write something on its rituals, the archaeological evidence, and limit it to the first millennium?" About the same time, I also had the privilege of meeting Professor James B. Pritchard, the curator of the University of Pennsylvania Museum. He read my thesis and encouraged me to expand upon it and get it published. I asked him, "Who would want to read this material?" He said: "Do it, and you will see."

I rewrote my thesis and then I went to Dar Al Mashreq, a Jesuit publishing house. As luck would have it, the Jesuits were looking for a series of books in English on Lebanese archaeological sites. After my book on Byblos came out, they asked me to write a book on Tyre. So the next year, I wrote about Tyre, and so on. I would publish a book every other year. I typed everything myself on my Royal typewriter. I would start writing a new book as soon as I was finishing one. What facilitated my research immeasurably is I have a photographic memory and a good grasp of the reference material available. I took Greek and Latin in school and was very familiar with the classical authors.

Nina Jidejian with her dog, Major.

Having written a book on coins, are you a collector?

No. But as a historian, I find coins useful in retracing history. In the past, there were no newspapers so coins were minted to commemorate important events in the ancient world. How else could you spread the news that the Romans had conquered or were successful in war? It was by the issuing of a coin! Coins were the propaganda tool of the old world. There was no portraiture or photography at the time so coins carried the effigy of royalty and conquerors, as well as representations of gods and myths. Coins, in essence, served as a record of the times.

Could you tell me about yourself?

I was born in Boston. I went to Iran with my mother and sister to visit my father. We stayed in Iran and I attended Sage Junior College. Then I came to Beirut where I met and married my husband, a man I admired very much. We shared forty-three years of married life. I lost him in the terrible war of 1989. My husband was a very well known and capable surgeon. He had a very strong personality and he was well loved. I lived, shall I say, overshadowed by him. But at the same time, I had my own interests and dedicated myself to doing research. I only began writing after our daughter, Denise, was in her teens. I was always a mother first.

You have researched Lebanon's history — wars and conquests — what was it like actually living through a war?

What affected me very much was the impact it had on the youth of Lebanon. Instead of attending school, visiting museums, learning about their cultural heritage, they were all huddled in basements trying to survive. They knew nothing about their history! To counter that, I wrote a four volume series entitled, *I Love Lebanon*. I am very proud of this series, which covers the history of Lebanon, beginning with the early Stone Age, because I feel I have done something for our youth. Events are seen through the eyes of the young people who lived here in the past, thus making the series more vivid.

Did you continue to write during the war?

No, I couldn't write at all. We were traumatized. We were surviving! We were just trying to get bread! We had to stand in bread lines. To get gasoline, you had to get into a gasoline line. When I think of all the lives lost, the war was all so futile. What was it for? What was accomplished? In Yugoslavia, there was territorial gain, but here there was nothing. The Lebanese have always been mercantile people and have always lived harmoniously together and with others.

As a historian, what city and time in history would you have liked to have lived in?

Perhaps the city of Baalbek during the Roman period because it was so well organized. Or yes! Byblos at the height of commercial relations with the Pharaohs, the Middle Kingdom, and the Kingdom of Byblos. That would be 1900 to 1600 B.C. It was a period of peace and prosperity, commerce and cultural exchange.

Do you have any desire to write a period novel set in one of the cities you document so well?

What motivated me to write my books was I wanted to preserve and consolidate scattered sources by collecting all the materials pertaining to one site in a single volume. Now, that I have done that, and done all the scientific work and everything is footnoted, I am ready for a new challenge. Yes, maybe even a novel! I feel I have paid back a debt to a country that has been very good to my family. When things were awful, here, and we were being shelled by the militias on all sides, I used to tell my husband, "Why don't we leave?" His response was always: "I lived in Lebanon during the good times; I am not going to leave now."

How do you think history will judge Lebanon these last seventeen years?

From a historical perspective, I don't think much has changed. In the history of Lebanon there were periods of great violence: Alexander came down the coast and Tyre was under siege for seven months. The people of Lebanon have survived many wars. These seventeen years of war are nothing new! When you review Lebanon's ancient history, it was always the wars of others that were fought here: the Egyptians against the Hittites, the Assyrians against the Egyptians. When the Persians wanted to attack Egypt, they came here to raise a fleet. Even the Greek and Persian Wars, which Phoenicia had no cause for involvement in, found the Phoenicians involved on the Persian side. I think nothing has really changed.

How did you cope during the war years, watching Lebanon self-destruct?

It was heart-breaking because the war was so futile. Nobody gained anything out of it. The Lebanese have always lived side by side. And all of a sudden this religious factor was brought into the arena: Christians were shelled here; Muslims were shelled there. It was unnatural! There was no rhyme or reason for it. First, it was heart-breaking, and then it became dangerous. We suffered. There was no water, no electricity, and the airport kept closing. What we did have, were shells falling and terrible insecurity. For me, when I look back on those years, oddly enough, the worst was having the airport closed; not seeing jetliners streaming in and out of Beirut. Aside from the silence of the skies and the lack of electricity at night, it was always depressing to read the obituary section in newspapers after a night of shelling. Every death was very much felt because even if you didn't know the person, chances were you knew a member of the family or a friend of the family.

My husband and I stayed here in our villa and, as you see, we were terribly exposed on all sides. The worst point during the war was 1989 when the fighting was just below us at the Presidential Palace at Baabda. The shelling is all done by computer. It's not like the good old days. Now, you just press a button. You don't even have to aim! General Aoun was shelling and he would send out twelve shells. Then, within a few seconds, we would receive double the amount. I could not keep track of how many times our windows broke. Twice, the house was hit while we were in it. Sides kept changing during the war: first, it was Palestinians against Lebanese, then Shiite militia against Christian militia, and so on.

I was almost killed four times. The first time was from a Palestinian position. They shot a "douchkah," a very small shell compared to what was later used. It was launched from the southern suburbs and our house stands out because there are no other buildings around. I was lying in bed when the douchkah came through the windowpane and hit the lamp, which was there merely as decoration because we had no electricity. The lamp saved my life because the shell ricocheted off of it.

The second time, I was saved by my dog. Instead of heading upstairs to wash my hands as I had intended, he insisted I feed him first. Had I gone to my bathroom the shell that entered the house would have hit me. The third time, was in 1987. I was in my bedroom at two o'clock in the afternoon, lying down, listening to the BBC radio broadcast, and a "grad" (a big shell), launched from a cannon located near the airport, hit our house. This is an old Lebanese house built with thick stones (from that experience, I know our walls are forty-eight centimeters thick). If the grad had come through the window, I wouldn't be here telling you this story because it would have blown up in the room. Instead, it blew up inside the wall. I saw the grad — it was red — enter into my room. There was a horrible sound as it hit the wall, and then it exploded. There was smoke everywhere. My husband was downstairs listening to the BBC. I entered the living room, covered with dust and fragments, and I said to him: "I want to leave Lebanon not tomorrow, not this evening, now!"

Did you leave?

No. We hired someone to repair the damaged wall and continued living here. Later, we learned thirty people had been killed that same day in Beirut due to Christian shelling, including a man we knew well. The shelling we received was a response to the initial shelling.

You said there was a fourth time?

Yes, the fourth was really the worst, because four people were killed in front of me. In the morning, an Eastern Beirut-based militia shelled the airport. Nobody dreamed that the other side was going to respond at mid-day. I drove down to Hadeth, the village right beneath us, to pick up something for lunch from the pastry shop. I had reached the village and there was a bus in front of me that had stopped to let off passengers. I waited, but the drivers behind me began blowing their horns impatiently. Then I realized a car coming out of a side road was blocking the path of the bus. I started to pass the bus and that saved my life, because as I was passing, four or five B-7 Korean Missiles landed and exploded.

There was a cloud of black smoke. I could hear people screaming and there were people lying wounded and dead. I remember, my car rocking back and forth. I pressed my foot all the way down on the gas pedal and the car would not move: all four tires had been blown out and the windows were shattered. I don't know how I passed the bus, but I did. I got out leaving the car in the middle of the street. It was absolutely chaotic, people were screaming and blood was everywhere. I ran past a few shops and entered the pastry shop. They saw me coming with blood streaming down all over me. They made me lie down on the floor and then they gave me a shot of arak to drink. I had pieces of shrapnel embedded in my thigh. My husband said I was lucky the shrapnel had not severed any major arteries. It's amazing how during life-threatening moments, God gives you strength and coolness to act. In hindsight, I don't know how I managed to get out of the car. More than anything, I remember the black smoke that was blinding. I remember the driver behind me was blowing his horn and almost at the very same instant as I was passing the bus and thinking: "I shouldn't be passing the bus," the shells exploded. My immediate reaction was: "My God, what have I done!"

After that, you still stayed?

Yes, in spite of everything we stayed. But after my husband died, I was in despair over the situation. I asked myself, "What is this shelling about?" I couldn't even get a doctor to come and visit my husband, a man who had saved so many lives throughout his long surgical career. Because of the shelling, I couldn't even get a doctor to sign his death certificate so he could be buried. Finally, it was signed by a French military medical officer at the French Embassy, which was located nearby. I left Lebanon for seven months and then I realized that bitterness is an emotion that destroys you. I decided to go on with my life and I wrote, *I Love Lebanon*, and dedicated it to my husband's memory.

How do you relax?

Just by sitting with my own thoughts, thinking.

HALA SALAAM MAKSOUD

PROFESSOR OF GOVERNMENT

"There are people who you somehow always knew were going to achieve something in life," says a childhood friend. "Hala Maksoud always fit that category. She is incredibly disciplined and passionate about her causes." Maksoud, descendant of a long line of Sunni Muslim political leaders, is a professor at the Institute for International Transactions at George Mason University in Virginia. Two of her uncles, Saab Salaam and Rachid Karami (who was assassinated in 1987) were former prime ministers of Lebanon.

Maksoud received her Ph.D. in government from Georgetown University while concurrently attending to diplomatic duties as the wife of Clovis Maksoud, the Arab League representative to the United Nations. A tireless activist and ardent Arab Nationalist, she is currently working on a book on Islam and Arab Nationalism. Maksoud and her husband are in demand as panelists, lecturers, and commentators on issues pertaining to the Arab world. Whether the Salman Rushdie affair, the Gulf crisis, the Oslo Agreement, the Lebanese conflict, or prospects of peace in the Middle East, they are always on the short list of experts contacted for their views.

A petite, engaging woman, who speaks with equal measures of passion and authority, Maksoud is involved in countless causes and organizations. She is president of the American-Arab Anti-Discrimination Committee, a past president of the Arab-American University Graduates, director of the American University of Beirut Alumni Association of North America, and is on the advisory board of the Middle East Policy Journal. She is an active member of the National Women's Studies Association, Women's Foreign Policy Council, and Political Science Society, as well as a founding member of the Committee for the Preservation of the Palestinian Heritage, Help Lebanon Association, and the Arab Women's Council.

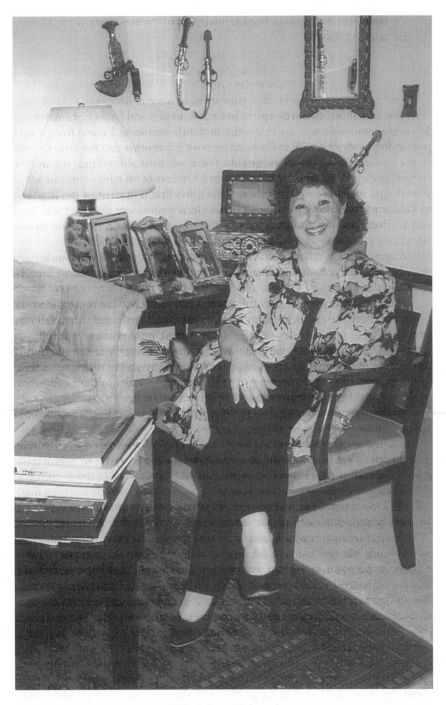

Hala Salaam Maksoud

We met at her home in Washington, D.C. as she was preparing to leave on a visit to Lebanon.

＊   ＊   ＊

Did you ever think you would grow up to be a social activist?

Yes. Somehow, my involvement in social and political issues came naturally. My first memories are of participating in demonstrations. I come from a very politically involved family in Lebanon on both my mother and my father's side. In the houses of both my grandparents, there was constant political discussion. In fact, my mother claims she experienced her first birth pangs with me while attending a meeting to elect Bishara Khuri, the first president of the Republic of Lebanon! Interestingly enough, he was elected president the day I was born and his election led to the independence of Lebanon. A rather timely coincidence! [laughter]

Coming from two very competitive political families, on both your mother and your father's side, did you feel caught in the middle in the political rivalry between both families?

The rivalry between both families was essentially centered on attaining the prime ministership. Somehow, my parents managed to deflect that rivalry by having us focus on the issues and the bigger picture rather than on the individuals. We were always told that had there been two chairs for the prime ministership, my uncles would have been the best of friends! But in the larger scheme of things, both my uncles were on the same side; especially in their support of Arab Nationalism: one representing Tripoli, the other Beirut.

I understand that you studied mathematics and it was at the Ph.D. level that you switched to government. Why?

I actually wanted to emulate my father and study engineering rather than mathematics. But, in 1960, women were not allowed to apply to engineering school. I pursued the next best thing: math and physics. I did my Bachelor of Science degree in physics and my Master's in mathematics. I was teaching math and thinking about doing a Ph.D. in mathematics when the 1967 war occurred. I am one of many whose lives changed as a result of the Six Day Arab-Israeli War.

In what way did the '67 war affect you?

It made me feel guilty. I felt that had my generation participated more actively in the political process such a debacle would not have occurred. Many of us became activists believing the earlier generation was doing things wrong and we had to take things into our own hands and partake in decisions on every level. It was a very intense period. I know a lot of marriages that were wrecked because the wife became too involved and the husband not enough, or vice versa. But there were also lifelong friendships that were forged.

You felt you were making a difference?

Oh, yes! It was an unbelievable time! I keep telling my nieces and nephews about that period. The intensity of our commitment was unbelievable! I don't think I can communicate to anybody who did not share in that experience how we felt. Our movement was perceived as part-and-parcel of the world movement. We were extremely aware of the Vietnam War and the counterculture movement in the United States, the student movement in Europe, and the youth movement taking place all over the world. We felt "this was our day" and we were going to change the world. We had an idealism that was unmatched and a cause that was bigger than ourselves.

As a professor of international relations and the wife of a former ambassador to the United Nations, do you still have faith in the power of diplomacy?

Indeed! Diplomacy is a lot more effective than guns where long term solutions are concerned. It is only through diplomacy that real peace is achieved. I believe in the power of ideas and it is through diplomacy — the art of communication — that ideas are exchanged. Our movement was all about ideas to improve society and the world. Ideas were the motor behind all our actions. Of course, there are a lot of disappointments. Sometimes, you wonder: "Why go on?" But in the end it is worth it. You have to live with yourself. However small your contribution, you have to feel you are contributing to the groundwork for lasting peace. Everyone counts when it comes to contributing to affect change.

When you were growing up, who were your role models?

I had a number of role models in my family. I admired both my grandfathers very much for their commitment to their principles, which they clung to at great cost to themselves. Both were well known nationalists who were imprisoned and exiled for standing up for their beliefs. I admired, too, my great aunt, Anbara Salaam Khalidi, who was the first woman to remove the veil in Lebanon. I felt a great deal of pride in her courage. I admired my mother for being able to be "modern, yet traditional" at the same time. I admired my father for his forthrightness, which I was sure had something to do with his mathematical training! Everything was clear and precise with him.

Have you any regrets about making the switch from mathematics to government?

No. But I apply my mathematical mind to my political thinking. My husband criticizes me for that because invariably I believe every political problem, like every mathematical problem, should have a solution. It is very frustrating for me to find out that some problems don't have solutions.

Tell me about your family?

We are extremely close. There are four of us: three girls and a boy. As the eldest, I was held up as an example to my brother and sisters. Consequently, my parents treated me with a lot of respect. For example, even as a small child, my mother involved me in minor and major decisions. I was being prepared early to be not only her daughter, but her friend. We were very close to my grandparents. Every day, after school, we would go to my maternal grandparents' house. When I look back, my fondest memories are of us as children gathered around the *canoon* (indoor charcoal grill) roasting chestnuts, listening to the stories and conversation of my grandmother, aunts and uncles. There was a real sense of family; a feeling that you belonged to a part of a larger whole.

Coming from a leading Muslim family, your marriage to Clovis Maksoud, a Christian, must have been revolutionary!

I don't think I would have been able to break that barrier had not many of my friends done the same. We gave each other support. After 1967, nothing was so sacred it couldn't be changed. We felt very strongly that we had to live up to our ideals. We were committed to a secular democratic state in Palestine. So we ourselves had to practice what we preached on a personal level. I always say, were it not for the social ferment in '67, I don't think I could have gone through with an interfaith marriage any time before or after that period.

Having given so many lectures on the topic of women in the Islamic world, what do you believe is the distinguishing factor, if any, between a contemporary, educated Muslim woman, such as yourself, and a contemporary, educated American woman?

I think it is in the priorities we set for ourselves. I like to think of myself as an achiever, someone who has goals, and who is as efficient as an American woman counterpart. But I, also, know that I can't live with myself if I don't live up to what my family expects from me. Family, above all, comes first with me. I don't think that family, friends and human relations come before a career with most American women. I think this explains the disintegration of American families. An Arab-American friend made an interesting observation. She said: "Arab women invest time in their families while American women invest money in health and life insurance policies." This, of course, does not mean that we love our families more than American women. It just means that we were raised differently, with a different set of priorities. In Lebanon, when we talk about "family," we include the extended family, while in the West, "family" basically implies only the immediate family. Also, there is a difference in the image Arab and American women have of themselves and their role in life. Arab women feel very strongly that they are the repository of values, that they are the ones who have to inculcate these values on to the next generation.

Does this world view apply to both Christian and Muslim women in the Arab world?

Yes, I think it is fair to say that Christians and Muslims in the Arab world participate in the same Arab-Muslim culture.

Did the war in Lebanon change your outlook on life?

Yes. It shook everything I believed in. Before the war, I believed there were ideas worth fighting and dying for. As a result of the war, I am not so sure about that any more. The war was too bloody. It wasn't worth it. Ideas such as "secularism" and "democracy" are still very important to me and I feel strongly about them, but they cannot be fought over. Before the war, I thought they could.

In 1982, you went on a one-month, twenty-two city tour of the United States to speak out against Israel's invasion of Lebanon. What were your emotions at the time?

I was running on automatic. I was so shocked by what was happening in Beirut. My parents, sisters, nephews, nieces, everybody I loved in the world were in Beirut, and Beirut was being destroyed. The news and the pictures on television were horrible and unbelievable. I couldn't eat, sleep or go out, without feeling terribly guilty since my family was being denied these basic things.

What, in your opinion, was responsible for the civil war in Lebanon?

It was mutual fear. I believe Christians feared that if Lebanon became part of an Arab patrimony, they would lose their identity, which they perceived in terms of a Western dimension. Muslims feared that if Christians controlled Lebanon, as they did, they would crush the Arab Nationalist movement. The fact of the matter is, it was Muslims and Christians together who put forth the ideas of Arab Nationalism in the first place. Also, I don't think one can ever over estimate what a wrench it was for Muslims to play a part in the dismantling of the Ottoman Empire, the only Muslim empire of the time. Yet, they participated in that dismantling because they wanted to belong to an Arab secular entity rather than a Muslim entity. Of course, the Christians of Lebanon were part-and-parcel of that whole movement as well.

What was the worst point for you during the war?

Losing the elements of a common discourse between Muslims and Christians. So many good friends of mine whom I grew up with were fighting on the other side. One day, I saw a very close friend, a dear friend of my parents, carrying a gun. I asked him, "Who are you shooting at?" He said, "Oh, I was just shooting across at West Beirut." It wasn't a person he was firing at, it was "West Beirut"! I asked him, "Don't you think, when you are shooting, you might be hitting me or my parents?" He said, "No, you just happen to be on the other side. I will get others." That shattered me. Real people were no longer assigned to targets. The extent to which people dehumanized the war was astounding. When faces, not religious identity, were assigned to victims of the war that is when it no longer became a Christian versus Muslim war and people started coming to their senses. There is a whole generation of Lebanese who have grown up without the benefit of interacting with one another. Consequently, it was easy for each side to dehumanize the other. By way of a small example, I was once standing in a reception line here at the Lebanese Embassy in Washington, D.C., and I heard the man behind me tell his wife: "Can you believe the woman in front of us is a Muslim!"

Are you optimistic about Lebanon's future?

You have to be; otherwise, you wouldn't do anything. There are basic human values I believe in which I think are worth struggling for, not fighting for, but worth trying to convince others about. My optimism comes from my belief in the goodness of humanity and man's persuasibility.

You don't feel words are meaningless?

No, on the contrary, I believe in the power of the word. I think that is where it all starts. Words and the ability to communicate through words are the source of my optimism. Selecting the right words can make the difference between success and failure — war and peace. Words are what move us all.

What was the difference between the way you felt during the '67 war and the Lebanese war?

Both were devastating, but the '67 war was devastating on an intellectual level. It didn't hit home. The Lebanese war did. The '67 war did not shake any of my basic beliefs, on the contrary, it reinforced my commitment. It made me feel guilty that I was not active enough; whereas, the Lebanese war shook my commitment and made me feel guilty about being too active in pushing the Lebanese system to the breaking point. Secularism is a great idea. I still believe secularism is the salvation for Lebanon. But you don't fight over it. You don't kill people who don't believe in secularism. The idea is not worth it if it ends in death and destruction — the very thing secularism is meant to prevent!

When the airplane you are on lands at Beirut International Airport, how do you feel?

I feel an inner calm. I no longer have to spell my name at every turn! I somehow feel I am back in place, like a missing piece that fits right back into the puzzle.

What is the source of your attachment to Lebanon?

It is definitely the people ... land never meant much to me. I am extremely proud of being Lebanese and being from Beirut, but I hate it when people talk about Beirut as the "Paris of the Middle East." I never liked the way Beirut developed as a city. Its modernity bothered me. What I loved about Beirut was not the architecture of the city or the beauty of the land, it was the fact that we were open to the world. Arabs from all over the Arab world could come, think, talk and write freely in Beirut. It was an oasis of cultural ferment. We partook in everything. Our antennas were hooked to the world around us. We competed in everything on a world class level. In ballet we compared ourselves to Bejart; in art, music and literature we compared ourselves to the best in the world. When Beirut was cut off from the world, we lost our compass, our basis of comparison. Before, we had standards of excellence at all levels to measure ourselves against. That was the greatness of Beirut. Nowhere else in the world did you have a city where there was so much ferment and so much concern about the rest of the world.

What changes would you like to see in Lebanon today?

Last year, when I visited Lebanon, I was extremely depressed not because things were not looking good but because I felt people were not thinking about the future. I think as a result of the war, "normalcy" has become an end in itself. People are so satisfied with the ordinary that they are no longer looking beyond themselves to the extraordinary. I can appreciate this state of mind after what we have been through, but I believe it has gone on long enough. We need to surpass mediocrity as an aspiration. I think, in Lebanon, we have the potential for greatness. We should not be satisfied with the way things are now. We must go back to measuring ourselves on an international level. In Lebanon now there is too much concern with rebuilding the concrete and too little about rebuilding the Lebanese citizen. You don't build and then have a society. You build according to the demands of the society.

What is the driving force in your life?

I have learned that the only thing that really matters is whether you can say with conviction at the end of the day: "I have done my best." That's what it is all about! When I lecture on the Arab world and do volunteer work, it is because

I feel that there is so much ignorance in the United States about the Arab world and Arab women. I truly believe that, if nothing else, my mere presence shakes stereotypes and misconceptions.

MISHKA MOJABBER

EDUCATOR AND POET

The first time I met Mishka Mojabber, director of the middle school of the International College (I.C.), one of Lebanon's most highly regarded preparatory schools, she was interviewing a bright, young boy seeking to gain admission to her school. The child's uncle made the near grievous error of stating that he had two nieces who also wanted to attend I.C. but the boy was an only child and therefore, to make her decision easier, he was only going to submit his nephew's school records. Mojabber, who had been listening solicitously up to this point, suddenly stiffened: eyes turning steely blue, voice lowering an octave, she informed the guileless gentleman: "At this moment, because of your remarks, should all three do equally well on the entrance exams, I would be more likely to accept both girls over the boy." The message rang loud and clear: sexism was not tolerated at this school.

Mojabber has a Master's degree in English Literature and a certificate in educational administration. She speaks fluent Arabic, Greek, Italian, French and English and is the author of a book of poetry about her wartime experience entitled Lest We Forget. *She began her career as an English teacher at I.C. and, from 1981 to 1986, worked as a consultant at the Educational Resource Center, an outreach branch of the school. In this capacity, she traveled to over twenty-five schools around the world that use the I.C. educational model, and spent a year in the Sultanate of Oman as well as a period of time in Kano, Nigeria, where she helped establish a Lebanese Community School. In 1986, she became chairman of the English department at I.C. A year later, she was appointed assistant director at the elementary school and shortly thereafter became director of the middle school.*

For the interview, we met in her large, sunny office on a busy day at the beginning of the school year. A petite, strawberry blond, Mojabber, with a knowing grin, admits she does not look the least bit schoolmarmish. But, during school hours, there is no question who is in charge. Mojabber, who is married to Paul Mourani, is the mother of a young daughter, Cara.

*   *   *

Are you proud to be Lebanese?

Very much so! Absolutely! I am Lebanese but my background is that of a true Levantine. My mother is Greek. My father is Lebanese. Both were born in Egypt. We spoke English at home because neither of my parents spoke the other's native language. I attended an American school in Alexandria until I was ten. Then we moved to Beirut, where I attended a British school. I spent five years in Australia, and attended university there. I suffered an identity crisis as a youth because I didn't know who I was: part Greek, born in Egypt, my native language English and I have an Australian passport! So who am I? That was very difficult to answer. Finally, I worked it through and realized, quite clearly, that my gut feeling is definitely Lebanese. I was sixteen years old and living in Australia when I discovered my identity. I relaxed after that! [laughter]

How did you arrive at that conclusion?

It is nothing tangible. It's the culture. For example, I love Arabic music, singers like Oum Koulsoum and Abdul Wahab, the way of life, the values, the cuisine, the commitment to family, friends, and education, and the openness Lebanese have towards other cultures and nationalities.

What drew you to teaching?

I returned to Lebanon and when I was working on my BA in Comparative Literature at AUB [American University of Beirut], the war broke out. I.C. had hired several American teachers who had to leave and replacements were needed. They contacted the English department at AUB and the department suggested several graduate students including myself. It was my last year and I thought it would be a great way to earn extra money because I had been planning to go to Switzerland to work as an interpreter. As it turned out, I enjoyed teaching so much I never left.

What is special about the I.C. program?

We have extremely competitive academic, extracurricular, and athletic programs. We are an American school in the sense that our board of trustees is based in New York. We are unique in that we have both an English Program and a French Program and both are equivalent: share the same building, have common teachers, and the second language in both programs is Arabic. In the English program, French is taught as the third language. In the French Program, English is the third language. The philosophy at I.C is that we are a nonconfessional, nonsectarian and nonprofit school. We have a very generous scholarship program. We believe in realizing potential where possible and respecting the dignity of students. Our discipline system is fairly unique; we are known for being very liberal. We believe in self-discipline rather than strict rules and regulations.

Did you experience unusual disciplinary problems with students after the war?

I don't think there is a correlation between the war and disciplinary problems. We have very few disciplinary problems compared to other schools. I think it's because we don't overwhelm students with rules and regulations. At the beginning of the year, we tell students, we expect you to respect each other and school property, and they sign, along with their parents, a contract to that effect.

Mishka Mojabber

Faculty and students have a very close relationship. I have an open-door policy with my students.

Lebanese society is very fashion-conscious. Do you enforce a school dress code?

We say we don't have a dress code but, in fact, we do have a uniform and it's jeans. [laughter] I had to draw the line at torn jeans and short skirts.

What happens if a student comes to school wearing a short skirt?

It happened twice during the school year. I called the girls in and explained to them why I objected to short skirts and asked them not to wear them again. I explained that they were attracting boys' attention in a way that might not be necessarily in their best interest. I told them: "You may be attracting the attention of a boy you like, but you will also be attracting boys you don't like, and you don't want to hassle with that. Besides short skirts are so uncomfortable. You can't sit without having to cross your legs and you have to keep pulling down on your skirt all the time."

Your job must be very difficult especially when you have to turn down students whose parents are determined to send them to I.C.

Yes, it can be difficult. I was threatened once with a gun. A woman, trying to enroll her daughter, came into my office and said: "Do you know what I have in my bag?" I said, "No, what do you have?" She said, "I have a gun." And she did! I called the police and when they came she told them: "I didn't mean to actually threaten her."

How did the war affect you?

I started teaching, in 1975, the year the war started. It was a major challenge. In retrospect, it was actually mad trying to run a school through those seventeen years of war. I don't know how we did it. I don't know if we could do it again. We never thought the war would last so long. In fact, after the first two years, we were sure the war had ended. And then it started again. It was the nature of my work that really kept me here. I would have left Lebanon a long time ago, but seeing those kids coming to school every day under the shells, ready to learn, and knowing that many of them had not slept all night, were living without electricity and water...well, I just couldn't leave. It was the children who gave us all so much hope. Certainly, they made me stick it out. Nothing else would have. Nothing else was worth it.

When there was shelling, how did you decide whether to open or close the school?

We would meet at six o'clock in the morning to evaluate the situation and decide whether we should send the school buses to pick up the students. Looking back, it is actually remarkable how few days we closed the school. Only in 1989 did we close for a substantial period of time (mid-March to October). But we reorganized the curriculum and students were able to make up the lost time over a period of two years. When we did close, we would prepare homework packets for the kids. They would pick them up during a lull in the fighting and then return the packets to be corrected. It kept the students busy at home. We had kids working on these packets in the south of the country, the north, Paris, London, and all over.

How did you personally cope during periods of intense fighting?

I live twenty minutes away by car. I found myself living in the school on several occasions. In March 1976, I came to school one day and I didn't go home until June. The situation had deteriorated that quickly. Most days, I couldn't make the drive home, so I packed a few things and set up house in a tiny little room on the third floor of this building. There were thirty-two teachers living in the school at the time, and we had quite a few student boarders as well. We really became one big family. I still see people I lived with back then and whenever we meet we reminisce about that period. There is a wonderful sense of community here and I think that is what has allowed this institution to grow and develop under rather trying circumstances.

Was the school ever hit by shells?

The main campus here in Beirut was never seriously hit, but several of our other campuses were destroyed and we had to close them down. We had buses burned, windowpanes shattered — damage of that sort. After seventeen years of war, you would think there would be nothing left. In fact, a lot of us grew up in this war; some of us even grew up as a result of the war. Miraculously, life went on.

In comparison, do you think life is dull now?

No, there is never a dull moment! I have yet to be bored.

Did the war change your life completely?

Yes, there is no doubt about that. A lot of things would have been different had I not lived through this war. On the bright side, I certainly would not have written a book of poetry. Writing poetry was one of the few ways I was able to maintain my sanity. I would write as the shelling occurred. The first thing I would grab when I headed down to the shelter was my notebook. In times of quiet and peace I was not interested in writing. Strangely enough, I was not as creative. It was only during moments of crisis that I would write poetry. It was a coping mechanism. I could ignore the sounds of shells exploding by concentrating on putting my feelings down on paper.

In one of your poems you write: "...This rain of shells upon the things we own, / These stalkers who break in / Through our very walls, / To foul our homes...." When did you write these lines?

It was something that happened in 1987. A man actually broke through my balcony wall from the building next door. I saw his head come through the wall and I asked him: "What are you doing? What do you want?" He looked up at me, his head framed by the hole, and he said, "Your balcony offers a good vantage point for sniping." It was surreal!

Some of your poems are very angry. For example: "...Implantation is sterilization,/Artificial insemination into schizophrenic wombs,/Breeding cloned clowns and puppets."

Yes, I was very angry. I was chosen to represent Lebanon on a Fulbright Scholarship. I went to New York and spent four months, during the summer of 1989, at New York University (NYU) as a Fulbright Scholar. It was right after the Israeli invasion (what came to be known as "the war of liberation"). It was one of the worst summers in Lebanon. One day, I turned on the television to listen to the news. There was a report about the shelling continuing in Lebanon and then they showed footage of my neighborhood and the street I lived on was hardly recognizable. The buildings were damaged and every car on my street had been completely burned. I managed to get through by telephone to Beirut and was told the apartment next to mine and the one underneath had been destroyed, and a fire had ignited in mine. I thought, my goodness, I've lost everything! I wasn't worried about material possessions except for two things: my notebook of poems and my family's photo album. Everything else I could replace. I vowed right then and there that if I went back and those items were safe, the first thing I would do was send the photo album to my sister in the States for safekeeping, and I would publish my poems. Thank God, I was able to keep both promises.

In 1989, I also took up smoking. I had never touched a cigarette before in my life. It was my first year as assistant director at the elementary school. We had 800 children in a five-story building and it had a basement where we practiced bomb drills. One day the shelling actually started and the drills were for real. That was such a harrowing experience. The magnitude of the responsibility hit me and I thought if anything happens to any of these kids, I will never forgive myself. I felt nothing was right, nothing was sure. The shelling started in March and it continued on every two or three days. There was a time when we had to stay overnight at school with forty or fifty children because their parents couldn't get through. It was a very stressful period. I thought: I'll take Valium, I'll start drinking, or I'll take up smoking. I just felt I had to do something to take my mind off the incredible responsibility I was under. I did not want to get hooked on drugs, nor did I want to become an alcoholic. Smoking, I figured, was the lesser of three evils!

In the first poem that appears in Lest We Forget, *you compare Beirut to a cigarette lit at the wrong end. Why that metaphor?*

Beirut in 1975 was the playground for much of the Arab world. There was a lot of glamour and money. Most of us living here thought that was the real Beirut, but it was not. We had this image of Beirut being "the Paris of the East." When the war broke out I realized just how artificial that image was, given the fact that people hated enough to kill each other the way they did. This was at the beginning of the war when everything was still pretty tame. All of our illusions were destroyed and that is why I wrote that poem. It was actually the first poem I ever wrote. The last poem in the book uses cigarettes as a metaphor as well. It comes full circle. I felt, at the time, a cigarette was the only thing in my life I had complete control over from beginning to end. With a cigarette you can light it or put it out when you choose.

You wrote a poem: "Souha Toukan was shot today, / And the roses / She sent me / For my birthday / Are still in bloom." Who was Souha Toukan?

Souha was a close friend. She was a well known painter in Lebanon and just the sweetest human being you ever met. It was tragic the way we lost her. She had a French friend visiting (this was during a time when the kidnappings were taking place) and she was worried about him going home alone. She told him, "I'm from the area, I'll drive you. If anybody stops us, I'll be able to talk to them in Arabic and they won't bother you." That night, there was no electricity and there was a road block along the way which she didn't see. She drove right past it and the armed men shot her.

Many people I know have been killed or been kidnapped and they have never reappeared. This has happened a lot in Lebanon but you never hear about those kidnappings in the news. I was kidnapped myself once. It was Christmas 1976 and I was leaving to join my family for the holidays in Greece.

I didn't think they kidnapped women in Lebanon?

I didn't think so either! I happen to be a Christian who has always lived in Beirut. Before the war there was never a "Christian East Beirut" or a "Muslim West Beirut." It was just one Beirut. I've never had any political affiliations so I didn't think I had anything to fear. I was coming to I.C. to park my car and take a taxi to the airport. There was a roadblock and I was stopped by a man carrying a Kalishnikov. He asked for my identification papers and I gave them to him. He said, "Ah, you are a Christian! What are you doing in these parts?" I said, "I live here. He didn't believe me. With his gun he motioned me to the side of the road. Then I was escorted to a nearby basement. I wasn't alone for long. They kept bringing in new detainees.

As it happened, I was doing an English program for Radio Lebanon and the basement where I was held captive was not far from the radio station. A colleague at the radio station saw me as I was being led down to the basement and he sent word to the kidnappers that I worked for Radio Lebanon, which was a very pro-West Beirut station. Several hours later, a man came to inquire whether I worked for Radio Lebanon. I said, I did and they let me go. They eventually let everyone else go as well. I later learned that the son of a prominent personage in the area had disappeared and they assumed he had been kidnapped by Christian forces. The irony was that he had been involved in a theft and the police were holding him overnight for questioning. It was one of the few incidents that occurred during the war that was not politically related!

How did that experience affect you?

I couldn't talk about what happened to me for the longest time. I was so shocked. I had always believed I was safe because I was a woman and I was not politically involved. I had lived in this particular area all my life. Had I been stopped less than a hundred yards back, everyone in the neighborhood would have vouched for me. Strangely enough, my cousin was stopped at that very same roadblock. What's more, he was politically involved with the leadership in West Beirut. He told his kidnappers, "I may be a Christian, but I am politically active on your side. Your enemies are my enemies." But because he was a Christian, they kidnapped him anyway. His identity card said "Christian" and that was that. When he was released, he was so disillusioned and disgusted by the experience, he got on a plane, flew out of the country, and never returned.

There are so many contradictions at play here. Even after what happened to me, I would never dream of leaving West Beirut and my neighborhood. I don't feel I or my family belong anywhere else. This is our neighborhood. We all know each other. Many Christians left the area but we remained. We were always protected by our Muslim friends and neighbors. At one point, kidnapping was so rampant, the neighbors would bring us bread so my father wouldn't have to go out unnecessarily. When you live together with your neighbors in the stairwell or in the basement of your building for weeks, sometimes months at a time, there are no barriers left. It is the closeness between people that has saved this country.

Do you feel guilty for having survived?

No. I used to feel guilty for not being politically committed during the war. But there was nothing that made sense to me. There was nothing black or white, good or evil. Positions kept shifting and everybody had blood on their hands. I could not identify with any political group. People were dying. I felt there had to be something worth fighting for, worth getting killed for. A lot of people were in that same situation. In retrospect, I find that it is just as well that I did not commit myself to anything. The commitment is really to the future; the past is nothing to be proud of. Certainly, not the years of war. The children are our future. They are our hope.

On the playground, have you witnessed any animosity among the children provoked by sectarian feelings?

Very little. The few incidents that do occur are very minor and are resolved by our addressing the fact that we are all one family. In class, we dwell on the fact that the similarities between us are much greater than the differences. When I was in the States on a Fulbright, we visited a school in New York and there was a teacher who did a wonderful, visual experiment with a group of ten-year-olds that I later repeated with my own students. She told them, "I want each of you to write a description of a lemon." They wrote: "It's yellow and oval in shape." She said, "Be as specific as you can." They wrote: "It is about three inches long and the rind has little dots in it." She said, "Okay, let me show you a lemon." She held up a regular looking lemon and said, "Is this a lemon?" They said, "Yes, that's a lemon." She said, "Okay, let me show you something else." She held up a tiny little green lemon that hadn't yet ripened and asked, "Is this a lemon?" They said, "Yes, that's a lemon." Then she held up a lemon that had been left out in the sun and was brown and all shriveled up and she asked, "Is this a lemon?" They said, "Yes, that's a lemon." She held up a giant sized lemon and asked, "Is this a lemon?" They said, "Yes, that's a lemon." Then she told them, "You see, many of these lemons don't fit your description, yet they are all lemons and that is the same way with people."

Did you have any role models when you were growing up?

Yes, many of my teachers. I think that is why I am so committed to education. I think education is the future of this country and I have a very clear and firm vision regarding education. I realize how much it affects your life. There were two teachers and a principal, when I was in elementary school, who were very much my role models. They were strong, intelligent women with a great deal of compassion and integrity. They were very firm and fair when it came to academics and they had clear moral codes that they lived by. That impressed me very much.

My father also was a wonderful role model. He had two daughters and he raised us no differently than if we were his sons. It was never: "Well, she is a girl, she doesn't need to do this." He never regretted not having sons. I never grew up feeling: "I am a girl and therefore it's a disadvantage" — ever. Whenever I have met discrimination in my professional life, I've met it head on. I think women have to work harder than men. But, that said, I don't think discrimination is much of a problem here. I think women who want to make it in this country, especially after the war, can.

If anything positive resulted from the war, it was the fact that it served as a leveler. Men left for jobs abroad because they wanted to provide for their families, and women had to take on responsibilities that were previously considered the man's domain. Women were forced to come out of their shells. In the past, they had to always consult with their husbands. Now, they make decisions on their own. Moreover, since a lot of men left the country, many more jobs were available for women to fill. Many more women, today, go on to university than did previously because with the economy as bad as it is everybody has to work. It is no longer enough for parents to say: "It's okay, she will get married." A woman today has to help her husband earn a living.

You don't think it's a man's world?

Not anymore. But I don't think the men know it yet! [laughter] We don't really have a woman's movement here, but I think we have been luckier than most societies. People were too busy surviving to say, "Who are these women who are taking over?" The war has been helpful in that sense. Women have a lot more to contribute. We don't have enough women in politics and I think we should.

Are you interested in holding public office?

It's definitely not something I would rule out if the office had something to do with education.

How do you relax?

I am an avid reader and that is one of the things that helped me survive the war. I play bridge. I paint. I take long walks. I love crossword puzzles, logic problems, games like "Trivial Pursuit" and "Pictionary."

When you travel and people learn that you are Lebanese, what is their reaction?

Most of them say, "You don't look Lebanese," which I resent. I say "Oh, how do you think Lebanese look?" and we go back to the lemon experiment. [laughter] They ask, "Are you really Lebanese?" I tell them, "Well, actually my mother is Greek." They say, "Ah, that explains it!" Well, if you know anything about Greece, you would know that most of the population has olive skin, dark hair, dark eyes. It's my father's side of the family that has the blond hair, the blue eyes and the fair skin. I tell them in Lebanon we have an incredible mix of people. The stereotype of a Lebanese does not apply. If you walk into any one of my classrooms, you would really be hard pressed to say: "Okay, this is a typical Lebanese."

LATIFÉ CHAMOUN MOULTAKA

PROFESSOR OF DRAMA

Her directorial skills have been described as "delicate and decisive as embroidery on lace." As Lebanon's first female theater director, Latife Moultaka and her husband, Antoine, a professor of Philosophy at the Lebanese University, are credited with introducing experimental theater to Lebanon. A woman of many talents, Moultaka graduated from law school in 1955 and practiced law for many years before devoting herself full-time to the theater. Together with her husband, she founded the Circle Theater in 1962, the Experimental Theater in 1967, and the Maroun Naccach Theater in 1981. All three theaters have been instrumental in developing a talented corps of Lebanese actors.

Moultaka, an accomplished actress, studied drama at the Sorbonne where she received a degree in 1972. She is currently a professor of Dramatic Arts at the Lebanese University. Her acting roles include: Antigone in Sopho-cles' Antigone, *Lady Macbeth in Shakespeare's* Macbeth, *Sonia in Dos-toievsky's* Crime and Punishment, *Electre in Satre's* The Flies, *Lady Anne in Shakespeare's* Richard III, *the mother in Camus's* Le Malentendu, *and Madame Dolfout in Brecht's* Arturo Ui. *Theatrical works she has directed include:* Crime and Punishment *by Dostoievsky,* Malentendu *by Camus,* The Lost Letter *by Caragiale,* A Dog's Will *by Souassouna, and* Ten Little Indians *by Agatha Christie. She has also adapted numerous works for the theater and directed for television more than a dozen episodes of works by Agatha Christie.*

A confident woman with a warm, engaging smile, and a twinkle in her eye, Moultaka is a talented pianist and the mother of three. We met at her third floor apartment in the Moultaka Building. As she talked, her cat, Natasha, (one of four cats in the household) snuggled contentedly on her lap while, in an adjacent room, the remaining three cats lounged around her husband as he graded term papers.

*   *   *

Could you tell me about yourself?

I was born in Lebanon to the Chamoun family, attended law school, and then practiced law for nine years. I met my husband Antoine Moultaka in 1957. He has always been involved in the theater and it was through him that I, too, became interested. I found the theater more interesting than the practice of law. Eventually, I consecrated myself entirely to the theater. I have been involved in theater since my marriage in 1959. I recall the first time I was on stage. I was a boarder at a Maronite nuns school. I was five-years-old and I had a monologue where I appeared alone. Even today, I can still remember the pleasure I had reciting my lines and being applauded. It was the first applause I had ever received! [laughter]

By nature, I am very curious and ambitious. I like to do everything with enthusiasm, and everything I do I enjoy. While studying piano, I adored prac-ticing. As a lawyer, I loved the law even though law was not my first choice. As a student, I had a passion for math and science and everyone thought I would become a doctor or a professor of mathematics. I made a *volte-face* and pursued a legal career instead. My father wanted to be a lawyer and as his eldest child I was encouraged to realize his dream. I am often told that I resemble him because I, too, have a very strong personality.

Your theatrical background must have been very helpful when you stood up in court to defend your clients!

[laughter] Yes, there was a point when I was pursuing the theater as a hobby while still a lawyer. I recall appearing in court one day and the judge, aware of my involvement in the theater, asked me: "Are you acting or litigating?" [laughter] Being a lawyer and an actor is a very effective combination! The law

Latifé Chamoun Moultaka

teaches you to be analytical and logical while the theater gives you courage to speak in public and trains you to project yourself.

What captivated you about the theater and convinced you to switch careers?

The fact that one can put aside one's natural inhibitions and become whatever your character demands. The theater for me represents freedom. I am by nature an extremely shy person. It was with great difficulty that I argued my cases in court. I suffered greatly because of my shyness. In the theater, I learned to transform my shyness into positive energy. The theater literally allows you to shed your skin. When you take on a role, you can freely express yourself in public in ways you would not dream of doing as yourself.

Are you more anxious when you direct a play or when you act in one?

Both give me anxiety! [laughter] But the nature of the anxiety is very different. As an actress, I only think about my character and my character's relation with the other characters in the play. I adore the work that is involved in creating a plausible character. Every time I get on stage as an actress I am afraid. That comes with the responsibility of having to give a good performance every evening. When you are a theater director the anxiety is totally different because you are responsible for everything: the lighting, the costumes, the staging, the actors, and the harmony of the piece. My vision, as the director, is the controlling force behind everything. I have to know what is the reason behind every movement, what it is I want to achieve, and how to get all the actors to see and comply with my vision. That is not an easy job! When I am working on a play, I become totally obsessed and consumed by my work.

Are you bitter about having lost so many creative years to the war?

I am not ashamed to say that I was traumatized by the war. It marked me deeply, so much so that I am unable to forget it. There were seventeen days towards the end of the war that were worse than all seventeen years of the war. The experience propelled me to direct my last play, "War on the Third Floor," which was about the plots and conspiracies that provoke wars in small, third-world countries. The play addressed why we Lebanese were susceptible to outside conspiracies. It addressed the fact that we are a country divided: Christians here, Muslims there, and that is what makes us vulnerable to outside influences. People can plot against us because we are weak. We do not know the meaning of nationhood. If we were truly united, no war could penetrate our boundaries and consume us. Theater, I believe, is most effective when it puts the world and reality into perspective. The setting of "War on the Third Floor" takes place in a bedroom — a supposedly very private place. I placed the bedroom in the middle and the audience was seated all around as were a few actors who were involved in the plot. The message was: Lebanon, like the couple in the bedroom, was open and exposed to the whims of outside conspirators.

Do you think theater can influence change in society?

At the beginning, I thought theater could, but now I am less and less convinced of that. Theater is like a mirror, all it does is reflect what is around us. It offers an emotional release, similar to how one feels when one talks about a problem in the open.

What prompted you to get involved in experimental theater?

We started with classical theater (Italian theater) where there is a stage on one side and the audience on the other side, but then we felt it was a form of theater unsuited to us as a people. It was a theater form imported from Europe. The mentality in Europe is unlike ours. There, the public comes to quietly watch a performance. Here, in the Arab world, our mentality is different. We don't just like to watch, we like to participate. If you go to a concert, you will notice that people just don't listen, they sing along! If a dancer is performing, people don't just watch, they get up and dance in the aisles! We, in the Arab world, have a very participatory mentality.

My husband and I felt — why should we limit ourselves to classical theater? Why don't we find a setting that complements our mentality? We did not want a curtain to separate the actors from the audience, so we experimented: we placed the actors in the center and the audience on either side. It was the first experimental theater in Lebanon. We called it *"le théâtre bilateral."* The audience on one side would take up a position and argue with the audience on the other side. Every evening, we would serve the audience wine and French fries and we noticed that the public very much enjoyed this setting. They felt involved. The actors, too, enjoyed the interaction with the audience in this setting and their message was better received.

My husband and I then founded the Maroun Naccach Theater. It had a mobile stage enabling us to dabble in all sorts of theater: Italian, Elizabethan, bilateral, central (with the audience all around the stage), and even panoramic (where we placed the public in the center and the actors played around them). However, when we moved away from classical theater, we discovered we also needed to change the way actors trained and performed. In classical theater an actor relies mostly on facial expression and frontal acting, but with our new theatrical setting (with the audience surrounding the stage) the actor's back is no longer protected. His entire body is exposed from all sides. He has to be as expressive with his back as with his face. It's a whole new dimension in acting and requires a new training process which we are exploring in drama classes at the Lebanese University. We are focusing on body expression and teaching yoga for concentration and relaxation. For the most part, the plays that I have chosen to direct, I have staged myself or adapted to fit the sensibilities of a Lebanese audience.

Is the war a period you want to forget or are you able to draw upon emotions from that period for creative inspiration?

Our house was shelled in 1990 and we went to live in France for one year and a half. We had no desire to do anything during this period. We were discouraged about everything. We felt we might never return to Lebanon and never do theater again. But once we recovered from our anguish, we returned, rebuilt our house, and tried to forget. The first thing I did was direct a play about the war. I felt it still weighed heavily on my soul. To get the trauma, the fear, and the anxiety I experienced, out of my head, I needed to communicate my feelings in front of an audience and argue with them. Directing "War on the Third Floor" did me a lot of good. I was able to reconcile with the past and become myself again. Now, I have no desire to talk about the war. It belongs to the past. The public, too, is tired of the war. They don't want to remember it. They want to go to the theater and forget what they endured for seventeen years. We are, now, in a healing mode.

How did the war affect you as an artist?

By nature, I am very sensitive. I am scared of many things. Even, now, if a door bangs I am unnerved. I was always frightened for my children and my husband. We endured some atrocious moments. Most of the time was spent in our bathroom because it was the safest place in the house. It had four solid walls. The fear and insecurity was so unyielding that there were several times we wished for death. The experience and the suffering we endured marked me greatly. We were reduced to the most simple state of existence. We spent so much time just thinking about survival and nourishment. During the entire period of the war, I did not direct anything and I only acted in two plays directed by my husband. The last, in 1987, was "The Old Lady's Visit" by Durrennmatt, a play about how people are corrupted by greed, which was a factor in the war. Some people grew rich and preferred that the war continue. They sold their country for money. I played the old lady, Madame Zahanassian, a marvelous role, which allowed me to release a lot of anger and frustration.

What is it like being directed by your husband?

We are almost always in disagreement and, what is more, we bring our disagreements home with us! [laughter] When he is directing, he is always telling me: "Forget that you direct. You are now an actress and that is all that you are."

How do you prepare for an acting role?

I enter into a secondary state. When I review the text, I divorce my personality and open up myself to my new character. At this point, we are in conflict. But by sheer immersion into the character, I slowly reconcile myself to my new persona. I take deep breaths, I sing, and do whatever my body needs to relax. Once I have a grasp on my character, oh la la, it is difficult to get out of character! For months, I am a different person. My husband and children don't recognize me. When I work, I work like a crazy person. Everyone tells me, "How do you keep up this pace?" By nature, I tire easily but yoga has saved me. I do yoga every morning and I attend yoga classes twice a week. I consider yoga my salvation.

Was it difficult being taken seriously as a female director?

No, on the contrary, I find that I get more respect and attention because I am a woman. I am sure that we will soon be seeing many more women directors. I have many talented students with great potential. They just need to be ripened a little bit more by experience and cultural knowledge.

Have any of your children followed your husband and you into the theater?

No. My eldest has a Ph.D. in theoretical physics and is at the National Center for Scientific Research at Montpellier, France. He was just sent by France to California on a scientific research exchange program. He is married and has made me a grandmother! The second is twenty-four years old and he is a great pianist. He studied in France and received first prize from the National Conservatory in Paris. He is a soloist and does concerts all around the world. My youngest, my daughter, is twenty years old and she is getting a degree in pure mathematics from the University of Orsay, in Paris. She is interested in a career in astrophysics. Thank God, from a family point of view, I have been lucky in life! I probably would never have been in the theater if it were not for my husband. He is always by my side: he critiques, consoles, and encourages me. I had a mother-in-law who was like a mother to me. She took care of everything. She would tell me: "Go take care of your work and don't worry about the children, the house, or the cooking." Without her I would not have been able to do what I did.

What have you learned that has made a difference in your life?

The realization that if you don't learn something new each day you might as well be in a closed dark room with no windows or doors. Life is all about new experiences, growing, learning, making mistakes and learning from those mistakes. You shouldn't be afraid to fail, you should only be afraid not to try. Regret is the bitterest of sentiments.

HILDA NASSAR

LIBRARIAN

Chief medical librarian at the American University of Beirut Medical Library, Hilda Nassar is a highly sought-after expert in the field of library automation. She is an instructor of library science at Lebanese American University (formerly known as Beirut University College) and at the American University of Beirut (AUB). "Ms. Nassar runs the library like a tight ship," says a former medical student. "You won't find a better organized, more up-to-date medical library or a more efficient and knowledgeable staff anywhere in the world." Indeed, it is due to Nassar's tireless efforts that despite the many years of war in Lebanon the Medical Library, today, is completely automated.

Nassar, a personable and energetic woman, received her undergraduate degree in 1970 from Beirut University College, where she majored in psychology. An internationally renowned consultant in automation, she earned a postgraduate diploma in librarianship from Ealing College for Higher Education in London and a Master's degree in 1980 from the College of Librarianship in Wales. She has helped establish medical libraries in Bahrain and Qatar, assisted in automating the World Health Organization Library in Geneva, and set up the Hariri Medical Center Library in Lebanon. She serves as a consultant to a number of local hospital and university libraries.

A frequent traveler, Nassar keeps abreast of the latest developments in library science by participating in conferences held around the world. A devoted daughter, she shares the responsibility of caring for her invalid father (a former AUB histology professor) with her two brothers. For the interview, we met at her spacious office at the AUB Medical Library.

*   *   *

Have you always enjoyed reading books?

Yes, ever since I was a child, I liked to read. Books are very precious to me. My mother used to read a lot. I would borrow books from the school library and if a book was too difficult for me, my mother and I would read it together. I was encouraged to read in French by my mother and in Arabic by my father. Now, I find that I prefer to read my professional work in English, novels and magazines in French, and poetry in Arabic! When I was young it was my dream to write a novel and I started writing one in Arabic, which is a very expressive language, but the story remains unfinished.

Did people read more during the war?

They may have read more newspapers but not books. From my own experience, I know, at the beginning of the war, I read a lot but after a while I only

Hilda Nassar

read newspapers. I couldn't concentrate long enough to read an entire novel. I was constantly worried something bad was going to happen. For instance, I always liked to attend movies and read the book before seeing it adapted to the screen. I don't do that anymore. I don't have the patience.

How did the war affect you?

It made me feel very insecure. Before, I was much stronger emotionally. I had more control. During the war, when the shelling would start, I would get very upset and cry easily. These days, I am feeling stronger. I don't know whether it is old age or because I am less on edge since the fighting stopped a couple of years ago. I now feel less fragile. I still cry easily but, I think, my war experience has made me more nonchalant about life. Now, when things go wrong I say, "Okay, fine, at least it's not the end of the world!" We saw so many people killed. When I see the news about other countries experiencing war, I remember what we went through and I think "*haram!*" (what a pity!) but it doesn't have the same impact on me as it did before. I don't like war. I don't like to read about it. I don't like to watch it on television. And I don't like to be reminded of it. Before the war, I used to read and discuss world news with my friends. I no longer do that.

How did you cope during the war years?

When the shelling would start, whenever possible, I would put on my Walkman and try to listen to classical music. I developed a tolerance for arak [a Lebanese liquor] and I would have a drink with my dinner to calm my nerves. I learned to do yoga to stay calm and my priorities changed. Instead of worrying about jobs, promotions, what to do on week-ends, I worried about basic necessities: food, water, and electricity.

During the war, I remember leaving the shelter and taking an eleven hour car trip to Aman, Jordan (the airport in Beirut was closed), to catch a flight to Paris to attend a conference. In many ways, the ability to get out and leave my fears behind is what kept me going. The worst time for me was in 1982 during the Israeli invasion. We were trapped. I had a conference to attend in Montreal and I couldn't leave. All avenues out of Beirut were closed. It was the first time I really thought I might die. I felt death around me. I was trapped with my father and my two elderly aunts. It reached a point where I was no longer concerned about my safety. I would go to my brother Nabil's house, which was nearby, on the AUB campus (he is the director of the AUB medical services) and have dinner with him and his guests. Then I would walk back home in the evening regardless of the shelling. The war made us all fatalists.

Tell me about yourself.

I come from a conservative Lebanese family from the mountain village of Ain-Ksour. I am the youngest of three. I have two brothers, Nabil and Khalil. My parents believed in education and sent me to College Protestant, one of the best schools in Beirut, where we were instructed in Arabic, French and English. I continued from there to Beirut University College.

What is it like to be responsible for a medical library?

It's a lot of responsibility and hard work. When I took over the management, I thought it would be easy! I used to always criticize the way things were done. I don't anymore because I know how tough it is. It is not easy being "a boss" especially for a woman because sometimes you feel like a dictator. As a woman your responsibilities are not just relegated to your work but you have to take care of your home as well. You can do one or the other well; not both, unless you are a super woman — I am not.

I don't relish managing a staff, especially after the war because people have changed so much. They have become very short-tempered and argumentative. During the war, we had to change library hours so people could get home before dark and before the shelling started. It is a five minute walk from my house to the library but there were many people on my staff who lived quite far away. The toughest part for me, when there was shelling, was to make a decision to keep the staff at work, send them home, or lead them to the shelter. My responsibility was to make sure no one got hurt. I had to decide whether it was safer for them to go home or stay at the library. I had the radio turned on in my office all the time so I would know what area was being shelled. Even when there was no shelling here in Ras Beirut, I had to follow the news because I had staff living in all areas.

We would be here only half an hour in the morning and then the shelling would start and I would have to send everyone home. Being responsible for the welfare of others is a heavy responsibility. Sometimes, I would stay at the library and send everyone else home. I had no problem taking responsibility for myself, it was my staff that worried me so much. Sometimes, there would be shelling for half an hour and then it would stop. I would send the staff home as soon as I felt it was safe for them to leave. It was really tough especially when we didn't have electricity. We couldn't operate computers or electric typewriters. We had no air-conditioning in the summer nor heat in the winter. During the Israeli invasion, in 1982, we didn't have electricity at all for three months. Students and doctors did all their research by flashlight. Now, we always keep flashlights charged for when the electricity goes out. At home, I had to constantly fill buckets of water for my family and I would go shopping every day since the refrigerator did not work without electricity. Having to regularly carry groceries and water up and down the stairs, aggravated an old neck injury I sustained in a car accident and made my ordeal all the more difficult.

Did you get a lot of shelling around here at AUB?

Oh, yes! Once, I thought I was surely going to die. I had just stepped away from my desk when a bomb exploded right outside my window. There was shrapnel everywhere. There was no warning that day. The president of the university had called a meeting and I ran down to the main campus and bombs were flying over my head. When I arrived at College Hall, I was told the bombing was concentrated on a parallel street from us. It happened to be the street where I live with my family. All I could think about was their safety. The meeting was not adjourned right away. We moved from the top floor to the basement. Finally, the meeting was canceled because we couldn't hear each other over the noise of the bombs.

Did you lose any of your staff during the war?

Yes, two women. One was hit directly from a shell. It was a Sunday afternoon in 1989. We were not working. The bomb hit the roof of the library and she happened to be walking by on her way home. The other woman died in 1988 of a heart attack caused by stress from the war. Three members of the staff resigned: two left the country and the third moved to the other side of Beirut.

Do you feel you are helping others through your work?

Absolutely! During the week we get quite a few emergency calls from doctors who need specific information right away. Sometimes we get half a dozen such calls in a single day. We have a special number for emergency situations where a doctor can get right through to me without having to go through the switchboard or my secretary. I keep all the important medical journals up-to-date because AUB is now going back to doing research. During the war, there was no time for research. We also have an excellent reference librarian, Aida Farha, who is a pharmacist. Scientifically, I am very curious and ambitious, I like to take the initiative. I learned how to use computers in library school in 1978 when I was in England. Computers at that time were just being introduced into the library science field.

What are some of the stranger requests or situations you've had to deal with?

Because this is a Francophone country some people assume we sell books because we are known as a "librairie." In French that means a bookstore while the French word for library is "bibliothèque." So they frequently ask me in a mocking tone: "If you don't sell books, what do you do?" I say, I just dust them!

[laughter] We have some very enterprising students here. I once caught a student at the copying machine using a coin attached to a thread. Every time he would make a copy he would reel the coin back up! A rather original way to beat inflation, don't you think?

How many years did it take you to become the head of the medical library?

Seven. I received my degree in 1979 and I became librarian in 1986. But on and off, during that time and even before, I was asked to be acting librarian in place of another person who had been acting medical librarian for a long time. She left and I took her place. After a year, I decided to put my foot down. I said, "Either I am in charge or I am not," and that is how I became medical librarian! A medical library is different from a university library. The needs are different. For example, journals are more important than books. We don't have many books. After a few years we give them away because in medicine, books become outdated quickly. We spend annually about $80,000 on books and more than $500,000 on medical journals. Our most important medical source is our on-line service, DIALOG, which includes material from the most recent medical journals. This California-based company has the most extensive data bases not only in medicine but in everything. During the war, DIALOG was our only link to the outside world.

Have you felt discriminated against as a woman?

Yes. When I used to travel as a consultant to Arab countries, I sometimes felt that they didn't take me seriously because I was a woman. But once I start working, they forget my gender, and I have no problem. The good thing about being a woman working in Arab countries is that Arab men are always very respectful and courteous to women. For example, when I attend meetings with doctors and medical directors, I am often the only woman present. The men always refrain from telling off-color jokes or saying anything that might offend me, which is perfectly okay with me! I am not too anxious to be regarded as "one of the boys."

What have you learned from your war experience?

I learned to depend upon myself, to accept help gratefully, and to help others. When we didn't have bread, our neighbors shared theirs with us and when they were short on supplies, we shared what we had with them irrespective of religion. I really understand now what it means when it is said: "Life is all about giving and taking." I also came to realize that people are basically decent, it is governments and politics that are the cause of so many of the problems.

How different would life have been for you had you not experienced war?

I lost many opportunities because the war dragged on for so many years. I am well known in my field and I had offers to work outside the country. I felt if I left, I would be abandoning Lebanon and my family. Now, my outlook has changed in so many ways. For instance, when I travel abroad to London or Paris, I find myself looking up at skyscrapers and wondering how do people dare live in those glass towers. What would happen to them if a car bomb went off. The war affected us all. I may appear calm on the outside but, compared to the way I was before the war, I have changed. When I travel, people ask me: "What is your nationality?" I tell them I am Lebanese and their response is: "Bang! Bang!" I never hide my identity. My parents and my education taught me to be proud of my country.

If you had a month off, how would you spend it?

I would love to have a house in the mountains, and spend my day reading and enjoying the view. If I hadn't gone through the war, I might have dreamed of doing something else. Now, all I want is solitude.

LAMIA RUSTUM SHEHADEH

PROFESSOR OF HISTORY

"Professor Shehadeh challenges your assumptions," says a student waiting outside her office, "and forces you to really think about history." Lamia Shehadeh, daughter of the late Asad Rustum, a distinguished Lebanese historian, is the director of the Civilization Sequence Program (CSP) at the American University of Beirut (AUB). This interdisciplinary program, part of AUB's core curriculum, explores texts dating from 2000 B.C. to contemporary times.

Shehadeh received her B.A. degree in 1961 from AUB in Ancient History of the Near East. After graduating, she married Issam Shehadeh, a medical school graduate. Both applied to Harvard and were accepted: he, to do training in nephrology at the medical school; she, on a scholarship to pursue a Ph.D. When told that there were no faculty members at Harvard who could advise her in her field, Phoenician history during the Greco-Roman period, she pursued instead a Ph.D. in Canaanite History, Religion and Literature and, as a minor, Ancient Near Eastern History, with concentration in two language areas, Northwest Semitic Epigraphy and Comparative Semitic Theology.

Shehadeh has written numerous articles and edited several books, including Asad Rustum: The Man and the Historian. *She is currently working on two books: one on the role of women during the Lebanese war and another on gender conflict in Lebanon. In addition to Arabic, Shehadeh is fluent in English, French, Hebrew, Greek, and many of the ancient Semitic languages including Aramaic. Throughout her career as an educator, she has taught a wide range of courses including: Ancient, Medieval and Renaissance Culture; Modern and Contemporary Culture; Biblical Hebrew; Religions of the Ancient Near East; Hebrew Prophets; Comparative Semitic Philology; Introduction to the Old Testament; and Society and Thought in the Classical Sources.*

I interviewed Shehadeh, a crisp, stylish woman, at her office in AUB's

Nicely Hall. Perusing a book I had lent her, she read aloud a quote from William Blake: "No bird soars too high, if she soars with her own wings," and smiling, noted: "'Soar' happens to be a favorite word of mine."

* * *

What was your reaction when the war in Lebanon finally ended?

After seventeen years of war, I remember that day clearly. It was 1991, after the elections, when peace was declared. We believed, this time, it was a "real" peace. My husband and I were in the car with the radio on and I turned to him and said: "Issam, we are still here. We made it!" It was something I honestly didn't think I would live to see happen.

Having survived the war, what do you now think is the most serious problem facing Lebanon?

Political survival. I don't believe that the fate of Lebanon has been decided. At the beginning of the war, I used to get excited and argue and discuss the political situation and then I did so less frequently and now I don't at all. I realize now that we are simply pawns in a chess game. There is nothing that I can say or do that will change that. So I am simply waiting and watching to see which pawn is going to be moved in which direction. The economic problem I think is secondary. It is an outcome of the current political limbo. Should the world leave Lebanon alone, the Phoenician blood will surge forth. We endured seventeen years of fighting and every time the world thought Lebanon was finished, all of a sudden like a Phoenix rising out of the ashes, Lebanon would reemerge. What the world needs to understand is that Lebanon will never die — not the Lebanese people!

It seems to be a point of controversy, today, whether Lebanese are descendants of the Phoenicians. As a historian, what is your position on this issue?

It's a point of controversy only because it has been politicized. I am a historian, not a politician. There is a difference between politics, history, and facts. We have two sides on this issue: one side insisting we are Phoenicians, not Arabs; the other side insisting we are Arabs, not Phoenicians. Both sides are wrong. It is a fact that this strip of land, Lebanon, used to be Phoenicia. It was also called Canaan and the inhabitants of this land called themselves Canaanites. The Greeks called these same inhabitants living along the coastline, "Phoenicians," which is the Greek translation for Canaanite. The cities: Beirut, Sidon, Tyre, Tripoli, Byblos — they are Phoenician names. Why should I forget that the original inhabitants of this piece of land were Phoenicians? They are definitely our ancestors. After the Phoenicians, there were many conquerors. This part of the world is the most ancient as far as history itself is concerned and many invaders came through: Babylonians, Assyrians, Egyptians, Aramaeans, Hittites, Persians, French, Ottomans, Seljuk Turks, and Arabs.

Fine, are we then none of these? Are we all of these? I don't believe there is any pure race, but we who live here are the product of those who came before us and this land was the land that was occupied by the Phoenicians. They were

Lamia Rustum Shehadeh

the original inhabitants. The geographical names and the archaeological remains point to that. Now, why is it that Egyptians consider themselves the descendants of the Pharaohs? The Egyptians are Arabs. Surely, they are not the Pharaohs. The Syrians do admit that the Aramaeans were their ancestors. What is wrong with that? The Greeks of today, are they really the Greeks of Plato and Aristotle? They are, after all, the inhabitants of that land called Greece. So why is it that there is an issue as far as the Lebanese are concerned?

What about Phoenician characteristics?

Yes! What I find especially fascinating is that the characteristics of the Lebanese are very Phoenician. It's uncanny! I've always wondered: Is it the climate? The land? The geography? What is it that promulgates these characteristics? There have been so many other people who have come through this land; yet, once they settled, they acquired the characteristics of the Phoenicians. For example, the Lebanese, like the Phoenicians, are still first and foremost merchants. The Phoenicians invented the alphabet; the Lebanese consider education the most important pursuit possible and they would sell everything they have to educate their children. The Phoenicians were good fighters. The Persians used the Phoenician navy to fight the Greeks. Today, the Lebanese are still good fighters (seventeen years of war attest to that). The Phoenicians explored the world and founded colonies wherever they went — Crete, Cyprus, Rhodes and Carthage. But no matter where they went they always maintained a special attachment to Phoenicia. Proof of which, they built Carthage in North Africa and called it the new city of Tyre. In a similar vein, today, the Lebanese continue to leave home and travel abroad in great numbers; yet, they still retain an unusually strong emotional attachment to Lebanon.

When you were growing up, what did you want to be?

Ever since I was a little girl I always wanted to be a teacher and obtain a Ph.D. like my father, Asad Rustum, who was the second person in Lebanon to receive a Ph.D. The first was Philip Hitti, the famous Lebanese historian who taught at Princeton University. I always told my father that I, too, was going to work towards a Ph.D. I was the youngest of four children and he would always nod his head in agreement but he never really thought I would follow through on my promise. Of course, at the time, I didn't realize that was his attitude until I was accepted into the Ph.D. program at Harvard. When he learned about it, he appeared totally surprised! I told him, "You mean you didn't really believe I would do it?" He said, "It's not that I didn't believe you could, I just thought you would grow up, get married, and you'd forget your dream."

How did you find Harvard?

The seven years I spent at Harvard were the best years of my life. What fascinated me about Harvard was that all these people, who were intellectually brilliant, worked long and hard and weren't ashamed to admit it. Just the opposite of AUB, where students would cram all night and then come to the exam saying: "I didn't study. I really didn't have the time." They would get a ninety on the exam and claim it was simply a matter of smart genes! [laughter] At Harvard, I found that students did not mind at all admitting that they had spent the whole night studying. In fact, they would vie with each other as to who had studied more!

After so many years in the States, were you reluctant to return to Lebanon?

Had I stayed in the States, I probably would have achieved much more academically, but here, in Lebanon, I became a richer human being. I have never regretted coming back. As director of the Civilization Sequence Program, I feel I am serving my community and serving the student body at AUB by helping to draw students out and encouraging them to think beyond themselves. Both my husband and I received offers to stay at Harvard but we felt we had to return to Lebanon. The first year back was very difficult. But once I started teaching, I began to readjust. I taught in a number of departments: English, Arabic, History, Religious Studies, and then I was offered a position in 1978 in the Civilization Sequence Program at AUB.

The Civilization Sequence Program was a real learning experience. It made me think about issues I would not otherwise have thought about regarding the human condition: man's fate, man's destiny, man's position in the world, the meaning of life. I liked the subject matter, the approach, and the method of teaching. It made me read books and articles I wouldn't have read had I remained in my speciality — ancient history. The program is epical in approach. Within the various periods of history, we study common themes and we see how during these periods man saw himself vis-à-vis God, vis-à-vis the universe, vis-à-vis his fellow man, vis-à-vis himself. We also try to show the interrelationship between Western culture and Arab Islamic culture.

On days when there was fighting in Beirut, what motivated you to leave your home and risk your life to come to the university to teach?

Teaching is what gave meaning to my life. Before we moved on campus, I would walk to AUB from my home. Sometimes it was eerie. I would find myself walking alone on what was normally a very busy street. My thoughts, as I was walking, were always: "Will I make it to class or will I not? Will I be killed or will I be kidnapped?"

It must have been terribly ironic teaching courses on civilization when yours was crumbling around you. What made you go on?

Continuing our work gave purpose to our lives. It was as if things were normal. When, in fact, our life was the enactment of Beckett's *Waiting for Godot*. You found yourself thinking constantly: "What am I doing here? What is the purpose of my existence?"

By "Waiting for Godot," do you mean waiting for peace?

Waiting for somebody to come along and save us. In the meantime, we cling to whatever we are doing just to make ourselves feel that we are here, we are alive. We had to give meaning to our senseless situation; otherwise, we would simply go crazy.

Is that why you risked your life to come to work?

Absolutely! In 1987, my husband and I decided to move on campus for security reasons. I shared my office with another faculty member, Nabil Mahtar, an extremely refined young man, who had a Ph.D. in 17th century English literature from Cambridge University. We both had early morning classes and we always came just a bit earlier to have coffee together and talk. One morning, I arrived and he wasn't there. I went up the hall to the office and inquired, "Where is Nabil?" They said, "He hasn't come yet." I said, "That's strange! He has never been late before." I went and taught my class and when I came out there was Nabil's wife. I was so relieved to see her. I said, "Where is Nabil?" She said, "What do you mean? He came here this morning!" It was then that we realized he had been kidnapped.

Less than two days later, one of my students found a piece of paper tucked under the windshield wiper of my car with the message: "Shehadeh, you are not wanted in West Beirut. Leave or you will regret it." At the insistence of the head of the department, I showed it to the dean and then I went home. My husband and my mother both insisted I leave immediately to the East side. I refused. I felt nobody in my own country was going to drive me away from my home. We compromised: My husband hired a bodyguard from one of the militias, and he would follow me from class to class and wait outside. Shortly thereafter, we moved on campus.

Do you have children?

I have a son. He was a little boy at the time. He is a young man now attending college in the United States. I remember during the worst of the shelling almost everybody left West Beirut, but we stayed. My husband wanted our son and I to go to East Beirut, where it was safe, and stay with relatives who kept calling and imploring us to come. My husband refused to leave his patients and I refused to leave without him. So we agreed to send our son with my sister, who had decided to cross over to the East with her family. Shortly after he reached safety, my son telephoned (telephones were still working then) and he started crying and saying, "Mama, I want to come home and die with you. I don't want to stay here." There was nothing we could say to console him so my sister took him to the demarcation line, separating East and West Beirut, and my husband waited for him on the other side and brought him home.

The last two years of the war, when the fighting was really intense, we would go down to the shelter (which had become a social gathering place) and meet with neighbors and friends. At night, while everybody slept in the shelter, we would go back to our apartment, have dinner, and sleep in our own beds. At first, when we had to go down to the shelter, during the day, I would get depressed and feel I was wasting my time. Then I decided I would take a book along and read regardless of what other people thought of me. Everyone else was playing cards, chatting, or listening to the radio. The radio was on constantly because every fifteen minutes there was a news bulletin and each station gave a slightly different version of the news. People were constantly switching radio stations to compare information. I would sit in my corner reading my book and nobody would bother me. They understood I needed to read. Books enabled me to take my mind off the shelling — to think about other things. It was important for me to come out of the shelter feeling that I had learned something new. It meant I wasn't wasting my life.

There must be nothing more frustrating than being forced to stay indoors on a beautiful day because a war is raging outside.

It's interesting that you would mention that. I remember, there was a lull one day in the fighting and I walked to the lower campus and I looked up at the sky. It was a beautiful day, warm and pleasant, compared to the dark, dank shelter — but it was desolate. I was completely alone (by that time AUB had only four families remaining on campus) and I said to myself: Which is worse? Being alone and dying above ground on a beautiful day or being with people and dying in a dark shelter? Which is better? Which is worse? I don't know.

Having survived so many years of war, do you feel your whole perception of life has changed?

Absolutely. It gave me a different vision of man, of death. Death became something one encountered daily, hourly. It wasn't that mysterious "thing" anymore. It became part of our everyday existence. You would hear that so and so died and the question, strangely enough, would be: What else is new? It also made me suffer and feel more for my fellow man. We shared a common bond of survival, understanding, compassion. It made me better understand and accept human weaknesses — something I hadn't before. It's interesting, I don't know why I didn't before. I used to feel: This is how things are. This is how it should be. Maybe it was a belief in the Protestant ethic that you should not give in to your weaknesses. You should always aim for perfection. I discovered it's part of our humanity to be weak. When I saw how vulnerable life around me was, I could begin to understand weaker people and I felt compassion for them rather than feeling, as I had in the past, that they were not doing or behaving the way I thought they should. So yes, I have become a much richer, one might charitably say, a wiser person.

Has it been a challenge being a female professor in Lebanon?

Quite! I introduced readings on feminism in the Civilization Sequence Program. At first, I approached the subject by assigning readings in fictional works and discussing how fictional female characters were treated and characterized. Then I decided to go for the jugular and assign readings on the treatment of women in nonfiction. I selected John Stuart Mill's essay "The Subjection of Women." Although it was written in the 19th century, it still applies; especially in the Middle East. Passages that did not address the universal issue of feminism, I left out. I would discuss the essay in class and then I would say: "Do you resent the fact that you are being taught by a woman?" I always took the male students off-guard when I asked that question. They could never reconcile the fact that when they spoke of their superiority to women they were being taught by a woman!

What sort of discrimination have you personally experienced?

I'll give you an example. Last year, I applied for a research grant to look into the role played by women in the Lebanese legislature. My intention was to draw attention to the fact that the Lebanese legislature discriminates against women. I was not given the research grant. I later heard from members of the grant committee, unofficially of course, that they thought my topic was emotional, based on persuasion and not scientific fact. They decided that since I wasn't a lawyer, I wasn't qualified to research the topic. The committee did not even ask me to appear before them to defend my proposal. It's only natural you become passionate when you work on something you really care about. For example, I am emotional about Phoenicia. I am emotional about Lebanon, and so am I emotional about the condition of women in Lebanon. That does not mean that my method is not scientific when I do research on any of these subjects. But that was a view the committee took for granted simply because I was a woman.

What are instances of discrimination against women in Lebanon that really offend you?

Well, look at the paradox: a single woman can have a business in Lebanon; however, once she is married, she cannot start a business without the approval of her husband. Another, if a third party takes out a life insurance policy in the name of a married woman, he does not need her approval, only her husband's approval. Who else is treated that way according to Lebanese law? The retarded, the underage, the legally insane. So a married woman in Lebanon is lumped together in that same category. On the subject of adultery: a couple caught in "the act" results in her going to prison and he going scot-free. If a man kills a female relative to save his honor, even if she is a very distant cousin, he is considered in the right; whereas if she does the same, it is homicide. This is referred to as a "crime of honor." I call it a crime of passion. He can kill her under two conditions: one is to catch her in the act, in that case he gets off scot-free, and he can kill her on the grounds of suspicion in which case he will be found guilty and receive a suspended sentence.

People in Lebanon don't believe that a problem exists. They believe women have their rights and when one brings up discrimination one is really making a mountain out of a mole hill. There are many women, I know, who say: "Well, this is how it is on paper but nobody practices that." These women don't understand that the minute you have recourse to the law, the law is against you. In the Personal Status Code, for example, women are considered mere chattel — nothing more than that. Again, I hear: "Well, husbands are not like that. They all treat their wives nicely and are kind to them." I say, yes, but then it's a favor! It's not her right. She has to please for this kind of treatment. Should the husband not be good, then what? The law is on the husband's side. The law is there to protect the innocent and that is why I believe the law should be changed.

How have you managed to balance a career and a family?

I have been fortunate enough to have a loving family, mother, and sisters, as well as the financial ease to afford hiring someone to help me. Having said that, I consider myself old-fashioned in the sense that I still do housework and take care of everything at home. Even though I am a feminist, through and through, I don't require my husband to share the work at home. When my son was a baby, I was the one who always fed him, bathed him, put him to sleep. I was the one who always woke up during the night to take care of him. After he started going to school, I arranged my classes so I would leave after he went to school and be home before he returned. Sometimes, I hear remarks said about me, that I am in charge, and poor Issam, he is the one who has to cook and do chores. When I hear that I smile and say, "Well, suppose you are right?" [laughter] People here can't understand that I can do both. They assume that since I am a full-time career woman, my house must be in shambles. When they visit and see it is not, they assume it must be because of my husband!

What is your definition of feminism?

I believe that since a woman is a human being, she shares with man her humanity. You might ask me: "Well, what is being human?" I would say to be human is to be free, to have dignity, and to be autonomous. Women are neither free, nor have dignity, nor are autonomous. By freedom, I mean freedom of opinion, freedom of thought, and the freedom to make one's own choices. A woman should be free to decide whether she wants to be a housewife or a physician; whether she wants to marry or remain single. Those should be her decisions to make. She shouldn't be forced into marriage. If she doesn't marry, she shouldn't be considered an old maid. A man is never considered an old maid. Why should a woman? A woman should be allowed to have the freedom to soar as high as she can. Not everyone can soar, but all human beings should be given the opportunity.

What is your preferred mode of relaxation after a long day?

I relax best when I listen to music. If I am uptight or depressed, I listen to Beethoven. A friend and I were arguing the other day. He said he can't listen to Beethoven when he is depressed, he has to listen to Mozart. I said, on the contrary, with Beethoven I am engulfed, transported to another world. I listen to Mozart when I am really happy. I dance to him. I used to listen to music a lot during the war. I would leave the shelter and sneak upstairs and turn on my stereo.

You had electricity?

When we lived here on campus, we had electricity. Your question reminds me of a time during a lull in the fighting when I was taking a walk on campus. This was during a period when AUB was a target. We received a total of eighty-five shells and our two cars were destroyed. Well, as I was walking, I met a friend who lived off-campus. She told me a ceasefire had been declared in her neighborhood. It did not apply to AUB because we were still getting stray rockets. She inquired how I was doing. I said, "Fine, considering we are still in the line of fire." She said, "Yes, but you have electricity!" I stopped in my tracks — stunned. It suddenly hit me how people's values changed! It didn't matter to her that my life was in danger. What was most important (because she lived in darkness) was that I had electricity. What was even stranger was that I could understand her point of view. This is what happened in the war. There was a distortion of values and, consequently, concepts and priorities changed.

Did you ever consider leaving Lebanon?

In 1976, at the beginning of the war, we left to live in Hershey, Pennsylvania. My husband received an offer from Harvard to join the transplant unit. At that time, the shelling frightened me and I wanted to leave. I couldn't stand feeling so insecure. But I had heard that the crime rate was very high in Boston and

I didn't want to trade one place of violence for another. I told Issam I would rather live in a small town. Shortly thereafter he was offered a position at the University of Pennsylvania in Hershey. I was delighted! I thought Hershey would be the ideal place for us. I had always read and seen movies about small towns in the States where everybody knows everybody, and people are warm and friendly towards each other. So we went to Hershey.

The first couple of months, I was fine. Hershey, as far as the landscape is concerned, is beautiful. But it's a huge area and there are only 17,000 inhabitants. These inhabitants are divided between the medical school and the chocolate factory. You don't see anybody! I would walk down the street and there would be no one else walking. In fact, people driving by would simply stare at me as if wondering: "What is she doing?" I tried to find work. I couldn't. I was told over and over again that I was overqualified. I tried to do volunteer work. Finally, I landed a position in the only museum at Hershey. I was put in charge of the Eskimo section.

My experience in Hershey was really devastating. I felt so alienated. I decided that I preferred the shells of Beirut to the peace and isolation of Hershey, Pennsylvania. I returned to Lebanon six months later with a new outlook. Once we came back, we never left. We made a decision that we were going to stay for the duration — for better or for worse. We were not going to emigrate. Consequently, every time the fighting flared-up, we avoided having to deal with such nagging thoughts as: "Should we leave now? Where should we go? How long should we be gone? What should we pack?" So many of our friends left Lebanon thinking the fighting would last only a few weeks or a few months. You can't live that way. You have to make a commitment one way or the other. We made a commitment to stay. I knew what it was like to be away.

GOVERNMENT, LAW, AND SOCIAL WORK

RANDA BERRI

SOCIAL WORKER

"We stretch a hand to those whom the war has disabled and left believing they are the living dead," says Randa Berri, president of the Lebanese Association for the Welfare of the Handicapped, established to provide social services, medical care facilities, and vocational training centers for those disabled by the Lebanese Civil War. Berri, wife of Parliamentary Speaker Nabih Berri, leader of the Shiite Muslim population of Lebanon, is a soft-spoken woman.

I met Randa Berri in her spacious office at the headquarters of the Lebanese Association for the Welfare of the Handicapped, located in the Barbour neighborhood of Beirut. Waiting patiently to meet with her, in an anteroom down the hall, were half-a-dozen sharply dressed businessmen and contractors.

Seated behind a large, finely polished wooden desk, inlaid in the front with the Koranic inscription: "In the name of God the compassionate, the merciful," Berri was wearing a pink and beige suit, her hair modestly covered by a matching scarf. Even though it was a beautiful, sunny day, the floor-to-ceiling, beige drapes in her office remained drawn. When members of her staff entered to speak with her, they approached with deference and spoke in low, muted tones. Throughout the interview, she rarely smiled, except when her eight-year-old son came to visit.

*   *   *

Could you tell me about yourself?
When I was growing up I read a lot. My father owned a publishing house and I read most of the books we published. The books covered historical, philosophical, religious and political subjects and were distributed all over the Arab world. My father was very young when he died in 1973. He did not have much of an education but he built a very successful business and was known for being clever and honest. My mother, too, is an exceptional woman, respected by everyone. She, as well, had little education. In all, we were eight children: five girls and three boys. My father attended school for eight years and then started his publishing house. After my father died, we carried on the business. From him, I learned that formal education is not everything. What really matters is what you learn from life.

Randa Berri

I married when I was twenty years old. I didn't get a chance to have much of an education but, like my parents, I learned from life and from every country I visited and lived in. Traveling, I think has made me very sensitive towards others. I like to be involved. I need to know how things work, including electrical and mechanical things, so when they break, I know how to fix them.

Why did you travel so much?

I am no different from many Lebanese. We are travelers. The world is our backyard. I, like most Lebanese, speak Arabic, English and French. We have integrated many nations into our society. Lebanon was the most educated and open country in the Arab world. We have always had excellent relations with countries around the world. You might say traveling is a "Lebanese routine"! and it provides us with a very broad education. Of course, it is a question of personality what you learn from your travel experience.

When you were growing up, what were your aspirations?

I remember walking to school from my house at about age thirteen. I would go to school, come home for lunch, and then go back to school. During the walk, to and from, I remember always imagining myself giving speeches and being surrounded by interesting, educated people. This fantasy was all the more astounding because I was a very shy and timid girl. I did not have the courage to speak up, even within my own family. I was always very quiet, reserved, and extremely sensitive. My two older sisters and my younger sister had much stronger personalities. I was always reluctant to ask anyone for a favor. Even if I needed something, I wouldn't ask for it directly. I would ask someone else to ask for me! So the subject of my daydreaming, as I walked, was very much out of character.

How do you explain your transformation and the fact that you are now living your dream?

Life is the best teacher. Also, wanting to achieve something in life is important. Early on, I made a decision that I wanted to be more involved. Before I married, I worked in our publishing house, with my sister, editing and signing book contracts with publishers and authors. I am the kind of person who can never sit behind a desk all day and do the same thing over and over. One of the things I hate most in life is routine. Even in my own house, I hate routine! I need to have constant renewal. I need to experience new things. To me routine is a rut. My husband is more routine-oriented than I, which creates matters for discussion in our marriage! I like to rearrange the furniture. I don't like to always sit in the same place in my house. I don't like to follow a set pattern. Routine for me is boring and, worse, it is controlling and leads to stagnation. I believe you must take risks and challenge yourself always. You must open yourself to change. Nothing comes about from routine.

How would you describe yourself?

As someone who never hurt anyone and who always tries to do her best for her people. I don't like people to respect me because of my position or where I sit — that means they only respect my chair. I think love is the most important part of my personality: love for others, for my family, for life, and for my country. I see the world through loving eyes and that helps me see things clearly. I am very sensitive and emotional. I freely admit that I am not made of strong stuff. Even now, at age forty, I cannot hear sad stories without weeping. I cannot watch television programs where children are in danger or dying. When that happens, I leave the room or I ask my husband to change the channel. I cannot stand to see a child abused, not even verbally.

It must have been very hard for you to live in Beirut during the war and to pursue the kind of work that you do. How did you cope?

I have three daughters and a son. The youngest, my boy, is now eight years old and my daughters are twenty-two, twelve, and ten years old. I used to spend sometimes two, three days in a row with the children down in the bomb shelter, crowded with people. It was so difficult. The air was full of smoke and there was no water for baths, nothing. Sometimes, when the shelling was very intense, my husband would insist we leave Beirut because he could not work when he was worried about our safety. My husband was a target because of the political situation. There were many attempts made on his life. But God was with us and that is how we survived. Faith is the most important thing.

Do you pray a lot?

I do my duty as a Muslim. I pray five times a day. I read the Koran all the time. I think my husband and I have a special feeling for life because of our faith. Our faith is our strength. When I speak about my love for life, that comes from my faith. It was not easy to leave my husband, during the fighting, but I had the children to worry about and he would not leave. He is a leader. I would only go as far as Damascus. I would spend a few weeks with the children there and then, when things calmed down, we would return. The longest time we were away during the fighting was two months.

Do you attribute your sensitivity to the pain of others to what you endured during the war?

I was always like this, but the misery and destruction caused by the war intensified those feelings. When I married my husband, I was afraid that I would not measure up to the requirements necessary to be the wife of a leader. I thought that his political and social obligations would be too much for me. It took my husband two years to convince me to marry him!

What finally persuaded you?

The fact that he believed in me more than I believed in myself. He felt I had what it would take to be his wife and to stand by his side. We worked it out from there.

How did you become a social activist?

My husband's position as a leader is what turned me into an activist. There was such a pressing need for social and humanitarian work. The war left behind a lot of orphans, as well as handicapped and wounded people. As the wife of a political figure, I felt, even though I did not consider myself an activist, I had to do something for those who were suffering. I didn't choose my work, it chose me. In 1984, I founded the Lebanese Welfare Association for the Handicapped to help the disabled lead productive and useful lives by establishing rehabilitation, educational, and vocational training centers.

What is a normal day for you?

My husband never complained in the past but now he and my children are complaining that they don't see enough of me. I believe you have to make sacrifices to help others. The Shiite of Lebanon have experienced not only seventeen years of war, but a century of deprivation. Some of us must sacrifice more than others to make up for that. We have to reconfigure our political, social, and health systems. Human rights are below zero. We have nothing! We must start from the beginning. Simple, routine work will not achieve the distance we must cover; nor will a routine way of life. What we need is exceptional people, exceptional effort, and exceptional belief. I believe not more than one generation should pay the price and that price should be paid by the generation I belong to. This is what makes me get up and go to work in the morning. I have taught my children to understand that their parents' work is important by involving them as much as possible in what I do. It also helps them understand why their father and I are sometimes tired and nervous. I tell them all the time that we are always thinking of them even when we are not with them.

You cover your hair with a scarf for religious reasons; are you encouraging your daughters to do the same?

No, because I didn't do it until I was ready. When I was young and unmarried, I didn't wear a scarf. My husband helped me to take that step. When they are ready, they, too, will take that step. I wear a scarf because I believe it is my duty according to my religious book, the Koran. But it was my choice. I don't believe a veil protects a woman one hundred percent, but it does offer some protection. There are many women who dress very conservatively; yet, their morals are not as modest as their dress! You mustn't judge people by the way they dress. Whether you choose to cover yourself or not is a choice based on your faith. If everyone wore a veil it wouldn't be a problem. It would be natural. However, even in Lebanon, I get stares. When I travel to Europe, I get an even stronger reaction. I don't insist that my daughters wear scarves. I don't want them to feel different from the rest of society or different from their classmates. Even if I insisted they wear a scarf, as soon as they are out of my sight, they could easily take it off. If they decide to wear a scarf, I want them to do so because that is what they want to do. Of course, not wearing a scarf doesn't mean that they are ignoring their religion.

Do you feel that there is a degree of resentment among men, here, at your association, because their boss is a woman?

I haven't felt that. Even though we are in the Orient, Lebanese men are used to cooperating and working with women. There are many Lebanese women who are involved in business. It is true that we haven't reached any major positions in politics, but I think that is due to our own fault. If men try to control us and take away our rights, we must stand up and win our rights. Of course, it helps to do so with their cooperation because, let's face it, the political and social system is in their hands. It has been that way for centuries. We cannot change things overnight unless we do it with their consent. I always say, how you get there is much more important than getting there, because you have to live with the consequences.

Do you think men and women are equal?

A woman is not a man and a man is not a woman. There is a difference. We must admit it. We are different physically and emotionally. That is why we are mothers. God did not give men what he gave women. I am a woman who can stay up all night with a sick child. I believe the majority of women, compared to the majority of men, are more sensitive and we, perhaps, have a greater capacity for love. We feel the pain of others' suffering more deeply and that is why so many women are involved in social work. God also made women more patient and detail-oriented. I think, too, women are more thoughtful when it comes to making decisions than men. A woman always thinks about the consequences. How a decision will affect others. A man, usually, thinks only about how it will affect himself. Have I got myself into enough trouble, yet?

If that is the case, women would make better leaders. Don't you think?

Yes, with the help of men, because women have the right outlook.

What social or political changes would you like to see evolve in Lebanon?

Our biggest and most dangerous problem is that the government is not equitable in its treatment of all Lebanese, especially the deprived classes. In Lebanon, you are judged by your religion. I was on television a couple of weeks ago and I was asked: "Do you believe Lebanon will change and become what you want it to be?" I said, "Sadly, no! Not as long as there are people in decision-making positions in government who discriminate along religious lines." There cannot be peace when there is such discrimination. All Lebanese, with no exception, should be judged according to their ability. Religion should not be a factor. People outside of our country see us all as Lebanese. We must learn to see ourselves that way, too, and not as Druze, Maronites, Greek Orthodox, Shiite, Sunni, et cetera. The Koran, for example, is the continuity of the Bible. That is what my religion teaches me. Religion is what is between you and your God. It is politics that ruins religion and separates people.

What did you do during the war years?

I was raising my children and I was asked to head the Lebanese Welfare Association for the Handicapped in 1984. I accepted the position because as the wife of a politician it is my duty to help my country anyway I can. I feel deeply responsible for my people. It bothers me when I see donor organizations come to Lebanon who are more interested in helping themselves than the people. These organizations have taught me an important lesson and that is no one can help you better than you can help yourself. During the war, I released a lot of my stress and anxiety by helping those around me. Every day, I felt I was being tested to prove my faith in God and in my religion. Every day, we lived with the hope that the next week or the next month a solution would be found to end the fighting.

Did you ever give up hope?

The last few years of the war I did. Hope was too painful. Every time a solution fell through it was heartbreaking. I made a decision never to count on hope because I could not take anymore disappointments. I would tell myself: I live here. I was born here. This is my identity. I cannot change my identity. I have to live here. This is my society, my nation, my country, good or bad. I have to continue on and I must give up hope; otherwise, I risk my health and my sanity. I must live one day at a time. It was that philosophy that pulled me through.

What was the worst point for you during the war?

There are so many! That is why I developed my philosophy. Thank God, I did not lose anyone in my family, but we lost a lot of close friends. It was difficult seeing strong healthy men go out to fight for our country and return missing a leg or an arm. Small children affected me the most. Many are the same age of my own children and seeing them handicapped depresses me. I have become used to seeing handicapped adults. I am able to joke with them and I try to lift their spirits, but I have not been able to do that with children. When I see a handicapped child, I cannot get the child out of my mind and it becomes difficult for me to continue working. All the volunteers and the staff here know this. Even though, according to my religion, I must accept everything, I find it very difficult to accept this. I used to cry every time a handicapped person came into my office. My staff would tell me: "Look, you have to have courage. These people are in pain and they are depressed. You cannot show that you have less courage than they. They have the problem. You don't! You must give them courage and hope." God knows, I try.

ZAHRA BISSAT

SOCIAL WORKER

"She is always there when you need her," says her nephew, Hytham Azhari. A serene, genteel woman, Zahra Bissat likes quietly to do good works and deeds. A life-long volunteer, she heads "Dar Al Salam" (House of Peace), a home for the elderly in her hometown of Sidon, Lebanon.

We met early one Sunday morning in her spacious Beirut apartment overlooking the Mediterranean Sea. Prominently displayed in her drawing room hangs an oil painting of her late husband, Muhammad Bissat, a successful businessman. A frequent traveler, she had just returned from India where she went to experience "the flavor of another culture," and was sorting through photographs of the trip.

When Bissat is not engaged in volunteer work, she enjoys flower arranging, painting on porcelain, and getting together with her large, close-knit, extended family. As we chatted, her four-year-old granddaughter, and namesake, played nearby. After showing me a portrait of herself and her late husband, where both are laughing and he is lifting her up in the air to reach something beyond her grasp, she observed with misty eyes, "This picture captures our marriage."

*   *   *

Who is Zahra Bissat?
I am the eldest of nine children. I lived in the city of Sidon, until the age of nine, where I attended an Arab kindergarten, and then the American Elementary School for Girls. I was very athletic and played a lot of sports. When I was in the fifth grade, we moved to Beirut where I was enrolled in an English school, which was strict and confining. I was unhappy there. I attended the school for three years and when I turned fourteen I became engaged to my cousin, Muhammad.
So you became engaged to avoid school?

[laughter] I was very happy to be out of that school! Now, I realize it was a mistake. In the Middle East, it is the custom to ask for the hand of a girl when she is very young. I was a beautiful girl and all the members of the family used to say: "Zahra is for her cousin, Muhammad." Whenever anybody came to ask for my hand, I turned them down because I believed my cousin Muhammad was to be my husband. Muhammad was nine years older than I. He, too, left school when he was young, which was shortly after his father had his first heart attack. Muhammad was the oldest of ten children and once his father became ill, he had to prepare to take over the family's import/export business. It would have been a disaster for the family if anything happened to the father and no one knew anything about the business. Muhammad, at the time, was studying to become an architect but was obliged to change his studies to business, which he did for two years before going to work for his father.

In the past, most of the commercial work dealing with sugar, coffee, and rice came through Egypt, so Muhammad spent most of his time there. Life was different in Egypt compared to today because Egypt then had a king. The lifestyle at the top was lavish and most of Muhammad's associates were influential and wealthy people. One was the minister of commerce, who had two daughters. Muhammad thought he would marry one of them. But my uncle (his father), feared that if he married an Egyptian, he would remain in Egypt and there would be no one prepared to look after the family. So he flew to Egypt and told Muhammad, "You will return with me to Lebanon and marry your cousin, Zahra, who is now old enough to be your wife." Muhammad said, "I like my cousin, but she is very young for me. She won't know how to conduct herself with my friends." His father said, "Okay, you don't have to marry her, you can marry someone else from Lebanon." Meanwhile, many people were asking for my hand but my response was always: "If I don't marry Muhammad, I will never marry."

You were only fourteen and you were sure you knew who you wanted to marry?

Yes, I knew. If I were older, I probably would not have been so stubborn. I would have said: "If he doesn't want me, then I don't want to marry him either!" [laughter] But I was young and I liked him. He was very good looking. Everybody in the family tried to change my mind especially when a nice young man, from a good family, came to ask for my hand. But still I said: "No, I will not marry anyone except Muhammad."

Muhammad returned and became engaged to a Lebanese girl. Just before they were to get married there was a death in her family and the wedding was postponed. They broke up soon afterwards. Days passed and then at ten o'clock one night, Muhammad said to his mother, "Let's go visit my aunt." His mother said, "Good, Zahra will be asleep at this hour." They came and my parents were not home. The maid woke me up and said, "Your aunt and her son are here and your mother and father are out." I was very excited. I put on a dress and I didn't even comb my hair. I went out into the salon very happy to see them. I offered them coffee and Muhammad took out a cigarette to smoke. I ran to light it for him. I was very nervous. I struck the match several times but it would not light. In a mocking voice Muhammad said, "Your fire is cold!" I replied, "No, it is not

Zahra Bissat

my fire, it is yours that is cold." He looked at me very surprised. I had grown up very quickly from the time he had seen me two years earlier when I was twelve. That very same evening, Muhammad borrowed his mother's ring and put it on my finger. It fit perfectly! He told me: "Go to sleep and we will come back tomorrow."

Muhammad returned the following day and spoke with my father, who agreed that we could become engaged, provided we wait three years before getting married so I could get my diploma. Muhammad agreed and began building our house. One year later the house was ready and furnished. He came to my father and said, "I can't wait two more years like we agreed, I want to marry Zahra now. She can continue her education. I will bring tutors to the house so she can study." Muhammad was very open-minded, he would have allowed me to continue attending school, but the law in Lebanon prevented married girls from attending secondary school. I could attend university but not secondary school.

My husband was a very active man. We had many friends and we were always entertaining. Muhammad was very good at mixing business with pleasure. I often traveled with him. During the day, he would attend to his business affairs and at night we missed nothing! We would attend musicals, operas, concerts. We led a very full life. The years I spent with my husband went by very quickly. He was only fifty-two years old when he died. When we married, his father was very sick. On his deathbed, he asked Muhammad to promise him that he would look after his brothers and sisters until the youngest, who was then three years old, reached the age of twenty-one. Muhammad kept his word to his father and I helped him.

I have only one son. When we married, Muhammad told me: "We are not going to have a large family because I have to raise my brothers and sisters. I can't raise two families. But for your sake, we will have one child." I accepted, because I also came from a large family and I understood his responsibility to his brothers and sisters.

When Muhammad knew he was not well, he became very strict with our son, Mustapha. He said, "If we spoil him, you will lose him. We have to be strong with him so he will grow up to be dependable." After Mustapha received his B.A.—it was during the war—he wanted to continue his studies in business and economics in Paris at a university which required that he know French, English and German. He already knew French and English, so we sent Mustapha to Munich to study German. During this time, my husband became very ill. We went to Europe to see specialists and they said it was too late for him to have a heart operation. Muhammad knew he had no time left and he began preparing for his death. He organized everything so his business would continue on after his death. He even took care of his own death formalities and selected his gravestone. He would tell me: "Don't worry, I will see to it that you are well taken care of and that your lifestyle will be the same as if I were alive. I don't want you to change your life at all. I want you to travel, visit your friends, invite them over, and if you meet a man you like, I want you to marry him."

What type of business was your husband in?

He was in the import/export business. We export fruit and import rice and coffee. My husband was forward thinking. He built a shopping center in Saudi Arabia and bought a barge to transport produce between Lebanon and Saudi Arabia. During the war, we had to throw away our fruit because we couldn't deliver it to the dock because of the fighting. We had to obtain fruit from Turkey and Italy to stay in business.

I understand that you are responsible for running a center for the elderly.

Yes, and I like to work with small children so they will grow up to be good people. When Muhammad died, I was very depressed. I didn't go out for five years. When I came out of mourning, I wanted to help people. I worked as a volunteer for whatever organization asked for my help: the deaf, the blind, orphanages, welfare organizations. One of the organizations I worked for was established to prevent begging on the streets of Sidon. Every month we would send a pension to those who agreed to stay home and not go out and beg. Today, Sidon, as a result, is the only town in Lebanon where you don't see beggars on the streets. Sidonians were so pleased with this that they gave money to the organization without even being asked. We accumulated a lot of money and discovered that many of the elderly people who were being paid pensions to stay at home had nobody to look after them. A group of us decided to get together and build a home for them. We called it "Dar Al Salam" [House of Peace].

The war started before "Dar Al Salam" opened. It was built on the top of a hill overlooking Sidon and all the various parties wanted to take it over for military reasons. It was only four years ago that the center was returned to us to be used for its original purpose. The Lebanese Army had been occupying the building and we asked them to leave, but they refused. I discussed our problem with Mrs. Haraoui, the First Lady, and she suggested I speak to the head of the army. I made an appointment with the general and I told him: "We want our center back." One week later, the army moved out. Now, we have all four floors of our center back. Originally, we started with thirteen volunteers, then we grew to eighty and I was elected chairman. After we had furnished the center, we made an announcement that all elderly people from Sidon who had nowhere to go could live at the center for free. Those who came from other regions were welcome but they had to pay a fee. We now have forty-two boarders and a waiting list. We have a staff of excellent nurses and a very dedicated group of volunteers.

During the war I traveled a lot. I went to Vienna and visited many homes for the elderly to see how we could improve our center. I discovered many of them had entertainment areas, restaurants, beauty shops, swimming pools, and they were located near parks to encourage residents to go for walks. I would come back and implement what I had seen. One of the first things we did was raise money to build a cafeteria so visitors would have a place to eat. It was a huge success and a revenue producer. Much of the kitchen staff is made up of volunteers. The profits now help contribute to the center's operating budget. Many visitors enjoyed the food so much they asked for take-out, which has resulted in a catering service for special occasions, weddings, and condolences. We also created a garden and the first playground in Sidon for children. The elderly can now watch the children play and supervise them.

How did you cope during the war years?

At the beginning of the war, I remained here with my husband and my mother-in-law. Muhammad sent all his brothers and sisters abroad and had them enroll their children in schools. When it was calm, we traveled to Europe but whenever there was trouble we returned to Beirut because Muhammad did not want his workers to feel abandoned. My husband would go under the bombs from Beirut to Sidon to pay our employees. When our employees were in danger, we moved them and their families to the mountains or wherever it was safe. We always looked after their best interest. Everyone who worked for us never wanted to leave. They were loyal to us and we were loyal to them.

What was your worst experience during the war?

We experienced so many terrible days that I have lost count. There was a parking lot next to our house in Beirut and sixty-eight cars were set on fire by exploding shells. At the time, the shelling was nonstop and we were trapped in our house. Every moment we expected a shell to land directly on us. As the cars caught on fire and burned, there was nothing we could do. I gave everyone a wet towel to cover their mouths and noses so they wouldn't suffocate from the smoke. All we could do was sit and wait for something to happen.

We felt we were going to die so many times. Once, I was in Sidon and I was worried about my father and my brother. It was Sunday and it is a family tradition with us that every Sunday all my brothers and sisters and their families come and spend the day at my father's house. I was in the car swerving between exploding shells and when I arrived at the house, my father and my brother were astonished to see me.

There are so many days and nights I will never forget. My mother was a very good mother...I cannot talk about her without becoming emotional, I am sorry.... I was not with her when she died. I was very sad because my son and his family were in Vienna and I wanted to visit them. My mother, for some reason, asked me not to go. I said, "I need to see them and I will be gone just for one week." I flew to Vienna, Friday, and early Sunday morning I spoke with my mother. Later that day, she died. I flew back to Beirut right away. When I arrived there was horrible fighting on the streets and we couldn't take my mother to Sidon to bury her. We couldn't even get out of the house to take her body to the hospital morgue. Imagine! We suffered a lot in this war.

What matters to you in life, now?

What really matters to me is to be loved by my family and to be kind to people. I like to help people. I never say no to anyone who asks for my help. Even if I am not in a position to help, I always try.

MONA HARAOUI

FIRST LADY OF LEBANON

Born in Jerusalem, Mona Haraoui, the wife of the tenth president of the Republic of Lebanon, Elias Haraoui, is admired for her courage and

The author (left) with the First Lady of Lebanon, Mrs. Mona Haraoui.

compassion. "*She is a rare friend,*" *confides a prominent doctor's wife.* "*I will never forget when my husband was dying, shells were falling everywhere and I could not get a doctor to come to the house to see him, yet Mona came, driving the car herself, to be with me.*"

Shortly after taking office on November 24, 1989, following the assassination of President René Moawad, President Haraoui announced the formation of Lebanon's Second Republic. Working alongside her husband, she does volunteer work and fundraising to support countless charities that assist children, the elderly and the handicapped. An inspiring public speaker, Lebanon's First Lady is comfortable delivering speeches in Arabic, French and English. As she travels to address world forums, she makes it her mission to meet with Lebanese expatriates, encouraging them to return to Lebanon and make a difference.

Passing through a phalanx of guards, a metal detector, then up an elevator, I am escorted to the drawing room where Mrs. Haraoui, an elegant woman with a warm smile and gracious manners, a filofax by her side, greets me. Orange juice, coffee and pastries are served in quick succession and then we are left uninterrupted.

*   *   *

Could you tell me about yourself?

My father died when I was very young. I wanted to continue my studies at the university but I didn't have the opportunity. I taught for two years and then I married. I am very ambitious. I always like to learn new things. I try never to look back on life. It stops your ambition. I believe you should always look ahead and anticipate achievements. My husband began his career in politics in 1972, as a member of parliament, and then he became a minister. In life you must climb the ladder one step at a time to reach the summit.

When you were growing up, did you ever think you would one day be the First Lady of Lebanon?

No. Even though my husband's family is very involved in politics, I never really thought that my husband would become president. My husband's father was a well-known personality in Zahlé and his older brother was a member of parliament. When his brother died, my husband succeeded him. Politics is not easy. You have to accommodate yourself to it. Your life is not your own. You are always surrounded by others. Fortunately, I like people and receiving visitors is second-nature to me.

Don't forget, my husband became president under very tragic and frightening circumstances. President Moawad had only been in office seventeen days when he was killed in a car bomb explosion and before him President Gemayal also met a tragic fate. I would have given anything for my husband to become president under different circumstances. The situation in Lebanon was horrible. What kept me going was my belief in God. I believe that when you have faith and you do good for your country, whatever happens, you can accept it.

President Clinton once was asked, if he were in a crisis, who would he want in the room with him? He responded: "My wife." What do you think President Haraoui's response would be to such a question?

Because the president and I think so much alike, I believe he would want to hear a different point of view. We have our cup of coffee together every morning and if I feel he is upset about something, I try to distract or cheer him up. I know his moods. If that doesn't work, we discuss what is bothering him. I believe a husband and wife should always be sensitive and responsive to each other's moods. That is the secret to a long and happy marriage! If my husband is nervous, I try to calm him and he does the same for me. When I travel, he feels very lonely so when I am at home I try not to go out too much, especially if I feel he is in need of me. We are very attached to each other. This is our thirty-fourth year of marriage.

As First Lady, what are your special interests?

Since my husband became president, it is very important for me to help those in need. I have formed a committee to coordinate relief efforts. At the beginning, we helped the poor by giving them food, mattresses, and blankets. Then it became apparent that many needed hospitalization. Seventeen years of war is not easy to survive and stay healthy. Through our work, we discovered that many people suffered from heart problems, diabetes and thalassemia [a

Mediterranean disease]. During the fighting, people couldn't afford to come to the city to be hospitalized so their health deteriorated. At the beginning, we focused our efforts on all those who needed hospitalization. Then, because there were so many, we were forced to concentrate on children up to the age of eighteen.

I am taking full advantage of my position and resources to help the children of Lebanon, especially those suffering from diabetes and thalassemia. Thanks to fundraising dinners, generous donors, and telethons, we have built the Chronic Care Center, a fully staffed and equipped medical facility which treats children who suffer from these two diseases without charge.

Do you think women are as capable as men?

Absolutely! When a woman decides to do something, she does it as it should be done. Why? Because we are not only as capable as men but we also put more effort and more devotion into what we do. When a woman makes a commitment to do something, she will do her best to see it through — that is not always true with men.

If Lebanon were a patient and you were a doctor, how would you categorize the condition of your country?

Lebanon is a solid country. Our homes are made of stone. People leave, but they always come back to the same village where their families have lived for generations. We have deep roots. We are attached to our country, to our mountains, to our trees, to our flag, to our way of life. Not many countries could survive after so many years of war and devastation. Life, before the war, was so easy even for the village people. They had their own houses, their own land, their own crops. They were happy. But with the displacement of the Lebanese people (many of who have become refugees in their own country), we now have so many who are very poor. Some left the country for good and many of those who stayed need help. To answer your question, we have stopped bleeding. We are improving, but we are still in critical condition.

Is that due to the fact there isn't much of a middle class left?

Yes, there is some truth to that. Because of the war, we suffered a brain drain in Lebanon. For a period, there were only two classes: the very rich and the very poor. Inflation combined with the devaluation of our monetary system depleted all the savings of the middle class. The middle class maintains the stability of a country. In a country where there are only two classes, it's hard to go on. But now doctors have started to come back, so have professors, engineers, et cetera. There is a lot of work available for everyone because of the reconstruction efforts. We are now in the process of regaining our middle class. We are also in the peace process and we are working very hard. We are asking the Lebanese people who work outside of Lebanon to invest their money in their country. I think many Lebanese will eventually return to Lebanon. There is a consensus that there will be no more war in Lebanon. We don't ask for donations. The Lebanese people are proud. They don't like to receive anything unless they can give something in return. We love our country.

Every time I have been on a plane that lands in Beirut, the moment the plane touches the ground the passengers clap, cheer and hug. I haven't seen that kind of reaction anywhere else in the world!

Do you know why they react that way? It is because we suffered a great deal; our country suffered a great deal. We are attached to our country. I, myself, used to clap and cry also. During the war, I traveled for ten days at a time to get some rest because we had horrific nights and days. It was impossible to sleep with the constant shelling. I used to cry and say: "Why God did you do this to us? Why are you doing this to us? What did we do? It's so hard to live like this." Sometimes, I felt we would not live to see the next day. Tomorrow seemed so far away...so uncertain. When I traveled and I saw how other people were living in peace and we were suffering trying to keep our country together and not abandon it, I would cry and cry. It was very hard. You don't realize what a luxury peace is until you don't have it.

When you travel abroad as First Lady, what questions are you most often asked about your country?

Lately, I've been to New York and Los Angeles to attend fundraising events. Many of the Lebanese I speak to have not been back to Lebanon since the war started. They are very curious about the living conditions, security, and quality of education. They ask: "How do you live? How are the people? Are the buildings still standing? How does the president manage with foreign troops in the country?" I tell them come to Lebanon and see for yourself. Perhaps, you will then ask different questions, beginning with: "How can we help?"

What do you dislike about being First Lady?

It is so formal! My life is not as spontaneous as it used to be. Before the presidency, I used to wear slacks and T-shirts. I was very sporty. People are always curious to see what the wife of the president is wearing. If they don't like what I am wearing, I will read about it the following day! [laughter] I no longer have the time to take long walks or do sports. It makes me a little tense having to wear formal clothes all the time. But you learn to make adjustments for each period of your life. For example, when my family lost everything, I accepted that and life continued. When we lived under the shelling, I accepted that. Now, that I am First Lady, I accept this life, too. I intend to do my best and set a good example.

It is amazing that after so many years of war, Lebanese society is still extremely fashion-conscious. What do you think accounts for this enthusiasm for fashion?

Lebanese women are very elegant. They like to dress. Our society is very different from other societies and other Arab countries for the simple reason that Lebanese men like to live well and they like their families to live well. Also, Lebanese women are well-educated: they are professors, doctors, lawyers, and now even members of parliament. Women are working in jobs outside the home to counter the effects of inflation. We are waking up and moving ahead! We are climbing the ladder to achieve political status. We didn't have it before, but we are now well along to achieving it.

Another element that surprises me is that after so many years of war the social fabric of this country is still very much intact.

Let me tell you why. The credit goes to the many Lebanese associations which were established by well-intentioned, capable women and men. Without them most of the people would have left Lebanon. These associations represented stability when everything else was in shambles. The people working for these associations worked very hard throughout the war and they were very able. Now, after the war, they are even more energetic. They are doubling their efforts to help those in need. Many centers have been established by these associations to assist those who have become handicapped as a result of the war.

When your children were growing up, what were your hopes for them?

As a mother, I wanted them to be the ideal children. Thank God, I have a girl and a boy. I taught them to respect others so they would be respected. I also taught them to be self-confident and to never imitate others blindly. My daughter is married to the minister of foreign affairs, Fares Bouez, and they have four wonderful children. She is cool, very simple, and adores her children. My son is happily married as well and he has a baby boy. He studied in the States for eight years and now he is back in Lebanon. He is very self-assured, intelligent, and independent. I've been very fortunate with my children. In Lebanon, even when the children grow up, marry, and travel, they never outgrow their respect for their parents. I do not like to interfere in the affairs of others, especially my children. From time to time, though, I will give them advice. If they take my advice into consideration that is fine; if not, it's their problem, not mine! [laughter] Like every mother, I want my children to be happy and live the Lebanese way, which is a fine way of life.

What do you mean by living "the Lebanese way"?

What makes Lebanon special is that we have a certain familiarity between families. The family, here, is very important unlike some countries where children are encouraged to leave home at age sixteen or eighteen because parents feel their children are grown-up and are no longer their responsibility. No! That is not our way at all! No matter how old our children are, we are always very protective of them. We fear for their safety and feel that we are responsible for them and they are a part of us. It's much better this way. Families are much happier when children have this sense of security. If you are living alone and are unhappy, you may do something crazy that you will regret. Whereas, if you live with your family, you can always go to your mother, cry on her shoulder, and unburden yourself. It is amazing how much better you feel when you have someone you can trust to talk things over with. When a mother says, "Don't worry!" she means it.

In the States, for example, psychiatrists and therapists are very popular. Why? Because people often don't have families to turn to and discuss their problems and anxieties. Here, in Lebanon, we rarely have need of such professions. I give you myself as an example. During the hardships of the war and the weight of my husband's responsibilities as president, I suffered, worried and cried a lot when the bombardment was heavy. But still, in spite of all that, I felt calm because I had my family around me. I never thought of going to a psychiatrist to tell him or her my problems. I had no reason to because I shared my fear and my problems with my children, my husband, and my mother. They would cool me down and reassure me.

How do you like to relax or unwind after a long day?

I relax by walking on my treadmill. Also, I try not to schedule too many meetings in the afternoon unless the meetings are with friends. When I am very tired, I enjoy listening to music. It helps me feel better, or I read. I read a lot at night. To tell you the truth, if I had a week to do anything I wanted, I would go to the beach and I would relax in the sun, wear shorts, read a book, and be as I used to be — simple — and no one would know me!

BAHIA HARIRI

MEMBER OF PARLIAMENT

Bahia Hariri, a member of parliament representing Sidon and the South of Lebanon, chairs the Parliamentary Committee on Education. Sister of philanthropist and Lebanese Prime Minister Rafiq Hariri, she is also responsible for overseeing the extensive philanthropic efforts of the Hariri family in the South of Lebanon, where she is known as an energetic, hands-on manager, who regularly pulls eighteen-hour workdays.

Hariri has always had a strong interest in education, having worked as a teacher and an administrator for many years. In 1979, she helped found the Hariri Foundation, a private, nonprofit educational organization established to rebuild Lebanon by developing its human resources. In its first year, while Lebanon was in the throes of its ruinous civil war, the foundation dispatched two thousand young men and women to study abroad. Today, many of these graduates, known as Hariri Scholars, and now numbering more than 18,000, have returned to Lebanon to rebuild the country and are making a significant difference in the private and public sectors.

Hariri, who is married to businessman Mustapha Hariri, is the proud mother of two boys and two girls. A soft-spoken woman who comports herself with dignity and grace, she is described by an associate as "a strong individual who wields power softly and gets things done without a lot of fanfare." For the interview, we met late one evening at her elegant and spacious home in Sidon. Her eldest son, Nader, a civil engineering student at the American University of Beirut, and an aide joined us.

*   *   *

Could you tell me about your background?

I was born in 1952 and brought up in a very average Lebanese family. There

The author (left) and Bahia Hariri.

were my two brothers and me. Education was always the most important thing for us. I studied to be a teacher and I taught school for ten years. I only left teaching in order to join the Hariri Foundation, where I felt I could make a real difference. I was a primary and elementary school teacher and I taught Arabic, French, and mathematics. When I helped found the Hariri Foundation, I had two children, Nader and Ghena. The foundation was established to assist students who could not afford the costs of an education. Our role is to provide interest free loans to young people who want to continue their education at the undergraduate, graduate and postgraduate levels. Our philosophy is to educate young men and women so they in turn will be in a position to educate others. The wealth of Lebanon has always been its people — that is our natural resource. Our intention is to gather our people back and together, rebuild our country.

All my work is in education. I founded the Rafiq Hariri High School in Sidon, where we now have 1,500 students. We also built a library, an infirmary, a recreational center and a university. Unfortunately, all this construction is in the Israeli-occupied zone in southern Lebanon. In 1985, we were obliged to close all the schools in the occupied zone but we later reopened them. It was because of my strong interest in education and my involvement with people from all backgrounds that I was elected to become a member of parliament, representing the citizens of Sidon and the South of Lebanon.

When you were growing up, did you ever dream that one day you would be a member of parliament and your brother, prime minister?

Never! I was not interested in politics but I was asked to enter politics and I felt I had something to contribute. I believe the education of our children is one of the most vital tasks of national recovery and development. I felt I could do more for the Lebanese educational system being on the inside of government rather than on the outside.

What did you want to be when you were a young girl?

I wanted to be a medical doctor but, instead, I went into education, which I have enjoyed very much. I like influencing students and preparing them to become responsible citizens with high moral and cultural values. I think that is the greatest challenge. I am now in a very good position as head of the education committee in parliament to make a difference for all Lebanese in improving our educational system. After seventeen years of war, all sectors of education have grown stagnant. We are now experiencing a period of activity and are working to improve Lebanon's educational program. I hope in the coming years to affect real changes.

Have you found it difficult juggling a career and family?

It is difficult but, thank God, my children and my husband are of great help to me. They understand the position I am in and they have been very accommodating. Otherwise, I wouldn't be able to balance a career with being a mother and wife. Of course, that said, I feel I am always trying to make up for the time I spend away from them.

What is your role as head of the Hariri Foundation?

I am responsible for the foundation in the South of Lebanon. Even now, I continue to assist in the student selection process, which is rigorous. To be a Hariri scholar you have to maintain a GPA of 2.5 and above. We look for students who are in need of financial support to continue their education and who are capable of doing well in college. I am also a member of the board of the Hariri Foundation in America.

What are your special concerns for Lebanon?

For me, the most important concern is public education because it is education that brings communities together and breaks down barriers. I have a lot of hope for the future of Lebanon. Were that not the case, I would not have become a member of parliament nor would I be working as hard as I am in parliament and at the foundation. During the extended period of war that we experienced, I worked for ten years through all the chaos. It was very hard for people to live a normal life but we are a country of optimists and we always had the hope that we would stay together as one nation.

The Hariri Foundation has given more scholarships than any other foundation in the world over such a short period of time. Why this generosity?

It is not generosity! It is a necessity. During the time that we founded the foundation many of our youths were on the streets carrying guns. We felt it would be best for the welfare of the nation that they be guided towards education and prepared for a constructive future that would benefit the country instead of a destructive end.

Is the Hariri Foundation trying to recreate a middle class?

Yes. We have only two classes now: rich and poor. If things continue as they are only the rich will be able to afford to send their children to school. The middle class is in very bad shape, but we have great hope that the middle class will once more thrive in Lebanon because they are the foundation of a nation. They are the ones who appreciate education and hold the jobs that build up a society. Fifty-five percent of Hariri scholars who completed undergraduate degrees went on to pursue graduate study in their area of interest and eleven percent completed doctoral programs. By far, the great majority of Hariri scholars select electrical and civil engineering as their major. Their knowledge and skills, along with those of fellow Hariri scholars who majored in biomedical, mechanical, architectural, industrial, manufacturing, transportation, telecommunications and system analysis engineering will enrich immeasurably the pool of talent upon which Lebanon must draw upon as it rebuilds its infrastructure. Moreover, when the Lebanese currency returns back to normal, it will be possible for the middle class to return to Lebanon.

If you were a doctor and Lebanon your patient, what category of care would you list Lebanon in?

Intensive care.

How did you cope during the seventeen years of war?

We remained here during the entire period. Whenever there was a break in the fighting those who could afford to would hurry back to Lebanon. The Lebanese people did not want war. I always had hope during the entire war because I have faith in Lebanon.

What type of advice do you give your brother, the prime minister?

It is generally my brother who gives me advice! He is my big brother and, since I was young, he has always been a very responsible and protective older brother. He is the one who gave people hope during the war by creating the Hariri Foundation to educate the youth. He understands how difficult it is to get an education when you have no money. When we were growing up my brothers and I went through very difficult times in order to afford an education. We suffered a lot. We are self-made people and we are still the same people we always were — wealth has not changed us. We have great faith in ourselves and in our ability to accomplish what we set out to do. We have not forgotten who we are or where we come from. To this day, education is the most important factor for us: education is what made a difference in our lives. My brother and I believe that the youth of this country, given the opportunity to have a good education, will also make a difference for Lebanon.

Why do you think your brother is taking on all this responsibility as prime minister when he could live very happily and very well as a private citizen?

He is a visionary. He is not someone who can stand by and enjoy himself while his country is suffering. I often pray to God to give him patience, strength and faith to carry on and bear through this period because no one but he can find solutions to our problems and bring Lebanon back to the way it was. That is what the people believe and that is what he believes. He is swift and decisive when it comes to making decisions and has the discipline and stamina to carry them out. Also, when those around him see how hard he is working, they are motivated to work equally hard.

How has being a member of parliament changed you?

It has put responsibility on my shoulders. Like my brother, I feel responsible for getting Lebanon back to the way it was. We are not dealing with ordinary problems that can be handled in an ordinary way. This situation requires faith, selflessness, and a strong desire to solve problems. We need to put our individual needs aside and work for the common good to achieve results. In the past, there were many who sacrificed themselves for the good of their country. Now, we feel it is our turn to do the same. Thank God, my family is well off and we are not in need of anything. In fact, our current position is less influential than the positions we held in the private sector. When my brother was an international businessman, his influence extended around the world. He chose to leave all that to work for his country. I will not say that he is the only reason Lebanon is returning back to normal, but he is certainly one of the reasons.

Did you expect anything different when you entered parliament?

No, because I was under an equal amount of pressure when I was working at the Hariri Foundation. But, now, I am in a position where my opinion counts more on a national level. Rather than asking for change, I am authorizing it! This year we accomplished a great deal. Since the war ended we have a lot more hope. We are now more open to the world and we are taking back our place in world forums.

What do you think when you pass block after block of destroyed buildings on the way to parliament?

I always think: when are we going to remove all this destruction? When is Lebanon going to be free of the war's ravages? The answer is: It will require at least ten years. We endured seventeen years of war and even before that we were experiencing problems that eventually caused the war. Rebuilding anything takes time. Patience is not only a virtue, it is a necessity in this case.

Do you think anything was solved by the war?

No, nothing. What we learned was to depend upon ourselves and the importance of remaining one nation. Also, I believe, our leaders are now more united and willing to work together to achieve a common goal.

I've noticed that the Lebanese people continue to enjoy life in spite of everything. Where does this optimism come from?

It comes from the way we were brought up and our way of life. The Lebanese people have always enjoyed living well, eating well, dressing up — the war has not changed that. An example of how the Lebanese people are undeterred by adversity is when the Israeli Army invaded Lebanon and was advancing to Beirut, people got into their cars and went on picnics! In any other city this would not have happened. It is this ability to go on leading our lives that has enabled us to survive seventeen years of war. The Lebanese people live for the moment; they don't think about tomorrow. This is not a new attitude; this has always been the mentality of the Lebanese people from way back. I frequently visit the homes of both the rich and the poor and, believe me, they are equally happy. This is our special quality as Lebanese.

What was the worst period for you during the war?

The Israeli invasion in 1982 — everything else was minor in comparison. We passed through many periods of fighting, but the Israeli invasion was the worst. During the invasion nothing affected me more than seeing the people thronging the streets of Sidon carrying white banners trying to save the city from utter destruction. Everyone came out, young and old, heedless to the danger to themselves in their quest to save the city. In my life, I will never forget this sight: the suffering and the incredible valor they showed in the midst of overwhelming odds. I am very proud of my people. For two weeks, I had over one thousand men, women and children — refugees fleeing from the invasion — living in this house with us.

The second thing that bothered me the most was after the invasion people did not know what to do: whether to return to the South or go north. They had no idea where to go...which direction was safe or what their end would be. Finally, when they heard there was no more shooting and the invasion was over, in less than twenty-four hours, more than 300,000 people returned to their homes. The people of the South are very brave. They have a lot of determination and they are attached to their land. Before the government began giving them aid, on their own, they began to rebuild. This self-reliance is a quality you don't find often — the Lebanese people know how to depend upon themselves and help each other.

Have you found it to be a disadvantage being a woman in politics?

Granted, a woman's role in politics is more difficult than a man's because she has two roles to play: a public and a private one as a mother and wife. Also, no one gives you a break or forgives you if you make a mistake when you are a woman. But I can say, without any reservation, that I have not felt that there is a difference between myself and my male colleagues and they have not done anything to make me feel otherwise. From the beginning of my working career, I have always worked more with men than women and I have always had good relations with my colleagues whatever their gender.

Do you think Lebanon is ready for a woman president or prime minister?

[laughter] I don't think a woman would have any problem in any position in government, provided of course she has the right skills.

How do you relax?

I relax when I come home after work, change into a loose fitting abaya, do simple chores around the house, and talk to my family. After a little while, I feel relaxed and ready to go back to work or to attend a function. On Sundays, I go out with my family for a couple of hours for fresh air and a change. Then, during the summer, I take a fifteen-day holiday and we all travel somewhere together.

ILHAM DARWISHE HOBBALLAH

MINISTRY OF TOURISM OFFICIAL

A matronly woman with a no-nonsense air of efficiency, Ilham Hobballah, a lawyer by training, is Lebanon's director of touristic accommodations, where she is responsible for inspecting and approving all tourist-related facilities, including restaurants, hotels, furnished apartments, tourist agencies, and nightclubs. "At the Ministry of Tourism the law is the law," says an experienced entrepreneur. "If you conform to all the regulations and your papers are in order, your request will be granted; if not, don't bother going to see Mrs. Hobballah."

On any given day, a dozen petitioners can be found outside her office waiting to meet with her. Hobballah's office is imposing: behind her desk hangs a portrait of the President of the Republic and next to it the red, white, and green Lebanese flag. Scenes of popular tourist attractions adorn the walls; books, brochures and magazines, featuring Lebanon, fill the bookcases.

As we chat, Hobballah's assistant discretely interrupts to consult with her and the telephone never stops ringing. Married to a director at the Disciplinary Council (Lebanon's court for civil servants), Hobballah, the mother of three, admits she is happiest when traveling with her family as a tourist.

*   *   *

If you had a month to spend anywhere in the world, where would you go?
I would want to see another world. I would go to America, which is another
world!

Can you tell me about yourself?
I was born in Beirut and my husband is from southern Lebanon. I did my
studies at the International College. Then I studied French and Lebanese law at
St. Joseph University. I worked for two years at the National Institute of Development. Then I was appointed to the Ministry of Interior, where I was responsible for the legal department, and I attended international seminars dealing
with the administration of municipalities. I was transferred to the Ministry of
Tourism, in 1982, and appointed chief of the Bureau of Travel Agencies. I was
responsible for licensing and overseeing all matters concerning travel agencies
in Lebanon. Two years ago, I was appointed director of the establishments that
cater to tourists. I am responsible for classifying the accommodations, licensing, and fixing price rates.

How do you fix price rates?
We do technical studies and then we fix the rates to reflect the services
offered by an establishment. There are many hotels in Lebanon that were once
classified as four star hotels but after almost twenty years of war some would
not even merit two stars. We are now working on reclassifying hotels. We have
the authority to review the classification of a hotel every year. I am very strict
about classifying hotels.

*In your capacity as director of tourist accommodations, it must have been
rather strange attending to your job during the war.*
True, there were not many tourists, but the Lebanese themselves continued to enjoy visiting their country and dining out. For many years, tourism was
largely dependent upon immigrants of Lebanese origin who returned to visit relatives. There are a few million Lebanese in Brazil alone. The Lebanese are very
attached to their family and their country, and they always stay in touch. Even
during the worst of the fighting, there was always a pile of work to be done. We
were always busy reviewing and issuing licenses for restaurants, hotels, travel
agencies, et cetera. Life continued in spite of the war. Replacing broken windowpanes and rebuilding damaged areas of our house was routine stuff. Sometimes, when I would leave the house, it would be calm or the shelling would be
far away. Then, on the way to work, the shells would start falling closer and I
would have to drive like crazy. Often, I would park my car — cars were too easy
a target — on the side of the road and run into a nearby building.

Now, when I look back, I think I must have been a bit crazy to go to work
under heavy shelling. It is a realization that I share with many of my countrymen who did the same. During the bad times, we tried to pretend that everything was normal around us. The children continued going to school, my
husband and I continued going to work and when the fighting was especially
bad, we stayed in the shelter. Once the shelling was over, we would leave

Ilham Darwishe Hobballah

the shelter and return to whatever we were doing. We lived that way for almost two decades.

How do you plan to attract tourists back to Lebanon?

It is a question of security. If things are calm, the tourists will come. As long as Israel occupies the South, we are in a state of instability. Before the war, the Cave of Gittah, considered one of the natural wonders of the world, attracted more than five thousand visitors a day, and that is just one of many tourist attractions in Lebanon.

Are you optimistic about the future of Lebanon?

In my line of work, I have to be optimistic. We often hear talk about the "Lebanese miracle." A testimony to that miracle is that we are still here! The Lebanese are a very resourceful people. If another country went through what we experienced, I don't think they would be in existence today. There have been many countries that have gone through difficult periods but I can't think of many countries that experienced a war that lasted seventeen years and demolished so much. Even during the war, the Lebanese miracle was evident when you saw children going to school and people going to work. My three children continued their studies and prepared for their examinations in the shelter. Now, both my boys are in the top percentile of their classes in universities in England. The oldest is going to graduate as a mechanical engineer, this year, and his younger brother has just begun studies to become a civil engineer. My middle child, my daughter, is studying computer engineering at the American University of Beirut. My children are products of the Lebanese educational system.

When you were young, what did you want to be?

When I finished law school, I applied to become a judge. It was my misfortune that a law had passed that disqualified me. It stated that women were not allowed to become judges. This law was in effect for a very brief period but it happened to coincide with the time of my application.

Has it been difficult pursuing a career and having a family?

It is not a question of difficulty but it is very tiring, especially for those of us who want to do everything well. Sometimes I ask myself if being a perfectionist is a curse! Aiming for perfection at home and at work is exhausting and can be very bad for a woman's health. We want equality, but a woman's work is never done. We will always have two jobs to contend with. When a man comes home, he rests; when a woman comes home, she begins yet another job. I have always taken into consideration the well-being and the happiness of my family. As the years go by, I feel that I have succeeded due, in part, to my sacrifice and devotion, and that of my husband, who stood by me in difficult times.

What have you learned from life?

That every day has the potential of changing the rest of your life. Overnight, my life as a mother changed. My eldest son, Ali, went with my husband to spend one week in Paris. Shortly thereafter, I received a telephone call from my husband saying he had decided to send Ali to London to continue his studies. Now, our younger son has joined his brother. I worry whether I have prepared my sons adequately for life in this world. I brought my children up to be honest, open-minded, and honorable. When I talk to my sons on the telephone and write to them, I often remind them to be careful, not to be naive, and not to accept what everyone says at face value. I think mothers everywhere are troubled by such worries.

Have you experienced discrimination as a woman in your job?

Nothing that I can't deal with! Among civil servants, the general consensus is that women who occupy senior positions in government are "aggressive types"! [laughter] At the beginning, people tried to unsettle me and discover how far they could go. I imposed myself immediately. I have earned the respect of my staff. They know that I only set the rules down once. I believe if a woman cannot assert herself, it is not worth the effort to be in a position of authority. That said, I really think everything depends on one's personality more than one's gender.

If you were a tourist planning to spend a month in Lebanon, how would you spend it?

Ah, there is so much to see and to enjoy here! Where would I start? I would begin with Beirut. I would go to the center of town, visit the shops on Hamra Street, stroll along the Cornich and sample the local specialties of push-cart merchants — hot chestnuts, iced cactus fruit, loquats, green almonds — walk around the grounds of the American University of Beirut, visit the National Museum; shop at the "Maison de l'Artisan," where there is a large selection of Lebanese craftwork — leather goods, pottery, brass, glass, textiles, cutlery from Jezzine, caftans, and ivory-inlaid tables and chess sets. After that, I would suggest you indulge your appetite with the delights of Lebanese cuisine at one of the many restaurants and sidewalk cafes. Then you can head off to either the beach or the mountains to hike, ski or visit the cedars. Noah, it is said, built his arc from the cedars of Lebanon!

There are so many day trips to take! You can go to the Bekaa Valley and visit the great Roman Temples of Baalbek, or to Tyre, the "Metropolis of Phoenicia," renowned for its maritime trade, Temple of Hercules, and its famous "Tyrian purple dye." One gram of purple dye was worth ten to twenty grams of gold, and garments colored in the dye were worn as a mark of imperial rank. You can visit the magic timelessness of Byblos, one of the oldest continuously inhabited cities in the world; the crusader ruins of Tripoli, the old vaulted souk and famous glass manufacturers of Sidon, a city credited with the very invention of glass, the excavations at Anjar where a Umayyad town is emerging, and Emir Bechir's Palace at Beit Eddine. When you have seen and done all this, come back to me and I will give you many more suggestions. There is much to enjoy in Lebanon! We have a rich cultural history and an entertaining social life. You will never be bored — you have my assurance!

ARLETTE TAWIL JREISSATI

JUDGE

Arlette Jreissati, president of Lebanon's Labor Court, is described by a colleague as "scrupulously fair, and capable of being tough and charming in three languages: Arabic, French, and English." A presiding judge since 1972, Jreissati teaches law courses at Saint Joseph University and Lebanese University.

As president of Mar Semaan Center Association, a welfare organization she helped found, she is deeply involved in social work. The mother of three adult children, she is married to Joseph Jreissati, formerly the president of Lebanon's Court of Appeals and, currently, director general of the Presidential Palace, where he is the president's chief counsel.

A warm, vivacious woman with a buoyant personality and a ready laugh, Judge Jreissati is a woman of great passion and conviction. Whether she is advocating the cause of Lebanon, speaking up for women's rights, skiing down a slope or hitting a tennis ball, she does so with enthusiasm and a generous dash of élan. We met late one afternoon in her apartment in the Beirut suburb of Ashrafiyeh.

*   *   *

Can you tell me about yourself?

I was a judge in 1975 when the war began, but I didn't work very much during the war because the court was often closed. We worked five out of twelve months. The rest of the time we spent in shelters trying to avoid the bombs. I felt there was so much misery around, I had to do something. So I began working in social welfare. We would collect clothes, wash and iron them, pack food and then, under the bombs, go to refugee camps and distribute what we had collected. The misery became so terrible that thirteen years ago, with the help of twenty friends, I founded a welfare association, Mar Semaan Center. It's well-known now as a Greek Catholic Association, but I am not Greek Catholic. I am a Maronite married to a Greek Catholic. In our orphanage, we have eighty-five children from all Lebanese communities. Misery does not discriminate.

The first center we established was an orphanage. It is now a huge building with a playground and a technical school for boys that teaches them carpentry. Seven years ago, we built a second center as a home for teenage girls and we established a technical school to teach sewing. We also founded a dispensary which we kept open during the entire war. It treated over four hundred people every month free of charge. Now, we are about to finish one of our biggest social projects: the first vocational school of its kind for girls in the region. It will prepare girls to either become nurse's aids or allow them to pursue a degree in hotel and restaurant management. What is especially exciting is the school will be covering medicine and tourism: two fields in which Lebanon has always been competitive.

Why have you and your friends decided to take the initiative on these projects and not wait for the government to act?

In Lebanon, social welfare was never a government initiative. What made Lebanon special was the private initiative. I believe strongly in the Lebanese people. Since the beginning of the war, nothing I learned in law school has been applied in Lebanon. As a judge, seeing human rights violated is very disturbing. It is ironic that Charles Malik — a Lebanese — was one of the great authors of the United Nations Declaration of Human Rights, written more than fifty years ago. Yet, today, we are not benefitting from those human rights. When a country is occupied, you cannot have free elections. We went without electricity, without telephones; we stayed in shelters, under bombs, for seventeen years to save our country. We will not accept to be humiliated and stripped of our freedom. We are a very proud people. Law and democracy originated from this land. The law school of Beirut, during the Roman period, was established here nearly 2000 years ago— a period in history when people from other lands did not even know the meaning of the word "law." The alphabet came from our ancestors, the Phoenicians. We gave civilization to the world. We are a six-thou-

Arlette Tawil Jreissati (left) and the author.

sand-year-old civilization with a long history of peaceful coexistence among different religions and we are being destroyed. It makes no sense! We just wish to be left alone in peace so we can rebuild our country.

I remember so many nights when it would rain down bombs. Then the next day we would go out, clear the debris in the streets, repair the damage, and make it look as though nothing had happened. I received many foreign visitors during the war and not one believed we could survive the destruction we endured. We survived because we helped each other. We shared what we had with all our neighbors and they with us. We were six families in this building, yet we lived together like one family.

Did you share similar backgrounds?

No, we all come from different regions of the country. Many of us have lived together for twenty-five years in this building. During the war, we constantly telephoned and knocked on each other's doors to see if anyone needed anything. We shared our water — everything. It was an unforgettable experience. One of my friends had three small children and I called her one morning and I asked her: How are you doing? Do you have enough bread? She said, "I had enough, but I shared it with the others in the shelter because I couldn't see my children eating and my neighbor's children going hungry."

Do you remember when the war began?

Yes, my youngest was two years old. It was very difficult for me to get used to the war. The first two years, I almost stopped eating because I was so frightened by the bombing. I lost ten kilos. I couldn't adjust to the war. One day, I said to myself: "Listen, my friend, if you are not strong enough to adjust you are not going to survive this war. You have to make a decision." I decided to adjust!

Would you say the war brought everyone closer together?

Absolutely! Look what happened in New York when you had a blackout ten years ago. People went on a rampage. They vandalized stores and private property. In Lebanon, we have lived not only with a blackout for seventeen years, but with no government, nothing — only militiamen and outlaws everywhere. How many crimes did we have during this period? Well, as a percentage, we had almost nothing compared to other very civilized countries with a government, a police force, and a strong army. I believe in the people of this country. I can go out at any hour of the day or night with all my jewelry on and no one will try to rob me. In spite of all the craziness, we have traditions and principles by which we live and conduct ourselves. Women, for example, were never kidnapped. Last year, my husband's aunt went to Columbia to visit her sister, and her suitcase was stolen right at the airport — in broad daylight — just a few minutes after she arrived! Here, in Lebanon, I have three youngsters and they go out dancing until the morning and I don't worry about them. Nobody appreciates the sense of security we have in this country in spite of seventeen years of war.

What do you think accounts for this stability in Lebanese society?

I believe it comes from our way of life and our relationship with people. We have a sense of permanence. Often, when we get married, we settle in an apartment and remain there for life. Everybody in the building welcomes you. Then you are invited to have a cup of coffee with your neighbors and you invite them for dinner; they invite you back and you become friends. After a few years you know everybody in the building, the shopkeepers on your street, and the people in the buildings next door. When everybody knows everybody you don't commit crimes or misbehave. It is understood that when I am not around, my neighbors watch over my apartment and look after my children and I do the same for them. During the war, I often went out at night with my husband because he worked at the Presidential Palace and we had to attend a lot of social engagements. I had three small children, but because of my neighbors, I felt it was safe to leave them. If bombing occurred in the area, they would take the children to the shelter and look after them until we returned. It is these strong ties between friends and family that make this country so fantastic.

Have you lived outside of Lebanon?

I've lived everywhere. In 1977, I lived in the United States for six months and I traveled all over the States. Three years ago, I lived in Paris for six months with my family in the most beautiful apartment in a very nice part of town. I consider France to be my second country. I am French-educated. I have a lot of friends and relatives who live in Paris. But even so, after six months, when I had to make a decision to stay in France and become a French citizen, I couldn't. Suddenly, I missed the sun and the sky of Lebanon, my friends and my neighbors, the people on the streets I would see every day, and I began to cry. I told my husband, I cannot breathe outside Lebanon. Even though there is no government, no electricity, no water — it's still paradise to me. We must go back because we will never find in any other country in the world the same quality of relationships among people that exists in Lebanon.

For many years, when I was a girl scout, we used to camp out in villages in the mountains. We would help villagers pick up litter off their roads or help elderly people clean their houses. It could be a Druze, Muslim, or Christian village — it didn't matter. They were always very appreciative of what we did and they would welcome us, offer us food, and we would become their friends. In Lebanon, traditions such as hospitality, maintaining a clean house, and respect for the elderly are considered sacrosanct.

What drew you to a legal career?

Initially, I wanted to become a dentist like my father. In school, I was considered brilliant! I was always the first in my class and I graduated from high school at the age of seventeen. But twenty-seven years ago it wasn't at all easy for a girl to become a doctor. There was only one woman dentist in Lebanon. My father approved of my becoming a dentist but my mother was opposed to the idea. She told me, "In our family, girls get married at eighteen and do not prepare themselves for a male career." She forbade me to take the entrance exam for medical school. When summer passed, I had to do something. All my friends were going to law school so I chose to join them and a year later I married. I was eighteen! [laughter] My husband is a judge and he is a very open-minded and cultured man. He told me, "I cannot live with a spouse who is not intellectually my equal. If you want to pursue your studies, I won't oppose it." And that is what happened. I was always pregnant when I was in law school. I had two children during my three years of study. I graduated first in my class and I received both French and Lebanese degrees. I was seven months pregnant with my daughter when I passed my final exams. It was a very hard period for me because nobody could understand why I was continuing my studies when I had a family to take care of. After graduating from law school, I spent two years at home and had my third child. My teachers wanted me to go to Paris and earn a Ph.D., but my husband opposed the idea because he thought I had already studied enough and had my hands full at home with three children.

Weren't you tired of studying at this point?

No, I just loved to study! I enjoyed school very much. I was very much encouraged by my teachers. My husband was also very helpful because he understood how important it was for me. We had to make a lot of sacrifices to do everything at the same time. Three children and law school is punishing! When my youngest was one year old, I took the entrance exam for judge school and passed with one of the highest grades. I studied for three years and became one of the first female judges in Lebanon.

Today, out of two hundred seventy judges, fifty are women. It's not a very large percentage but, nevertheless, it's amazing. During the war, a social revolution occurred in Lebanon. Nobody realized what was happening. It happened so quietly. Women did not protest for their rights on the streets, they just calmly went on pursuing their studies at universities. Because of the economic crises and the devaluation of the Lebanese currency, a man could not afford to get married unless his spouse worked, too. So now almost sixty to seventy percent of Lebanese women continue their studies to prepare themselves for a job. It's a revolution! The economic situation has changed the old mentality that a woman's place is at home with the children. I have two sons and a daughter. My daughter, this year, will be graduating from medical school.

Is she going to be a dentist like her grandfather?

No, she will be a doctor in six months — a very good doctor! One of my sons is a lawyer and the other received a B.A. in public administration from the American University of Beirut. He is now pursing a second B.A. in business administration and working at the same time.

What does your mother think about her granddaughter becoming a doctor?

She is very proud of her and she is now proud of me, as well. A month ago, I chaired a conference on women's rights and it was the first time my parents had ever attended one of my conferences. When they were leaving, the priest of our village came up to them and said, "You should be very proud of your daughter." So my mother called and said to me for the first time, "Your father and I are very proud of you!" It took a long time for her to understand that I had the same rights as a male child to realize myself. She never helped me with my children because she was against my studying and working. At the beginning, when I decided I wanted to continue with my education, she told me: "You want to study? You study alone. You bear your burden alone." I told her, "Okay, I will bear it alone because I want to be somebody. I need to realize myself." She didn't understand my need at the time, but now, twenty years later, she's proud of both her granddaughter and me.

Why do you think your father encouraged you and your mother did not?

It has to do with the mentality of mothers in this country. They, I believe, are the ones holding back the progress of women's rights. Mothers are educating their children like they themselves were educated some twenty or fifty years ago. They raise their sons differently from the way they raise their daughters. A boy has to be strong. If he cries, even if he is hurt, they shout at him and tell him: "No, you are a man and a man does not cry. You must fight and be strong." But if a girl cries, it's considered normal. They tell her, "It's okay, you are just a girl. You are acting the way a girl is suppose to act." Unlike my mother, I raised my daughter just like I raised my sons. When my daughter was ready to attend university, I told her, "If you want to pursue your studies and get a job, I will help you. If you want to get married and continue your studies, I'll take care of your children. Whatever you choose to do, I will support you." I believe that if all mothers have this attitude, women cannot be held back.

What was your first year as a judge like?

They tried everything with me that first year! People didn't accept me as a judge; even my male colleagues felt I had no business being a judge. They considered women judges to be of a lower order! But I proved through my work that I was just as capable as any one of them.

Who has had the greatest influence on you?

My husband, whom I admire very much. I am very proud to be his wife. I married when I was very young and I didn't know anything about life except going to school and being with my family. He was seventeen years older than I. He was, and still is, one of the most respected judges in the country. I saw how people looked up to him and that is partially why I decided to become a judge.

It must be interesting having two judges in the family.

[laughter] It is marvelous training for learning how to live peacefully together at home! We often collaborate. I ask for his advice and he, for mine. Most of the courts in Lebanon are collation courts. Collation courts are composed of three judges and every case is decided by all three judges. As judges, we are used to collegial work. It's very stimulating when you exchange ideas and have to defend and support your arguments. Only at the lowest courts such as small claims court do judges decide on cases alone. Those judges are called unique judges. So as judges, we are used to arguing, sharing our experiences and ideas, and arriving at decisions together. After twenty-seven years of marriage, what really matters is that we love each other and enjoy sharing everything together.

Who was responsible for disciplining the children?

In our house, we believe in compromise and equilibrium. I am now perhaps harder with the children and he is more tender with them. I think that has to do with age! [laughter]

What is it like being a judge in Lebanon?

Judges in Lebanon do not stay in one field. They are moved around. For twenty years I worked in civil and commercial cases and now I head the labor court. We have a rotation system which requires all judges to rotate three weeks during the summer to decide on urgent cases. During my summer rotation, I frequently find myself working on criminal cases. I put quite a few people in jail; consequently, I have come up against a great deal of political pressure. Even in civil cases, where there is money on the line, one is exposed to political pressure and a certain amount of danger.

In England, judges wear white wigs in court so when they are on the street they won't be recognized. Perhaps wigs should be standard issue to judges in Lebanon!

[laughter] Here in Lebanon we are used to danger. I am not afraid of death. If I were, I wouldn't have survived seventeen years of war. During all that period I went on with my job and with raising my family. My husband is a very strong-willed man and in spite of the war he wanted us to live as normal a life as possible.

Most evenings, under the bombs, we would have dinner together as a family, drinks in the shelter at seven o'clock with the neighbors, and then we would play cards, listen to music or the news. I believe, like most people in this part of the world, in fatalism — what is written is written. You will die when your time comes. I had a friend who survived the war and then died falling down a staircase. My sister-in-law survived all the bombardment in Zahlé and then died at age forty from cancer.

What was the worst point for you during the war?

Some periods of course were worse than others. We could breathe between rounds. We would have a series of heavy bombings which would last a week or two and then a cease-fire. Then it would begin all over again. You couldn't survive in an area where there was heavy bombing, so you would leave. Then when it stopped, you would return to what was left. That happened often. Once, two of my children and I were held hostage for ten days in our house by militiamen. We were considered the enemy. They forbade us to leave the apartment or to even talk to anyone. My husband was at the Presidential Palace and couldn't reach us. It was the most difficult period of my life. I wasn't afraid for myself but for my youngest son. They kept warning me that if they saw him at a window they would shoot him. We did not have bread or water. I had to beg the militiamen to let me send out for food and water.

Why were you detained?

Because my husband worked at the Presidential Palace. This actually happened twice during the war. The first time was during President Amin Gemayel's presidency. He was fighting against the Lebanese forces and we happened to be living in an area controlled by the Lebanese forces. Another time, I had to spend forty-eight hours without my children, not knowing what had become of them. Those were very difficult days. My children were at school and the bombing began. My husband and I had gone to work that morning and we were caught on one side of the fighting and the children, on the other. I couldn't sleep. I was just crazy. Luckily, friends of ours, who were on the other side, learned of the danger the children were in and picked them up from school. They hid them for two days until we managed to get through and bring them home. A similar experience happened to us after President Amin Gemayel completed his mandate as president.

How did you cope when you were held hostage in your own home?

I was very nervous. I put music on to keep the children calm, and I played cards and games with them. My neighbors were just extraordinary people. They protected us. When the militiamen came into our house, my neighbor's husband came up and told them: "Her husband is not here. If you want anything, speak with me."

Did the militiamen know you were a judge?

Yes, they knew. They were youngsters — sixteen-, seventeen-year-olds carrying machine guns that they kept pointed at us. There was nothing we could do about it. There was no law to turn to. Law did not exist for seventeen years during the war. It was a very frustrating situation. I was a judge; yet, I could not apply the law. I had outlaws in my house, threatening me and my children, and

I could do nothing. After ten days, I told myself, we can't survive any longer in this situation; either my children and I die or we escape. I took a risk and we escaped into an area where there were bombs falling and mines planted everywhere. I thought it was better to die than to live without freedom. When my husband saw us, he couldn't stop crying. He had given up hope of ever seeing us again.

How has the war changed you as a person?

It's strange; I don't feel hatred for anyone. I pity those militiamen because they paid dearly for what they did. They lost their futures. They cannot integrate back into society. Most of them are addicted to drugs. It is our leaders who made us believe we were fighting a civil war. Christians believed Muslims were going to murder them and Muslims believed Christians were going to do the same to them. It just wasn't true. I was born and lived in West Beirut in a Muslim area until I was married. I had a lot of Muslim friends at school and university. I still have those same friends. We never were divided or separated during the war. I helped them when they were in my area and they protected me in their area. During seventeen years of war, I never once avoided an area of Lebanon because it happened to be a Muslim area. I used to go to the airport, under the bombs, to pick up medicine for our dispensary. I would show my judge identification card and they would let me pass. I was never asked whether I was a Christian or a Muslim.

What has changed in me is now I am much harder. My emotional threshold has risen considerably. I don't react to problems like before. I am not as sensitive. Death does not frighten me. I have had to face it for so long. In the past, when I lost somebody, I would mourn for years. When I lost my sister-in-law I cried a lot. She was like a sister, but then I said to myself: How is crying going to educate and take care of her four children? I learned, if you want to overcome adversity, you must be strong. Difficulties do not overwhelm me anymore. I know how to face them because I had to face so many during the war and find solutions. I slept in shelters, on mattresses, on dirty floors. I even got used to taking a bath with a small jug of water. Now, I appreciate life much more because I no longer take anything for granted. I appreciate the fact that I can walk down the street without the threat of bombs exploding, that I can go to work and lead a normal life with my family.

Are you optimistic about the future of Lebanon?

When I work in the social welfare field with people from all sides, I believe that nothing will stand in the way of this country and that sooner or later we will regain our freedom and our independence. As an intellectual and a citizen, I am not proud of the politicians or the militiamen, but I am very proud of the Lebanese people and the solidarity we have shown for each other in times of great difficulty.

Do you remember when the war ended?

Yes! Isn't it strange that the day after an agreement was signed abroad, the next day in Lebanon nobody hated each other? Isn't it strange that for more than ten years we weren't able to go out on our balcony because there were snipers in the building across the park from us? For ten years, our shutters were closed because we didn't dare open them. Then suddenly, one day, there was an external decision to stop the fighting in Lebanon. I woke up and there were no more bombs, no more snipers, no more hostages. Suddenly, we could go anywhere. Just like that...a snap of the finger! I remember thinking to myself: Where did all those snipers, those murderers, who used to threaten us, go? We could never cross the street without running. Then an agreement is signed and — poof — no more war, no more snipers. I am convinced there is an international *chef d'orchestre*, outside Lebanon, overseeing everything that is happening here and giving orders to both Christians and Muslims.

If you believe that, you must feel helpless affecting change?

We are helpless. But I am convinced, at the same time, that if we are strong enough not to emigrate, to believe in our country, and to keep on fighting every day for our principles, we can make a difference. By being a good citizen and applying the law, I can help my country survive and recuperate what it has lost. My children believe as I do. My son lived in Paris three years preparing for a Ph.D. When he returned to Lebanon, he refused to go back. He is now working here. My children refuse to emigrate or take another nationality. They believe in this country, especially the warm human relations that exist here.

Without traffic signals or traffic signs, I think what keeps the traffic flowing may indeed be attributed to "warm human relations"!

[laughter] Yesterday evening, I was driving with my sister-in-law to visit my aunt. I went down a one-way street and three cars were coming at me. I couldn't pass, so I stopped in the middle of the road and told them you have to go back. They said, "Why?" I said, "It's one-way and you are going the wrong way." All three cars were driven by men. They said, "We will not go back." I said, "Well, don't waste your time waiting for me. I am in the right and I intend to stay right here and enforce the law." One of the men told the others: "This woman is crazy." Then they started insulting me. I can't repeat what they called me! I turned off my engine and I waited. A woman walking by said, "Please Madame, you have cars in front of you, why don't you back up." I said, "No, I will not go back." Eventually, the three cars backed up and I passed. When I am in the right, I am not afraid. As a judge, I must apply the law wherever I go. I cannot do otherwise. If everyone acts responsibly, people will understand that they have to obey the law.

Do you feel you have a balanced life between work and family?

I am well organized. It's helped me to survive. I write down everything I must do that is important. But sometimes some small incident might happen and destroy the balance for a few days. I have learned from the war that you have to live life to the fullest every moment. We don't own the future and the past is the past. So you live for the moment. I don't like to waste time. If I am not in court, I am either with my family or working on a social welfare project. You have to do what makes you happy and what fulfills you. I am a passionate woman in everything I do. I work hard, sometimes sixteen hours a day. When I put my head on the pillow, even when there were bombs, I would fall asleep right away.

I believe what is going to happen is going to happen. I am not a heart attack candidate or a nervous breakdown risk! [laughter] I believe the most important thing is to be sincere and to be at peace with yourself and with God. When I say: "There is no problem"—my husband claims that is my favorite expression—I always find a solution!

NIMAT ASSAAD KANAAN

MINISTRY OF SOCIAL AFFAIRS OFFICIAL

Nimat Kanaan, director general of the Ministry of Social Affairs, is the highest ranking woman in the government of Lebanon. A broad-shouldered, imposing woman, Kanaan is deeply committed to improving the lives of all Lebanese, especially those injured and displaced by the war. "She is a woman of immense compassion and great fortitude," says a colleague who heads up a nonprofit organization.

Born in Baalbek, Lebanon, Kanaan is the mother of three daughters. She is married to Kamal Abi-Abdullah, a former general in the Lebanese Army. Kanaan received her B.A. in 1958 from Beirut College for Women and, six years later, an M.A. from the American University of Beirut. She has worked as a government employee in the social services field for more than thirty years and was appointed director general of the Ministry of Social Affairs in 1993.

Kanaan heads up a number of committees, including the Technical Committee at the Social Training Center, the Committee for Joint Projects between the Lebanese government and the World Food Program, the National Committee for Illiteracy, the National Council of Health, the Child Care Development Project (sponsored by the Lebanese government and UNICEF), the Committee for Developing Basic Services, and the Data-Bank Committee (which monitors Lebanese and non–Lebanese voluntary social welfare organizations working in Lebanon). She is vice-president of the National Committee for the Handicapped as well as the Higher Council for Childhood. Kanaan is a member of many other organizations, including the National Committee against AIDS.

We met in her office, on the fourth floor of a bullet-riddled building, the Ministry of Social Affairs. The interview was punctuated with telephone calls and frequent interruptions by her assistant. Kanaan, well coiffed and immaculately attired in a crisp suit, handled each new emergency with aplomb.

*   *   *

Nimat Assaad Kanaan

Who is Nimat Kanaan?

I was born in the Bekaa Valley, the offspring of a Muslim father and a Christian mother. I graduated from the American School for Girls in Tripoli. Then I received my B.A. degree in Education and Psychology and my M.A. degree in psychology and social work. I wanted to be a doctor, but my parents did not accept that. They said, "It takes a long time to prepare to become a doctor. You will become old and never get married." I was too young to argue with them. Instead, I taught English and, at age twenty, I applied for a job in government and began work with the Office of Social Development, which was created in 1959. There was no Ministry of Social Affairs at that time. I began as an ordinary clerk and within three years I became head of a department. Eight years later, I became the first woman director of social services.

I consider myself a strong woman. I know what I want. At home, we were raised very strictly. My father was a military man and my mother, a very "correct" woman. We were always encouraged to do our best in everything we pursued.

In 1974, before the war, I was nominated to become director general. It was unheard of for a Muslim woman to take a man's place to represent our sect in the government. Consequently, I did not win the election. But I did not give up. I continued working as if nothing had happened.

When the war started, I felt caught in the middle because of my background. Moreover, I am a Muslim married to a Christian. I felt torn apart. My parents were living in the western part of Beirut and I lived, here, in the eastern part. There were times when I used to think the war was against me personally. I was determined not to give up and to fight with the only weapon at my disposal: government. I refused to let the government be divided. During thirteen years of the war, I would cross the Green Line — the demarcation line between East and West Beirut — from home to work and work to home. In the western part of the city, I would hear people say: "Christians are bad. They are doing this and that to us." I would say, "No! You are mistaken that is not true!" Then I would come back to the eastern part and hear the same thing said about Muslims. I never had peace. Those years took a toll. I began suffering from a skin allergy. I didn't know what was happening to me. I traveled abroad to seek help. I remember one doctor in England asked me: "Where do you come from? How do you live? What do you do in life?" When I told him about my life in Lebanon, he said, "Enough! I know what your problem is. You have a very bad physical reaction to the stress you are under."

I used to come to the office with my face horribly swollen. I thought I had skin cancer. I tried so many medications but nothing worked. It was useless. Every day, I would wake up to the sound of bombs and I would go to work under the bombs. Sometimes, I would work in the western part and sleep at my parents home. There was only one outlet between East and West Beirut and often I would discover the outlet was closed. I would find myself sandwiched between bombs in front of me and bombs behind me. Through it all, I continued going to work and visiting our offices on both sides of the Green Line. My husband would say, "For what?" He used to wait for me at the Green Line because there were so many gangsters during the war. He was always afraid that I would be killed, kidnapped, or something. He is a general in the army and he would tell me: "You are going to die! You have three daughters. What are they going to do without you? You are a mad woman! You think you are going to single-handedly stop the war? It's not your affair!"

What would you tell him?

I never answered.

What motivated you to continue working?

I wanted to stop the war. I didn't want my country to be divided. I used to come early, every day, to work at the Office of Social Development. Even though I wasn't director general, I felt responsible because so many people depended upon me to lead them. When the staff knew I was coming to one part of the city or the other, they would show up. If I didn't come to work, no one else would. At the Office of Social Development, we look after all the social institutions: the orphanages, the orphans, the destitute, and the handicapped. That is why I could never be comfortable sitting at home, sipping coffee and chatting with friends when I could be helping others. I am very proud of the fact that the orphanages stayed open during the entire war and orphans had a place they could call home.

During the war, were you viewed as a mediator because of your interfaith background?

No, nobody wanted mediators! I used to tell everyone, "I am the only true Lebanese among you because I don't take religion into account when I make a decision. It does not dictate my behavior towards others." In Lebanon, it is said, one is first a member of one's family, then one's village, then one's religious group, and then and only then does one consider oneself Lebanese. We are very independent in all aspects of our lives, which is good and bad. It is good because it engenders self-reliance and enthusiasm but, at the same time, it results in selfishness and a lack of coordination. After seventeen years of war, we must try to coordinate our efforts and work as a team in all social, economic and industrial endeavors.

How have you managed to juggle a career and a family?

My husband says I work forty-eight hours in a normal day! Since I was very young, I have never sat around with nothing to do. I have never been bored! My agenda has always been full. I don't like to waste time. I also don't require more than three to four hours of sleep. I get up at six o'clock in the morning with my youngest daughter who is still in school. I prepare breakfast, make lunch, then I take my bath. I am at the office around eight o'clock in the morning and I return home quite late. Sometimes I don't see my husband for forty-eight hours and we live in the same house! I leave him messages and he does the same for me. He appreciates my work, but sometimes he says: "Look at the director generals in other ministries; they don't work as much as you do. You should give your family part of your time, too!" I humor him. I tell him, "You are eating well, you are sleeping well, your shirts are pressed, your daughters are grown up and your eldest is a civil engineer! What more could you want?" Also, I am fortunate, my sister, who is a widow, looks after my family when I am not home. My husband is a great help, too. He took an early retirement from the army because of friction within the ranks based on sectarian differences. He wanted no part of it.

How did you become director general of the Ministry of Social Affairs?

When the war was over, the government wanted to have nominations to fill the empty posts and my name was suggested for the position. I was acting director general of both the Ministry of Social Affairs and the Ministry of Health. I let it be known that if there was anyone better qualified to fill the position at Social Affairs, I would gladly step aside. In spite of my being a woman, they finally appointed me in 1993 to the post.

What are your priorities as director general of Social Affairs?

My priorities are to advance the role of social institutions and nongovernment organizations, take care of the handicapped, and promote rural development. We want to stop immigration from rural areas to urban areas. We need to build a social infrastructure to support the Lebanese people, especially women and children who have had to endure such a prolonged and traumatic experience. We need an adequate budget to meet all these responsibilities. Last week, I went to parliament to discuss next year's budget. I told the members: "You are investing money in so many projects but you are not thinking about the poor, nor are you thinking about the pillar of society — the middle class. Construction of the downtown of Beirut is not going to bring back the middle class. Good schools, reliable health facilities, a stable currency, job opportunities — that is what is going to bring the middle class back." We have a foreign educational system in Lebanon. We need a national, unified system of education that teaches our children Lebanese history, not French history. I warned them if we continue on our present course, we will return to the war we just emerged from.

Do you have any desire to enter politics?

I come from a very large family in the Bekaa, not a political family, but one that is very influential. In my family there are four girls and a boy. My brother, the youngest, was born handicapped. My eldest sister, who I admire very much, has a Ph.D. in law and is a judge. My next sister married an ambassador from Latin America who was of Lebanese origin. He died a year after their marriage. They had one son, who is now a lawyer. I am the third, and my youngest sister, who has a master's degree, worked at Radio Lebanon but left, during the war. She is now living in London where she owns and operates a company which offers translating services. During the last election, I was asked, "Why don't you take part?" I feel I can help people much more from my current position than by being a member of parliament. There are no female ministers and, thus far, all the female members of parliament are related to male politicians. Men, here, are not used to dealing with a woman who has authority. Should I be elected, I would want to rise on my own merit.

How do you escape from the pressure of your work?

I would say by sleeping, but that would not be true because even when I sleep, I dream about my work and I wake up tired. I used to jog but I no longer have the time. When I finish my homework at eleven or twelve o'clock at night, I read for a couple of hours.

Do you regard the war years as having been wasted years?

No. I found my real self during those years and I accomplished what I set out to do. However, if you ask me: "Would I have preferred not to have gone through those years?" I think the answer is quite obvious.

NAYLA MOAWAD

MEMBER OF PARLIAMENT

Nayla Moawad had been First Lady of Lebanon for seventeen days when her husband, René Moawad, was assassinated on November 22, 1989. She is

*currently a member of parliament and serves on the parliamentary commit-
tees of finance and education. Prior to her marriage, Moawad was a journalist with l'Orient, a Lebanese newspaper published in French.*

*When not attending to parliamentary work, she heads up the René
Moawad Foundation, founded in 1990 to perpetuate her husband's lifelong
commitment "to help build a promising future for the people of Lebanon." In
keeping with this goal, the foundation has established a clinic, a mobile dispensary unit, held summer camps and sports tournaments for orphans and
underprivileged children, awarded scholarships, distributed medical equipment and medicine, sponsored cultural conferences, and reforested 10,000
cedar trees.*

*I interviewed Nayla Moawad, the mother of two grown children, in her
elegant apartment in Hazmiyeh, a suburb of Beirut. A slender, immaculately
groomed brunette, Moawad had spent the day attending commemorative
events marking the fourth anniversary of her late husband's assassination.
Still ahead on her schedule, although it was already late in the evening, was
a radio interview and a formal dinner.*

*   *   *

Do you foresee one day running for president of Lebanon?
There is this mentality in Lebanon that if you seek election to parliament
it is because you are aiming for a higher position. Attaining a "position" is not
my aim. My aim is to be in a position to implement my convictions and my husband's convictions. I want to belong to a nation I believe in and feel proud of.
I am a dreamer. When I am asked: "Are you running for president?" My response
is always: Why not?

*People have described you as a woman of great courage and strong convictions.
Who is Nayla Moawad?*
Sometimes, I don't know myself! But I have always taken action on things
that I feel strongly about. I am convinced that if you are brought up with a certain sense of responsibility, you live up to that responsibility. I had a very active
childhood. My father was a lawyer and I was the youngest of three girls. I attended
the Franciscaines Missionnaires de Marie School, which was a wonderful school
run by French nuns. They made us feel as though we were all part of one big
family. When I was seventeen, I was asked to lead the girl scouts at the Naz-
erette School. The Nazerettes were a very conceited group and some of my scouts
were older than I. One day, one of the girls asked me what was the difference
between their education and mine. I told her the Franciscaines nuns taught us
to love our country, our land, our family, our friends and simplicity. Those are
still the same values I cherish, today.

I spent one year in Cambridge, England, studying English. Then I returned
to Lebanon and earned a degree in French literature. The editor-in-chief of
l'Orient newspaper had read an article I had written on the girl scouts and asked
if I would be interested in working for his paper. At the time, it was very rare

Nayla Moawad (left) and the author.

for women to work, especially an unmarried girl from a good family. My father was furious until the owner of the newspaper called him up and said, "Don't be cross with your daughter, we will look after her." Journalism was wonderful for me. It helped me break down many barriers.

Who did you admire when you were growing up?

My aunt, Alexandra Issa El-Khoury. She was the president of the Lebanese Red Cross. She was a wonderful role model. She was so disciplined! She would leave her apartment every day at 7:50 in the morning and come back at 1:40 in the afternoon. We lived in the same building and when we would see her, we always knew exactly what time it was!

Did your interest in politics begin as a result of your marriage?

I have always lived in a political environment. I come from a political family in the mountains. My uncle was a member of parliament, my father ran for elections, and I was a journalist which in and of itself draws you into politics. My husband was a *zaim* (a traditional leader), and the town he came from,

Zgharta, was a very clannish, close-knit milieu. He had very modern ideas and wanted to improve things quietly without announcing that he was making major changes. Nevertheless, the measures he undertook were considered revolutionary at the time.

He was first elected to parliament in 1957, during a time a revolution was taking place in Lebanon with clans and families fighting against each other. Zgharta, in the north of Lebanon, was a very violent place. In 1957 and 1958, even though Zgharta is not a very big village, there were 180 murders committed. My husband was against violence and he took practical measures. For instance, the secondary school in Zgharta was located near the center of town. One day, I said, "René, it's ridiculous; why didn't you build the school in an open space where children could have room to play?" He said, "My dear philosopher, in this very spot where we now have the elementary school about two hundred families once lived in one-room shacks. Every family had ten to twelve members and all had guns. We were coming out of a civil war and experiencing daily incidents of violence. The only way to bring peace to Zgharta was to help these people get away from each other. The opportunity to build a school provided the perfect excuse to move these people and at the same time provide them with some government compensation so they could afford to relocate." My husband believed in social and economic development as a means to implement peace.

René was the first leader coming from a clan mentality to believe in creating government institutions for public services like electricity, water, telephones, schools — the basic infrastructure. I remember, after he became president, we were driving to the airport and we passed a shantytown that had sprung up. He stopped the car and said: "This area is a social powder keg. It is unfair to have people living in such conditions. The first opportunity I have I will open roads, bring electricity, telephones, build schools and dispensaries, so people can live decently and there won't be any cause for anger and hatred." He had so many plans for Lebanon.

When you married René Moawad did you think he would one day be president?

When I married him he was one of the pillars of Shihabism. Fuad Shihab, president of Lebanon from 1958 to 1964, was one of the few true "neutrals" in Lebanon. He believed in state institutions and founded the modern state. He established the central bank and social security. He believed that institutions would protect and bring the Lebanese people together and make them patriotic and nationalistic. He wanted them to feel protected by national institutions rather than by a *zaim*, party or community. Shihab recognized that Lebanon could endure only by becoming an authentic nation state rather than continuing as a disjointed piece of territory that tribal chieftains divided and redivided among themselves. He believed very much in social justice and human rights. The first important social laws in Lebanon were voted in 1959, under Shihab's mandate. Before I married, I was very much a Shihabist. I always quarreled with people who were not. I belonged to a group known as "the Monday Group" because we would gather every Monday and dream of changing Lebanon. René, at that time, was a strong Maronite leader and one of the main pillars of the movement. When we married, apart from the fact that I was in love with him, I respected and shared his ideas and aspirations. I had great admiration for him because he was set in his beliefs; yet, at the same time, he was supple and diplomatic.

Was your marriage an equal partnership?

I strongly believe a wife should never represent her husband on a political level. I am horrified when that occurs. A first lady should remember that she is only married to the president and is not the president. With that said, I have always felt responsible for my husband's constituents in Zgharta and I believed I had an important role to fill. We were living in Beirut and we would travel back and forth spending our weekends in Zgharta. It is a rhythm I continue to this day.

I was very much involved with women's issues. I believed we could automatically improve so many things if we could improve the lives of the women of Zgharta. It is a known fact that the Zgharta women are very strong-willed and it is the women who are largely responsible for pushing their husbands and sons to fight and seek revenge. I felt they would be less contentious, if they had other things to distract them. A few months after we got married, I told my husband: "I can't stand to see the women gossiping all day. I am going to gather all the women of the family"—there were about three hundred—"and see if we can do something together." He said, "Don't forget you are in Zgharta; not in Beirut!" I gathered all the women and we decided to create an artisana. At the time, it was unheard of for women in Zgharta to work because it was viewed as a sign that their husbands couldn't support them. I can't tell you what a scandal I created! All the men came and complained to my husband. They would say: "My wife lives like a queen, she is very happy at home and she does not need to work." I am sure that women working in Zgharta would have eventually happened, but I hurried the process along. I also opened a dispensary at a time when people thought going to a dispensary was admitting to everyone that they couldn't afford a doctor. People were extremely proud but, now, after the war, they are less concerned with pretension.

As an outsider, did you have a problem being accepted by the women of Zgharta?

I went through some rough periods! I am from Bécharré, a rival village. The fact that René, who was the leader of the village, married someone outside of Zgharta, did nothing to endear me to the people of Zgharta! They, of course, eventually accepted me but it had a lot to do with the fact that I had the full support of my husband.

In hindsight, do you wish your husband had never been president or involved in politics?

It's a temptation my children and I sometimes indulge in. But, no! Politics was his life. He was one of the very rare politicians in Lebanon who did nothing but politics. He was a lawyer but he never worked as a lawyer with the exception of a few associations that he advised. His life was politics. When he was elected president, he knew he was in danger, accepted the danger, and faced it as though it were his mission. I don't think he would have been happy in any other capacity.

Were you worried about his safety?

Always, even before he was president. When he was elected, my anxiety level increased exponentially. I felt a terrible unease. I had a feeling I could not express even to myself. When people came to congratulate us, I would always tell them, "Please pray for us, pray for René." My husband, on the other hand, was extremely determined and happy. He was optimistic that he could make a difference. I remember, at one point, telling him: "As a Lebanese citizen, you give me hope." It was truly as though God had taken him by the hand and led him up to the point where he was elected president because there was no one better suited for the job. He was the perfect leader for Lebanon. All his life, René was a man of dialogue. He believed strongly in institutions and was an experienced administrator. He had been minister of communications, public works, and education, a member of parliament for thirty-two years, and chairman of the finance committee. All through the war, he was the only person able to travel to all areas of the country and help everyone, including those who were against him politically. During the war, he negotiated the release of over four hundred people who had been kidnapped by different groups.

I remember, during the Israeli invasion, the bombing from airplanes was so heavy that I begged him not to go to his office. He agreed, but then he received a telephone call from his ministry informing him that one of the buildings storing Lebanese historical art had been hit and was burning. Like a mad man, he rushed to the burning building and saved about nine hundred fifty cultural artifacts. That was so like René! Nothing deterred my husband. We would be under intense shelling and he would act as though there was nothing unusual happening. He was always a very reassuring presence. I think it is very symbolic of René's life that he died for his country.

Do you find it strange that your husband was assassinated, November 22nd, the very same day President Kennedy was assassinated years earlier?

There are a lot of parallels between the two. René was not as young as President Kennedy, but he was highly respected and charismatic. He had this wonderful ability to make you feel safe and secure in his presence. In France, they call President Mitterand "*la force tranquille.*" I think that very much applied to René. After he was gone, so many friends and colleagues told me: "We never realized we would miss him so much. Lebanon is not Lebanon without him."

I remember the sequence of events so clearly. Monday, we came back from the North, from Zgharta, and we had a chance to talk together. He was assassinated Wednesday. During the seventeen days he was president, I hardly saw him. He was working from six o'clock in the morning until two o'clock in the morning. During our talk, I pleaded with him not to leave the house on the twenty-second to attend Independence Day ceremonies. I told him it was an invitation for murder. He said: "The last fifteen years you have worried every time I went out under the shelling. Had I not nourished friendships with all the active forces in this country, I wouldn't be able to work with them, now, to rebuild Lebanon." He was right. From the moment he was elected president, our house was filled with people. Men, who days earlier were ready to kill each other, were in our house laughing and talking. My husband was a peacemaker.

What do you miss most about him?

René and I were very close. People who knew us both always thought of us as a team. We had a wonderful dialogue, a big complicity. We complemented each others strengths and weaknesses. After he was assassinated, it was as though a big rock had suddenly given way. The children and I felt we had lost our security.

Do you think your husband would be disappointed in the Lebanon of today?

It is much easier to criticize then to take action. Having said that, I don't believe René would be happy with the situation today. There are many things that could be better. I fear we are returning to a society with shocking differences: The poor are getting poorer and the rich display their wealth with a terrible disregard for those in less fortunate circumstances. There is so much more corruption. Everything seems to hinge on who you know in power. I have always believed in the value of leading by example. Unfortunately, I don't see role models in our leaders. A good leader must remain close to his people but, at the same time, keep a certain distance. This distance I speak of is not a social, class, or money distance — it is a distance nurtured by dignity and authority. There must be respect for the leadership; otherwise, psychologically, it's like seeing a cardinal dressed in jeans.

René was very much for legality and dialogue. I can't tell you how often I would hear him say: "Always keep a channel open! If you disagree with someone invite him or her over for a meal and discuss your differences." I believe a leader's role is to bring people together. Even with the family in Zgharta, when people were rude to me, he would never allow me to react. He would say: "It's the way they have been brought up. Remember, it's my family and you can't be judgmental about family. You have to gather the family together." As a leader you have to absorb people. There is an Arabic proverb which says, "The big container absorbs the smaller container."

What do you consider to be the most pressing issue facing Lebanon?

First of all, the economic and social situation is very fragile. I am fearful if things continue as they are, things will implode. One of the reasons for the war that began in 1975 was the social inequities. In the past, Lebanon had a very prominent middle class and this middle class was the backbone of its democracy. It was the only Arab country that had an upper and a lower middle class made up of professionals and intellectuals. When they speak of "Lebanese enterprise and know-how," these are the people who made Lebanon. In the seventies things began to change: An economic and social gap between the classes began to grow. Money was pouring into Lebanon from the Arab world and Lebanon was becoming more sectarian. It lost its social face, its nonpartisan equilibrium.

We need to establish good Lebanese public schools and remind ourselves that we are coming out of a war. Miracles don't occur overnight. We must be sober in our spending. But you can't teach people to be conservative if their leaders are not. Today, there is no middle class and that is very dangerous for democracy and stability in Lebanon. Furthermore, the rich are spending money in a very ostentatious manner. I think that is very wrong. The example should come from the top. To build a nation, you must start with the people: educate them, provide them with an infrastructure, and allow them their dignity. The most important thing is social justice and equality among all citizens. It is very dangerous just to rebuild Beirut and ignore the other regions of the country. That creates conditions for another explosion. If you cannot have equality for all citizens then the "haves" should be particularly conscientious about keeping a low profile.

Your successor as First Lady, Mrs. Haraoui, is focusing on children's diseases and working to build a children's hospital. Had you remained First Lady, what would your focus have been?

As a member of parliament, my priorities are health and education. In parliament, I head the special committee on the rights of children. I believe strongly in the rights of children and human rights. One of the things we are trying to accomplish is to make it mandatory for all couples intent on getting married to have a check-up and obtain a medical certificate to avoid the risk of having children with mental or physical diseases. I am very concerned about education. I am on the parliamentary committees of finance and public education. For me, social equality is extremely important. I think it is essential that every citizen be given a chance to obtain a good public education because without education you cannot succeed in life.

How has your life changed since your husband's assassination?

I have definitely become much more active. I describe my situation to friends as being in a battle and seeing the person holding the flag in front of you fall; without thinking, you pick up the flag and continue. I try to avoid days when I have free time to think about what has happened.

Do you feel you have more or less influence as a deputy compared to when you were First Lady?

The Lebanese people have been very faithful to the memory of my husband. According to protocol, at formal engagements, I come first, in the pecking order, after the wives of the president, prime minister and speaker of the parliament because in addition to my being a former First Lady, I am a member of parliament. Of course, I know I was elected for no other reason than the fact that I am the wife of an assassinated president. But I think seeing me in parliament has accustomed the Lebanese people to having women in parliament.

As a female, has it been problematic being taken seriously in parliament?

Not at all. Carrying my husband's name has given my voice added weight. I have not had to start from scratch to prove myself. For two years, I was the only woman in parliament. Journalists would ask: "How do you feel being the only woman among so many men?" It never felt strange because most of the deputies were friends and colleagues of my husband going as far back as twenty years. Although I have a literary background, not a legal background, I know what people want and I know how to criticize a law that does not benefit the ordinary person. In the last session of parliament, I sat next to a very bright lawyer whom I would often ask for advice on issues. One day, he told me: "I am very good at making laws but you understand people's aspirations and needs." That is true. I am a good listener and I keep in touch with people. Some weekends over a two-and-a-half-day period I easily receive over two thousand people.

Did you experience any discrimination being the only woman in parliament?

There are those who think women cannot be in politics. That has not been my experience. For instance, during elections in northern Lebanon, my name was the first one listed on a ballot with twenty-eight names. I was the only woman on the ballot and I am a Christian; yet, I won overwhelmingly in all the Muslim areas.

I hate gender discrimination. Very often journalists ask me questions like, "Do you get along with your colleagues?" For me, being a man or a woman makes no difference. The difference is if you are capable or not. I am aware that as a woman you have to be extra careful not to say anything silly because then they will simply say, "What do you expect? She is a woman!" You have to always be on your toes.

Were you appointed or elected to parliament?

The first year I was appointed because of special provisions in the Taif Agreement. They were concerned that candidates would be assassinated while campaigning so they made a decision that if they couldn't proceed with elections, deputies would be appointed. I was appointed along with other deputies on June 19, 1990. I was the second woman in Lebanon to be in parliament. The first was Myrna Boustanny, in 1963, but she did not intend to continue. I, on the other hand, intend to stay on.

Do you enjoy campaigning?

During the last election, I did not campaign. I was still in mourning and wearing black. I stayed home and people would come to see me from dawn to dusk. I am in a rather unique position. When my husband was elected president, the whole of Lebanon came to congratulate us. Shortly thereafter, he was assassinated and they all came to extend their condolences. If I want to return visits, I have to visit the whole of Lebanon. I can't just limit my visits to constituents who are sick or in mourning. To assist me, I have designated representatives in the various communities to attend occasions in my place when my presence is required.

Were you in Lebanon during most of the war?

Yes. We would travel when there was peace and return when there was trouble. You have to have lived through the war to understand why people have changed and how best to lead them. René was the head of his family and as such we could never be away when things were rough in Lebanon because when members of your family are suffering you cannot go abroad even if you can afford to. You must always be with your people during the good times and the bad times. Responsibility has a price. When my husband was elected president, I thought about my girl scout days. How they would tell us when we were promoted to the next rank that with this honor came added duties, expectations and responsibilities.

What have you learned that has made a difference in your life?

I have learned to view life as a school which you must attend daily for better or worse. I have learned that you cannot face life without love and forgiveness; that you cannot live with anger and bitterness. I never thought I could live without my husband. I have learned that you can survive even your worst fear. His death came as a terrible shock to our children. Each reacted differently: My daughter, Rima, became disgusted with Lebanon — she is better now — and my son, Michel, wanted to remain in Lebanon rather than return to Paris to continue his studies. I think if I did not love my country and my people so much, I wouldn't have been able to cope.

Are you proud to be Lebanese?

Definitely! And I have paid a heavy price for that. I am proud to be Nayla Moawad. I share with my people the pain and anguish of having lost a loved one because of war. Nobody can give me lessons about sacrifice. Because of my husband's death, I have been given a certain moral authority to gather people together. And because of that, I must always be careful to bring only honor to his name. Otherwise, I would be compromising his blood.

LAURE MOGHAIZEL

ATTORNEY AND HUMAN RIGHTS LEADER

Laure Moghaizel, attorney, wife, mother of five, is one of Lebanon's most eloquent human rights advocates. With her considerable legal skills, she is a tireless proponent for the rights of women and those unjustly treated. She and her husband Joseph, a member of parliament with whom she shares a legal practice, are the founders of both the Lebanese Association of Human Rights and Lebanon's Nonviolent Movement.

Moghaizel's activism can be categorized under three headings: national, regional and international. On the national level, she belongs to numerous organizations and is a founding member of the Committee on Political Rights, Committee on the Amendment of the Penal Code, the Lebanese Association of Women Jurists, Lebanese Association of University Women, National Council of Lebanese Women, and National Association of the Family. On the regional level, she is a vice president of the Federation of Arab Women, a member of the Arab Association for Women and Development, and a member of the Alliance for Arab Women. On the international level, she was first

Laure Moghaizel

vice president and legal counsel of the International Council of Women, a member of the International Federation of Women Jurists, and a member of the Federation of Abolitionists.

Moghaizel has published numerous articles on the condition of women in the Arab world, and has represented Lebanon at national, regional and international conferences. She speaks fluent Arabic, French and English, and has been honored by her government and countrymen for her steadfast advocacy of human rights.

I telephoned Moghaizel to set up an appointment to meet with her and caught her just as she was stepping out of her office. I didn't appreciate how pressed for time she was until, some twenty minutes later, I turned on a television set to watch a live panel discussion on women's issues and there, staunchly defending the rights of women, was Laure Moghaizel!

We met early one morning in her law firm's library, reputedly one of the best private libraries in the country. A slender woman with neatly styled jet black hair and a grave demeanor, Moghaizel appears strong and in charge; yet, her calm demeanor conceals a great sorrow. Her daughter, Jana, a brilliant Sorbonne-educated linguist, was one of the 150,000 innocent victims killed during the Lebanese Civil War. Eight years later, Moghraizel, still dressed in black, is a mother in mourning.

*   *   *

I am amazed at the number of associations you belong to. How do you find the time to practice law?

For my husband and I, our work is our enjoyment. I cannot live without working. I was in the hospital for two months for major surgery and I very much missed my work. For years, our office and our house was located in an area that was under heavy bombardment. We were unable to practice law because for a long time there really were no laws to uphold. So instead, during this time, Joseph and I founded many movements against the war, including the Nonviolent Movement. I am fortunate to have a husband who is a feminist and who himself is engaged in public issues and activities. We have parallel interests and we often work together. For instance, at this moment, while I am being interviewed, Joseph is moderating a debate on human rights. If my husband enjoyed playing cards and attending cocktail parties, it would have been very difficult for me. Fortunately, we share not only mutual interests but mutual respect for each other's work. This has made all the difference in our marriage. We have now been married forty years. We are the parents of five children and it is a joy for us to have our children participate in our pursuits.

What is an average day for you?

It begins at six o'clock in the morning with a big breakfast. Joseph and I start our professional work at half past seven. We lead a very simple life. Usually, I reserve the morning for my professional work, the afternoon for volunteer work, and the evening for family. Some evenings we enjoy attending cultural events and reexperiencing the Beirut of old.

How many of your children are lawyers?

Only one! Our family is a democracy. We didn't insist that the children become lawyers! My eldest daughter is a professor of education at St. Joseph University; my second daughter, Jana, was in linguistics. She died, in 1986, a victim of the war as so many Lebanese were. The majority of the people who died in the war were civilians caught in the crossfire. The fighters were hiding in the trenches and shooting, but the civilians had nowhere to hide.

Our apartment is on the top floor of a building located on the demarcation line, dividing East and West Beirut. We often had the militia in our building because they wanted to shoot from our roof. Under the circumstances, we made a conscious choice to continue to live our lives as normally as possible. My daughter, Jana, was finishing her doctorate in linguistics and had just published a book in her field when she was killed. She was twenty-eight years old.

All of our children share our belief in nonviolence. In 1987, my husband and I organized, along with the Handicapped Association, a nonviolent march from the north of Lebanon to the south. It took us four days and we slept on the roadside. The marchers included fifty people in wheelchairs as well as blind people. We marched for human rights, peace, and a unified Lebanon. My children would appear along the route and hand me an apple or a boiled egg, insisting I eat something. It was easy for me to be involved in such things because I had a supportive husband and supportive children who collaborated with me. The whole family pulled together. I have learned so much from my children. Most of them have Ph.D.s and they help me stay up to date with life. When we lost Jana, life appeared absurd and devoid of worth. My husband and I plunged into our work, even more than before, because if you have a goal to achieve the pain is easier to endure. I will always be dressed in black for Jana.

What made you stay in Lebanon?

Joseph and I are committed to working for the unity of Lebanon. It was never a choice for us to go abroad or move from our apartment. We are both Christian Catholics who very much believe in the nonconfessional unity of this country and so we stayed with our five children. Our youngest son, Nagi, was born handicapped. Our life revolves around our work and our family. Joseph and I work together as a team. We were that way before our marriage. Our children have only strengthened our commitment to Lebanon. They learned early to be independent but, even so, I was the kind of mother that the French call *"une mere poule"* [a mother hen]. After I would come back from the office, I would take off my suit and slip into some overalls, play with the children, give them their baths, and help them with their homework.

What activities did the Nonviolent Movement undertake?

During the war, we collected 70,000 signatures for peace in Lebanon. We mobilized a blood drive to transfer blood from East Beirut to West Beirut and vice versa. We exchanged the blood at the demarcation line, under the bombs. In 1988, we had a sit-in for peace and unity in Lebanon. We sat in the streets of Beirut all day and all night with the fighting continuing around us. There was no electricity for street lights, so we used candle lights.

Could you tell me about your background?

I was brought up to do things out of a sense of duty and commitment and not for recognition. I will always be grateful to my parents for the sacrifices they endured to send my sister and I along with my two brothers to college. Every day, in everything I do, I think of them; especially of my mother, who was a feminist before the word existed. I attended law school at St. Joseph University and was one of three girls in a class of one hundred boys.

What drew you to the law?

I suppose it was my family's influence. Here in Lebanon, if one's family thinks their child is "a little" clever, they say: "Oh, he or she will make a fine lawyer." When I was growing up, I was told that often enough that I believed it! [laughter]

What are your feelings concerning feminism?

Women today don't like to be called feminists because they think of "feminists" as being old, ugly, radical women who wear tattered shawls and have a hint of a mustache! Admittedly, the original suffragettes from London were guilty of certain excesses, but we are now benefitting from their excesses. I have a lot of veneration for these feminists. Now, at the end of the twentieth century, I think women have outgrown feminism. We should no longer be feminists but humanists. It is very important that we work with trade unions and political parties because women's concerns and issues are an integral part of the human problem. I believe in this approach and I feel this approach is more in keeping with the aspirations of the younger generation. For instance, I don't see my daughters working strictly for feminist causes because they live and work in a world with men and women. We should all be humanists.

What is the focal point of your work, today?

I think men and women have the same destiny. When one fights for women's rights one is fighting for the rights of all human beings. There is no difference between men's and women's rights. I don't believe the rights of each is in opposition to the other. Even though I've devoted a lot of my work to women's causes, I prefer to describe my work in the larger framework of human rights. My husband and I founded the Lebanese Association of Human Rights. Due to the efforts of the association, the preamble of the Lebanese Constitution was amended to state that Lebanon is an active member of the United Nations and, as such, is bound by the Universal Declaration of Human Rights and all international conventions in all fields without exception.

My legal studies have given me the opportunity to help improve the situation of women in Lebanon and internationally. I was elected first vice president of the Paris based International Council of Women (ICW). It was a great honor because there are nine vice presidents and the first vice president is elected based on the number of votes she receives. I didn't seek the office but countries, including Belgium and France, nominated me to be president. Israel mounted a campaign against my nomination. They were not against me personally, they understood that my work for ICW was for all women, but they were against my nomination because my husband and I are also engaged in the struggle for Palestinian rights. The Israelis circulated an article that appeared in an international newspaper stating that Joseph had defended Palestinian victims. There is nothing to be ashamed in that. Joseph defended them even without remuneration as he would have any other wronged people. Unfortunately, politics and justice don't always mix. I withdrew from the election. I thought it would be in the best interest of the organization. Besides myself, there was only one other candidate nominated for president of ICW—Helvi Sipila, assistant secretary general of the United Nations, from Finland. As a gesture of solidarity, because of the circumstances of my withdrawal, she too withdrew from the election. As a result, the former president was asked to stay on for another term and, in spite of everything, I was elected first vice president.

Are you bitter about that experience?

No, but I am saddened.

What motivated you to become such an outspoken advocate for women's rights?

In the early fifties, when I studied the laws that affected women in Lebanon, I saw that Lebanese legislation, on the whole, was up to date except for the laws that still discriminated against women. I decided to wage a campaign to correct that. My strategy was to single out those laws and go after them one by one rather than all at once. In seeking to change the law, our basic reference and justification was always international instruments such as the United Nations Convention and the Declaration of Human Rights.

I was not the first to demand women's rights. Earlier in the century, there were pioneers like Iptihage Kaddoura and Saniya Habboub. Their demands for civil and political rights, however, were not specific. They were made in general terms. Consequently, the deputies and parliamentarians did not give their requests serious consideration. Learning from their experience, I thought it best that we be specific in our demands. I decided to begin with political rights because in most cases political rights are the easiest to argue and win. Moreover, that year, 1949, women were winning their political rights in many countries. I thought it was important for the momentum of the movement and morale that our first initiative be successful. I wanted to move from success to success.

How did you mount your campaign?

I began by appealing to Lebanese women's associations for assistance. They responded by electing a committee of nine women — myself included, I was still a law student — to work on their behalf and represent them. Most of the women on the committee, though advanced in age, were marvelous pioneers. I prepared a brief arguing that women be given the right to vote and presented our case before the court. In 1952, only educated women with high school diplomas were given the right to vote. I was truly revolted by this law because the government did not give women the opportunity to go to school. I told the legislators that we did not want political rights; we just wanted article so and so of the law to include the word "female" next to the word "male." Our persistence paid off and finally, in 1953, we were successful in amending the law giving all women the right to vote.

After that victory, I thought it was time to work on the inheritance law. In Lebanon, we did not have any civil laws legislated for inheritance. All of us, Christians and Muslims alike, followed the Muslim law of inheritance which did not treat men and women equally. We elected a committee made up of Muslims and Christians to draft an inheritance law that all could agree upon. I presented the study prepared by the committee. Unfortunately, our Muslim colleagues were immediately criticized in the media for daring to tamper with Muslim Shariah law, and were forced to resign from the committee. We continued on without them and ratified a civil law providing equality in inheritance for non-Muslims. I was saddened that the law did not apply to all Lebanese because I believe in the unity of this country. Our laws should apply to all citizens; otherwise this country cannot exist. When dealing with human rights, you cannot say the law applies to one person and not to another. But in 1959 when the civil inheritance law was passed, we decided it was best to have half a victory than no victory at all.

From there, rather than addressing civil law dealing with marriage, I decided to work on the issue concerning the nationality of married women. Before 1960, when a Lebanese woman married a foreigner, she automatically became a foreigner herself; yet, if a Lebanese man married a foreigner, his wife automatically became Lebanese. To correct that we passed a law giving Lebanese women who married foreigners one year to decide if they wanted to remain Lebanese or change their citizenship.

Currently, we are working on a mother's right to pass on her nationality to her children. In Lebanon, children inherit only their father's nationality. A mother can only pass her Lebanese nationality to her children in two cases: if the child is illegitimate and she recognizes him before the father, and if she is a foreigner and after the death of her husband, who is also a foreigner, she takes on Lebanese nationality. But if she remains a Lebanese citizen, in spite of her marriage to a foreigner, and her husband dies, she cannot pass on her Lebanese nationality to her children. Also, if she is Lebanese and marries a foreigner and after the death of the foreigner she decides to reactivate her Lebanese nationality, she still cannot give her nationality to her children. It is an outrage when Lebanese law favors a foreign woman over a Lebanese woman in matters regarding nationality. We are asking for equal treatment for all women under the law.

Do you find yourself constantly fighting against discrimination?

One must always stay alert; if not, certain rights can easily slip away. For example, in 1974, I and several women lawyers worked to annul an old law that forbade a married women from leaving the country without the written authorization of her husband. Last week, I received a call from a woman who said she went to get a passport and was told she needed her husband's authorization. I told her go back and tell the official that no such legal requirement exists! She declined to do so because she needed her passport to travel and did not want to risk antagonizing the official. Next week, I plan to go to the passport office and request a passport. If they ask for my husband's authorization, I will demand that they show me where in the law that is required. Then I will take them to court!

As the president of the Lebanese Association for Human Rights, what are the priorities on your agenda?

I, along with activists from various Lebanese women's groups, have called upon the government to live up to its commitment to uphold human rights, including women's rights as dictated by Lebanon's membership in the United Nations Council for Human Rights. We demand four laws be amended: the law stating that the credibility of a woman's testimony is equivalent to one-third of a man's; the linkage and subordination of social security pensions for married women to the husband's pension; the reduction of prison sentences and acquittal of men who commit crimes of honor — where a man kills to save his honor, a situation recognized mainly in Mediterranean and Arab countries; and the law requiring a woman to secure the permission of her husband to work or engage in commerce.

I was asked to attend several parliamentary meetings on this subject in 1972, before the war, and one deputy told me: "Do you know this law was imported from France? We are not better than the French, therefore, why do we need to change it?" I told him, "Yes, Mr. Deputy, you are right, the law is from France, but it represents French law in 1807 and was thrown out by the French before the turn of the century!" I proceeded to inform him that in France and other western countries when that law was enacted the property of a woman automatically transferred to her husband upon marriage. However, during this same period, in Lebanon, no such transfer took place upon marriage. This was thanks to Muslim law which stated a husband had no legal claim on property brought into a marriage by his wife. So we were the beneficiaries of a French law that did not apply to us, yet has remained in our law all these years!

Other areas that need work is the discrimination against women in the penal law system. In instances of adultery, men and women are not equally punished. Women are punished much more severely while men sometimes are not punished at all. Lebanon's laws regarding this matter are no worse than those of other Arab countries; however, when I want to amend a law, I always compare our laws with those of other Arab legislatures. It often disquiets Lebanese politicians when they discover other Arab legislatures are more enlightened than our own.

Now, the big problem in Lebanon is the personal statute laws which deal with matters concerning marriage, engagements, paternal rights, pensions, alimony. Every Lebanese follows the conventions and laws of his or her religious community. We have seventeen different communities in Lebanon. Fortunately, we don't have seventeen sets of laws because some Catholic communities have similar laws. Nevertheless, to a greater or lesser degree, all personal statute laws are discriminatory against women. It is a case of not only inequality between men and women but inequality among women themselves. My rights as a Christian Lebanese woman are different from my neighbor's rights as a Muslim Lebanese woman because many of our laws are based on the dictates of our religion. In a democracy, I believe, it is important to have standards, rules and regulations that apply to everyone. If every religious sect follows a different set of laws, it creates a lacuna in the national unity.

Is there no civil law that pertains to all citizens?

We are trying to enact that, but it will not be compulsory. We want to at least provide Lebanese citizens with the choice of having a civil marriage. Currently, in Lebanon, you cannot have a civil marriage: you either marry in a church or a mosque. If you insist on a civil marriage, for it to be legal, it has to be performed outside the country.

What do you consider to be the most urgent issue facing Lebanon today?

The economy is a big problem. There are not enough volunteer workers in Lebanon because many can't afford to work without money. Another big problem is education. As parents and educators, we have "a lost generation" that we must integrate into society. This generation knows nothing but war. They have witnessed nothing but violence, hate, and human rights trampled. We must re-educate these youths and show them that there are values worth upholding in this world. It would be a disaster for Lebanon's future if we don't reclaim this generation. They are our collective responsibility. The economy I believe is beyond my control, but I feel these youths are not. It is important that every Lebanese feel that he or she is responsible, that the streets stay clean and the laws — traffic included — are upheld. It is an ability to adhere to small things as well as big principles that form a worthy citizen able to function on a national level. On the international level, we must bear testimony to the horrors and destruction of war. Our plight should serve as a deterrent against war for others. There is a lot to do.

What really matters to you in life?

I believe in simplicity, what the French call *transparence*, and, above all, sincerity. What motivates me is love for others. Those are the things that Joseph and I have tried to teach our children. Life is simple when you have nothing to hide and there is no vanity. I detest vanity. Our family will never be the same because of this war. If anything the war has taught us that material things matter very little. So many things are less important now. The death of our daughter devastated us, but Joseph and I would have been even more crushed if Jana had died fighting as a member of a militia. We have never had to be ashamed of our children. We have the peace of mind that comes with knowing that our children share our values, convictions, nationalistic point of view, and love of our culture.

Are you proud to be Lebanese?

I am not proud to be Lebanese when I hear the remark that we live in the "Switzerland of the Orient." That is not a true statement. Lebanon, like it or not, is a developing country. We have a lot of catching up to do. We need lessons in modesty. Yes, we are descendants of the Phoenicians but that alone is not going to help us out of this mess. We must get a toehold on civilization and learn to assimilate into our own culture what we have learned from the West. Most of all, we must overcome our differences as Lebanese and work together for a common goal.

What has shaped you into the person that you are today?

I am nothing. Allow me a different approach to the question. When I lecture on human rights, I always say that when the history of civilization is written, they will not write about Napoleon or Alexander or Genghis Khan, they will write about Gandhi, Martin Luther King, Marie Curie, Jean Dunant. These are the people worthy of remembrance. They are the true role models.

ANISSA NAJJAR

SOCIAL WORKER

Anissa Najjar, a petite woman with a serene smile and gray hair worn up in a bun, becomes a veritable force of nature when she addresses herself to the subject of Lebanese nationalism. An educator and a trailblazer in the field of women in rural development in Lebanon, she is president and founder of the Village Welfare Society, an organization she helped establish forty years ago.

Perceiving village women as the custodians of Lebanese culture, Najjar's aim is to improve their status by providing them with economic opportuni-

ties that will stem the flow of villagers to the city, and thus safeguard age-old traditions for the next generation of Lebanese. To accomplish this task, her organization has built and staffed dispensaries and schools in needy rural areas, provided social services and vocational training, undertaken relief programs for families displaced by war, coordinated agricultural projects, and marketed handicrafts.

A graduate of the American University of Beirut (AUB), Najjar is the author of Literacy of the Mind, a course of study designed to transform village women into leaders and productive members of their communities. Married to the late Fouad Najjar, a government minister who died in a car accident, she has two surviving children. Tragically, her daughter, Sannah, a graduate of AUB and a newlywed, was killed during the Israeli invasion of Lebanon.

✳   ✳   ✳

In your life, who has had the greatest influence on you?

My mother, she just turned 102 years old yesterday. We were cutting her birthday cake and my niece asked me: "What should I wish her?" I said, "Wish her a second hundred years!" Except for an ulcer, my mother has never been ill. I come from very sturdy stock. All my uncles and aunts are in very good health. My Uncle Halim, who is now ninety, has white hair but he is still a tall, handsome man. All through school, girls were always very friendly with me because they wanted to know my uncle. He is a graduate of UCLA. As a child, I used to read to my grandmother the letters he would send her. Once, he wrote that he was asked by a Hollywood director to be an actor and he asked his mother, "What should I do?" My grandmother was a very intelligent woman; she told me: "Go get some paper. Write him that we sent him to America with one personality; we don't want him to return with ten!" So instead of becoming an actor, he got his degree in agricultural engineering.

What did you want to be when you were growing up?

I wanted to be a doctor. I took premed courses but it was so difficult to travel between home and school. I would stay in the library until eleven or twelve o'clock at night and my brother had to accompany me to school and then back home. In those days, it was considered not only dangerous, but shameful for a girl to go anywhere by herself. I felt I was putting an unnecessary burden on my brother. Finally, I decided it was useless becoming a doctor if I had to be chaperoned all the time. I quit taking premed courses and received my B.A. in social sciences and education.

As an ardent nationalist, what do you perceive to be the stumbling block to Lebanese nationalism?

I think the problem has always been with our government. It has never been a real government that represented and served all the people. Lebanon with its diversity does not allow for a stable government because there isn't one government that is leading on national grounds. The government operates on sectarian grounds according to sectarian demands. This, of course, results in fragmentation of goals since every sectarian group has a different set of goals. If we were led by our leaders on national grounds, we would be united in our efforts. Because we are so divided, we are open to meddling from outside and thus we find ourselves continually in this divided state. Ever since my childhood there has always been a presence saying: "Remain as you are: sectarian." This is how we are controlled. What you see in Lebanon is a simple exercise in divide and rule. For example, in secondary school, I attended Ahlia, a school founded with national aspirations, but the French mandate did not accept the school as it was. They insisted on providing us with two salaried French teachers to teach us French. Why? Because they could not countenance our studying English. They thought that would make us pro–British.

Have there been recent leaders who have sought to unite the country?

Unfortunately, it is a fact that whenever anyone gives a nationalistic or patriotic speech they are discouraged from continuing to do so by outside forces. Something or someone close to them is immediately targeted: If the speaker is Shiite, a Shiite village is hit; if he is Christian, a Christian village, et cetera. The message, of course, to all is: "Beware don't speak out about nationalism."

Are you ever fearful for your own safety?

My father died when I was four years old, my brother was six years old, and my sister was almost a year old. We grew up without the security of having a man in the house. I was afraid of so many things, darkness, strange sounds, et cetera. My uncle had a hunting dog who would come and scratch at our door and the sound always frightened me. If I wanted a drink of water at night, I would be afraid to leave my room and get it. My mother used to encourage me by saying if you go alone and get a glass of water I will give you something special. I would go trembling but eventually I became very brave and learned to overcome my fear of many things...including the darkness.

What was the effect of the war on women?

Women won their independence during the war. In 1954 a poll was taken asking parents if they would allow their daughters to work outside the village: 100 percent said "No." In 1970, 56 percent said "No," and in 1991 only 31 percent said "No." This change occurred because of economic conditions brought about by the war; women had to work. It was no longer something that was considered in terms of being socially correct or incorrect.

Do you feel that you have the support of the government in your efforts to help women in rural areas?

I head the Women's International League for Peace and Freedom, the Village Welfare Society, and the Children's International Villages, all nonsectarian organizations. As soon as I ask for something at the Ministry of Education, they say: "Certainly madame, you will have everything you ask for." After I leave nothing ever materializes. Why? Because I am a Druze! I have no credit. Although my activities are nonsectarian, I have encountered this attitude for years. If those in power don't repair this attitude, the war is going to resume. There is something so unintelligible about the whole sectarian business! Tell me, how important is it when you are dealing with another person what his

Anissa Najjar

beliefs are? If he believes in Satan or God, what does it matter? It doesn't change a thing! But there are those who believe that it does. So we continue to live like this. When I went to work for the villages in the South, where there are a few Christian villages but many more Shiite villages, some of the members of the Village Welfare Society would say: "Why should we go to the South?" I would reply: "Why shouldn't we? They are Lebanese, too! And besides, if you help others you will never need to use Max Factor products, because you will never have wrinkles." [laughter] I'm not sure which provided the greater motivation!

Tell me about your work with the Village Welfare Society.

We started the organization in 1951. I spent a great deal of time thinking about our divided society. I concluded the problem was with the mothers in this country. I thought to myself we have the wrong mothers! They are not teaching their children well. I decided to do something about that. I thought I would begin work in the villages, where people have not been spoiled by politics or by missionaries. It was a practical starting point. I took a small group and we visited several villages and we started asking questions. I discovered that the parents, in spite of the fact that they were illiterate, wanted to educate their daughters. We found a one-room school in Mount Lebanon being taught by a very old, crippled teacher. They had hired her because they could afford her. She required only a few Lebanese pounds a year, a small supply of food staples and, during the winter, every child would bring her a piece of wood for heating. It was a poor village but they managed to cut this deal and the teacher was happy and they were happy.

Was this a co-ed school?

No, it was a girls' school; the boys had their own school. A girl's education was not considered a priority because girls could get married without an education, but boys needed jobs to get married and therefore their education came first. The government school consequently accepted boys only. The villagers had to create a private school for their daughters so I knew there was some initiative here. I asked questions such as: "Do you want your daughter to go to college?" The answer invariably was "No, it's enough for her to know how to read and write." I would ask the women: "Who takes care of the children, you or your husband?" They would answer: "What does he know about these things. He goes and works and I take care of everything." I asked: "What would you like your daughters to learn?" The answer was almost unanimous: Everyone wanted their daughters to learn how to sew.

When we learned that sewing skills was what they wanted for their daughters, we brought in a dressmaker and all the girls came to learn how to sew. Sewing was our master key. During the sewing classes we would slip in information about hygiene, nutrition, social knowledge, agriculture, et cetera. We found the girls to be very receptive to learning. Rather than work to repair mistakes, we decided to start a new school for them. We had a good grasp of what was lacking in the educational curriculum and realized we needed to create a special program. The government's educational program was a failure in the sense that it only taught the "three R's." It taught nothing about how to be a mother, how to raise and take care of a family. I thought this had to change. I started creating a syllabus by collecting articles and asking people to write articles on certain subjects. I assembled all the material in a textbook, which I called, *Literacy of the Mind*. We covered everything that the government's program missed, such as handicrafts, health, nutrition, hygiene, home economics and art. Imagine a program devoid of all these subjects that are so important in your life as a woman! When you get married, you have to know how to dress, furnish a house, prepare a meal for your husband and guests, and look after the health of your family so you don't spend a fortune visiting doctors every time a child sneezes.

Did you help all the villages in the same way?

No, we tailored our assistance to capitalize on whatever was available. For example, one of the villages we assisted was located in an area with very little water. The villagers were barely earning an income because they had no agriculture. So we introduced flowers, like carnations, which require very little water. They also had a lot of Batum, a tree which if you graft with a pistachio tree produces pistachio nuts. I brought them fifty plants of early grapes — vines that yield fruit in June. We managed to generate a source of income for the villagers by selling grapes, pistachios and carnations for them. They were also very good weavers and we helped sell what they wove.

In another area, which had good agricultural conditions, we started a canning project so the village women could preserve fruit and vegetables for the winter months and sell what was extra for pocket money. We provided a pressure cooker and let them borrow it to do their canning. But we insisted they pay a nominal rental fee for its use. I don't believe in charity. It is important that they understand nothing is free. Everyone has to earn a living. We also taught them how to bottle tomato juice. We had volunteers who sold the preserves and the tomato juice and the villagers rarely could keep up with the demand!

I remember in one village, only the daughter of the *mokhtar* [the village headman] knew how to read and write; the rest of the girls were illiterate. The parents were not concerned that their daughters couldn't read or write; they were only interested in their being able to sew. I told the teacher: "Teach them how to sew, but emphasize that they have to be able to read directions in order to sew." At the end of the day the girls went back home very unhappy and told their parents, "We can't possibly learn how to sew if we don't know how to read." As I had hoped, the parents came to us and said, "Why don't you open a school and educate our daughters. And that is how we created our first school! It was very important that the villagers ask us to set up a school and not the other way around.

What motivated you to get involved in rural welfare work?

During school vacations I used to go and live in the villages. I liked the honesty of the people and the simplicity of village life. By background, I am a Beiruti. My family has a family tree that goes back six hundred years. I am a pure Beiruti and Phoenician. If you see my uncles, they are very Phoenician-looking. They all have the long noses of the Phoenicians. We are a Druze family and we don't believe in intermarriage. The Druze have always been the natives of this country. Most people don't know anything about us. They often speak very naively about our religion. I know everything about Christians and Muslims but they know very little about us.

In my "Literacy of the Mind" program I teach the rights of Christian, Muslim and Druze women, and the religions of all three. People have to know about each other. You cannot live together in peace if you don't understand each others' ways, rituals and customs. If I see Christians look at a statue and cross themselves, I know it is their way of worship and it doesn't mean that they are pagans. If I see Shiites doing Ashura [a passionate rite of self-flagellation], I understand the history and the tradition behind why they do it. As a Druze, there is a reason why sometimes I pray very fervently and sometimes I don't. Cultural understanding is so important to human understanding. It is a field that is not touched upon in the educational system. If real peace is to be achieved among the Lebanese, we have to teach cultural understanding in the schools.

I am curious, what do people say about the Druze, besides their being very secretive?

They say that we have certain practices. We pray late at night. Our prayers start Friday evening. We go to the mosque and there is a wall between the men and the women so there are no distractions. Those unfamiliar with our practices spread ridiculous rumors that after midnight Druze men and women mix and make love. They don't know our religion! It is a mystical religion, which very much deals with the afterlife. We are regarded as heretics by orthodox Muslims, because we believe in reincarnation and the transmigration of the soul. In our religion, we are taught to do good with no thought of recompense here on earth. Our compensation will come in the afterlife. One is not allowed to smoke or drink alcohol. Also, we do not have counselors: you alone are responsible for yourself and for punishing yourself when you commit a sin.

I once heard someone ask my neighbor, Abou Amin, an old Druze man, "Where are you going?" Abou Amin responded: "I am going downtown, if God wills." Hearing his response, I remarked to my husband: "If he is going downtown, why does he say, 'If God wills?'" My husband said, "Because if he changes his mind or dies along the way, he would be a liar. He is being very cautious. He doesn't want to commit a sin."

What is the goal of your "Literacy of the Mind" project?

To teach values. My son one day came from school with a small piece of chalk. I asked, "Where did you get the chalk from?" He said, "I found it on the floor at school." I said, "Then the chalk belongs to the teacher and you are a thief." He was six years old and he looked at me and said, "I, a thief?" I said, "Yes, tomorrow morning you will give the chalk back to the teacher. Now, go bring your pencil and I will teach you your lesson." He said, "I don't have a pencil." I said, "Go look in your younger sister's school bag. He went and started shouting, "Mama, Mama, Mona is a big thief." He found two sticks of chalk in her bag. Mona came and I asked her: "What is this chalk doing in your bag?" She said: "The teacher chose me as a monitor, so I keep the chalk."

Honesty is a very important value to teach your children. A mother should be constantly on the lookout for every opportunity to teach a child good morals — that is what builds character. If you train your child well that training will last a lifetime and you can be proud of your achievement. I believe in women. It is not both parents, it is the mother who raises the children. Fathers rarely have the patience to spend time with their children. I believe in the saying: "If you teach a boy, you teach one person, but if you teach a girl, you teach an entire family." I believe education puts women and men on equal footing. Their roles may be different but they are equal. He has his role and she has hers. If the husband earns the money to buy the food and the wife has the knowledge to cook a meal, they are both equally important to the family unit. If she doesn't cook, he doesn't eat! Many people think it is degrading to be a woman or to do "woman's work." I am proud to be a woman, proud to do "woman's work," and proud to perform my role well. I don't think men are better or more accomplished than women. Men don't enjoy what we enjoy by way of sincerity. We take pleasure in sacrificing for others and our reward comes with that knowledge. The goal behind the "Literacy of the Mind" program is to create not only women leaders and role models, but mothers who will raise a whole new generation of open-minded, healthy, intelligent and happy children. Can you think of anything more important?

RABAB SADR CHARAFEDDINE

SOCIAL WORKER

"Social work is spiritual nourishment," says Rabab Sadr Charafeddine. Described as "a woman who works like an unknown soldier in the service of her country," Charafeddine, for the past thirty years, has been a prime mover in the field of social and humanitarian work in Lebanon, heading up welfare associations in Tyre, Baalbek and Beirut. As the sister of Imam Musa Sadr, leader of the Lebanese Shiite community and the founder of both the Muslim Shiite Supreme Council and the Amal Movement, she continues his work since his mysterious disappearance on a visit to Libya in 1978.

We met at the Institute for Girls in Beirut, a technical training center offering instruction in secretarial and sewing skills. As I was ushered into Charafeddine's office, a Shiite cleric, dressed in a black robe and white turban, and his wife, covered in a black shroud, were leaving. We were joined by Charafeddine's twenty-four-year-old son, a recent graduate of the University of North Carolina, who gamely volunteered to act as our interpreter.

Hailing from a family with strong clerical affiliations in the Muslim Shi-

ite community, Charafeddine, a modest woman who covers her hair with a scarf, is currently researching a book on the role of women in Islam and Christianity. The mother of four sons, she is married to Hussein Charafeddine, a member of a distinguished family of ulema.

* * *

In presenting you with the Order of the Cedar, the First Lady of Lebanon, Mrs. Mona Haraoui, said: "You are a credit to your country having planted the seeds of honor, love, forgiveness and affection in the hearts of those around you." How is it possible to do that in a country that has been so bitterly divided after so many years of civil war?

In truth, only a person who doesn't know the Lebanese people would ask such a question. If you've lived in Lebanon, for any period of time, you would know the hostilities did not affect or change the basic decency of the people. In the days when there was fighting between the religions, they still couldn't separate Muslim and Christian neighbors from each other. There has always been a deep abiding friendship and understanding among the Lebanese people irrespective of religion. Proof of which, we are still one nation. We will not be divided. I remember the day the road opened between East and West Beirut, no one from either side hesitated to cross over to the other side. The war did not change the Lebanese people, nor did it change their values or their character. You cannot destroy the compassion that people have for one another.

Could you tell me about yourself?

I come from a religious family with a long history of service to God and our community. On both my father and my mother's side going back to my great, great grandfathers, we have been a family of clergymen and religious scholars. I was born in Iran. My father is of Lebanese origin and my mother is of Iranian origin. I remember, as a child, our house was always open to visitors. Everybody came: presidents, ministers, clergymen, scholars, the most powerful and the most humble. Our door was always open to those in need. My uncles on both sides are also clergymen and religious scholars. I came to Lebanon with my mother when I was sixteen years old to visit my brother, Imam Musa Sadr. He had been invited, in 1959, by the Shiite community in Lebanon to take over the duties of Imam Charafeddine, who had passed away a year earlier. Imam Charafeddine himself had selected my brother to take over from him since he was getting on in years and wanted someone capable to replace him.

The same year I arrived in Lebanon, I married Imam Charafeddine's grandson, Hussein Charafeddine. I have lived in Lebanon ever since. My husband is an educator and a writer. My native language is Persian so I had to learn Arabic. I am not the kind of person who enjoys going to coffees and on visits. I like to help others. In 1962, with my brother's guidance and sponsorship, I began by helping women in the South by doing social and humanitarian work. Imam Sadr believed that women should play a role equal to that of men in society. I am in charge of our social institutions in Tyre, which devote special attention to the

Rabab Sadr Charafeddine

sick, the needy, orphans and the elderly. Our institutions also provide day care services for working mothers, and we are now planning to provide free meals for students.

Where does the funding for your humanitarian work come from?

From donations, and we raise funds from exhibitions and *iftars* [Ramadan fast-breaking meals] attended by people of all religious denominations. We have a factory which produces carpets, sheets and towels, enabling us to be self-reliant and not dependent on donations for our social work. The factory also provides us with an opportunity to employ widows and the needy so they do not have to depend on charity. From 1962 to 1978, under the leadership of Imam Musa Sadre, we worked very hard to establish institutions to help those in need. Then, in 1978, Imam Sadre was kidnapped. In his absence, we are continuing his work. It has been difficult with hostilities ranging between Muslims and Christians, Sunni and Shiite, Shiite and Druze, et cetera. In spite of the hardships, I will not leave, nor will I quit. Nothing, except death, can stop me from carrying on his work. We have put to rest the lies and dirty rumors people spread about Imam Sadr. If one believes in God, no one but God can hurt him.

Are you referring to the whispers that Imam Musa Sadr was a foreign agent?

There were many mischievous rumors spread by those who disliked Imam Sadr for trying to help the weak and create a better society. Imam Sadr's goal was to build a strong and just society made up of responsible and educated men and women. I am working to carry on his dream. The war in Lebanon was designed to kill justice. We have put our faith in justice, backed it by strength, and thus have succeeded in protecting and helping our people. Many of us read the same book, but we don't all get the same message. Thankfully our community is prospering and we are raising and nurturing a new generation to appreciate and better understand the true spirit of Lebanon.

When you were growing up, who were your role models?

Three women are my inspiration: Khadijah, the wife of the prophet Muhammad, who was wealthy in her own right and helped the prophet spread the word and ideology of Islam; Fatima, the daughter of the prophet and the wife of Imam Ali, the first imam in the Shiite Muslim religion. She, too, helped spread the ideals of Islamic thought after the prophet's death. And Zainab, the sister of Imam Hussein, the son of Imam Ali and Fatima. During the struggle between two Muslim factions, she was the woman who made sure Islam continued to thrive. Also, my father and then later my brother, Imam Sadr, were my role models.

As a young girl, did you have a sense that your brother would become an imam, and be described by some as "a man unlike other men"?

Yes, he was always special, considerate and thoughtful. There were three boys and seven girls in my family. I was the youngest of ten children and I naturally looked up to him since he was much older than I. But it wasn't until I started working with him, seeing how people from all walks of life were drawn to him, that I realized he was not just special because he was my older brother.

When you were growing up, what did you want to be?

I always knew I was going to be some kind of administrator or manager. When I was young, they would call me "the organizer." I was always arranging activities, even though I was the youngest in my family and among my cousins and my sisters' and brothers' children, I was always the leader and everyone listened to me.

How did you manage to continue your humanitarian work during the war?

It was very difficult. Those of us who wanted to instill hope were overtaken by those who had weapons and wanted to commit violence. In the best of times it is difficult to implement ideas into action. Imagine what we were up against! The headquarters of the foundation is in the South and we have branches all over the country. Each branch has a director and each director was influenced by the war in a different way. The war had a destructive influence on values and norms. Some people grabbed guns and started shooting for no reason. They were wild and unwilling to listen to ideas or work for the common good. The absence of authority has affected not one but several generations of youth who grew up in this war. I feel my mission is to redirect and influence the values and goals of these young people by introducing useful projects to them and teaching job skills that will enable them to earn a living.

Are there ever times when you watch the news and think: "If my brother were here things would be different"?

Yes, of course! A day didn't go by during the war that I and many others didn't think such thoughts. The worst time of my life was the fifteen years of the war following his absence. We experienced the Israeli invasion, kidnappings, and it seemed that every negative thing that happened on earth was blamed on the Shiite community. It is unbelievable what is happening in this world! There are those who are traitors, who lie, steal, kidnap, kill innocent people, and then say it is done in the name of Allah and Islam. Our people are not like that! If Imam Sadr were here they would not dare make such claims. He was a strong leader.

How did your life change after your brother was kidnapped?

It changed a lot. The stability in my life is gone. There is no one I can rely on to listen and solve my problems. He left behind a hole. He was not just a brother to me, he was a teacher, a leader, and a father. I was raised at his knees. Everything I learned was from him. I was very young when my father died and he, among my brothers, was the one most involved in my upbringing. I always felt comfortable and protected in his presence. He had a strong but not intimidating personality. He was a tall, large man; yet, very gentle. Children felt comfortable with him.

What do you believe is the goal of religion?

The foundation of all religions on this earth is to teach, help, and be of service to people. This is why we are closer and more attached to our religious community than our political party. The pull of religion is stronger than the laws of governments and organizations. People of the book, religious people, have much more influence over their followers than politicians.

Do you believe there is now more equality in Lebanon among the various religious communities as a result of the war?

The war did not achieve a single thing in Lebanon. Absolutely nothing! It did not give people more rights. The war destroyed the character of all the sects. We went backwards a hundred years.

Before the war, only the president presided at important occasions. Now, you see all three leaders — the president [a Maronite Christian], the prime minister [a Sunni Muslim], and the speaker of parliament [a Shiite Muslim]— appear as equals.

Yes, on the surface that is the way things may appear but in reality it is far from that way. After seventeen years of war and the death of so many martyrs, one would hope for more. So many mothers lost their sons, so many wives became widows, so many children became orphans — for what? What do we have to show for this sacrifice? Three leaders, from three different religious communities, who appear as equals on television. We should have achieved so much more. Those who led the fighting have attained high positions for themselves, but they have not achieved what they promised their people. Today, if you need to get something done at a government department, no matter how small the matter, if you don't know someone or if you don't give a bribe, nothing will get done. In the past, there was corruption but it was hidden under the table; now, it is out in the open and an accepted way of doing business.

You don't think the war lessened class stratification?

On the contrary, it augmented differences. Before, the stratification of society was more nominal. It was based more on traditional values and lines of authority that no longer exist. The war made so many people lose their values and their sense of devotion to their country.

On a different front, how do you manage all your obligations as a mother, wife, administrator and a public figure?

I have four boys. My children and I grew up together! My oldest son is thirty and my youngest is nineteen. I was fortunate my responsibilities came gradually. Before my brother was kidnapped, I had a very manageable schedule. I would do social work in the morning and be home in the afternoon to help the children with their homework. As my responsibilities have grown, so have my children, and they no longer need me as much. My husband has always encouraged me to do social work. He has never said to me: "Don't work, don't go out, don't do this or don't do that." My children understand my commitment and appreciate what I do. They often help me with my work and everyone helps out at home. We have an equal opportunity household! My boys have no problems with washing dishes, setting the table, or hanging the laundry. I look upon my work as a mission to serve. I am not working to win any popularity contests.

Have you considered running for a seat in parliament?

I am very fortunate to have the love and respect of Lebanese people from all regions of the country, not only the South. I love my life of service; especially the fact that I can help women and children. I don't believe success in social and humanitarian work should be traded for political power. Both fields are not compatible. People today are tired of "nice" words; they want deeds. As long as there is breath in me, I will do the work my brother started and continue to soothe and comfort those who have experienced great sorrow. I understand sorrow.

MEDIA, COMMUNICATIONS, AND BUSINESS

SUADE KARUDE AL-ASHI

BROADCAST JOURNALIST

"In Lebanon, I am considered a superstar," says Suade Karude Al-Ashi with a twinkle in her eye. Ashi, a news anchor on Television Lebanon, also produces television specials on notable personalities and routinely interviews politicians and celebrities for her popular weekly program, "Thursday Salon." She is noted for her stylish clothing and a penchant for asking probing questions. In 1995, she was presented a gold medal by Lebanon's First Lady in recognition of her accomplishments as Lebanon's most acclaimed newscaster and ideal mother.

As I groped my way up several flights of stairs, during a mid-morning power outage, I spotted Ashi, radiant in a cool, summer frock, waiting for me at the entrance of her elegantly furnished apartment in the heart of Beirut. Like her television persona, in person Ashi is engaging and charismatic. A perky brunette, she is married to television writer and producer, Ahmad Al-Ashi, and is the mother of two sons and a daughter. Her eldest son Mazin, a freshman at Beirut University College, joined us in the living room. Whenever Ashi searched for the mot juste in English (her third language), she would glance at her son whose fluency in English enabled him to cheerfully offer up a number of alternatives.

* * *

Can you tell me about yourself?

I am Lebanese and I love my country deeply. I began working in television at age nineteen and from my first day on the job I have loved my work. I can't think of a more satisfying profession! I have been doing television for twenty years and I am still learning, still striving to be more successful.

What is your definition of "being successful?"

Success has no limits. It is not something that you finally grab. It keeps eluding you. But it provokes you to dream. Many people tell me: "Stop! What more do you want?" I don't see it that way. There is always so much more to achieve. That is what gets me up in the morning!

When you were growing up, what did you want to be?

When I was in school, I enjoyed public speaking and I have always been very outspoken in the face of injustice. I am anything but shy. Even as a little

Suade Karude Al-Ashi

girl, I was always asked to sing or recite poetry at important occasions. My teachers and everyone around me predicted that I would have a career that was very much in the public eye.

Did you have a role model?

There really were no women I admired on Lebanese television, but on Egyptian television, I admired Leila Rustum and Himat Mustapha: Leila, for her interview skills, and Himat for the way she delivered the news.

How did you begin your career in television?

I was nineteen and I asked a family friend who headed Radio Lebanon if I could work at the radio station. He said, "Let's see how well you can read." He handed me a newspaper and I read it and he said, "You are good but you need practice." I started reading out loud all the time, taping my voice, and listening to myself. Then I went and took the Radio Lebanon reading test and I was hired. I worked in radio for two months and then I was invited to be a television newscaster on Television Lebanon.

Do you remember the first time you appeared on the air?

Yes, I was scared to the point where I was actually trembling. I felt I had this huge responsibility to do well. The program was about the history of Egyptian film and I had to interview celebrity writers, actors and directors. It went fairly well because afterwards I was asked to do news bulletins, which then led to children's programs and a whole series of social, cultural and political programs.

What type of programs do you prefer doing?

I prefer news programs and political interviews and that is actually what I do most. I head the news bureau at my station and I have complete control over what I read on the air.

I saw your two-hour special on President and Mrs. Haraoui. You asked some very personal questions. How do you determine where to draw the line?

I believe if I am going to do a special, I might as well make it as interesting as possible by asking questions that will make people sit up and listen. My television special with the President and First Lady was broadcast live. I insisted on that. If it were taped, the President would have called and requested that we cut out certain parts. In this business there is no room for the faint of heart! When I decide on something I am not afraid. If I were, I wouldn't have lasted all these years. Fear is a real enemy. If I believe in my cause, I become fearless. For the special with President and Mrs. Haraoui, I thought it was a good idea to show how the President thinks, what he likes, interview members of his family, his friends, and find out what they think about him. I was pleased with the results. It played well! It wasn't conventional. Everything that is conventional is boring. The audience wants something extra. People would not respect me if I didn't have the courage to ask the tough questions. If I interviewed the First Lady and asked her the same questions all the other reporters ask, I wouldn't have a story. I ask the questions people talk about.

How did you convince President Haraoui to do a live broadcast spanning several hours?

It was easy. I went to see the First Lady and I told her I wanted to do an interview with her. I had previously done a very successful interview with Mrs. Haraoui for my "Thursday Salon" show, but the President was not included. I asked her, this time, if I could do a brief interview with both she and the President and ask them questions about their family and life in general. She said we'll see. After a week of working on the program, I called Mrs. Haraoui back and told her I thought it would be better if we filmed the President as he watched the broadcast and record his reaction to it. She said she would speak with the President and they both agreed to do the special. I don't think they realized it was going to be a two-hour, live broadcast!

The camera kept panning President Haraoui as he waited to be interviewed and he appeared restless. Weren't you worried that you were taxing his patience?

No, I was doing exactly what I intended to do!

Where does your sense of confidence come from?

It's true, I have a lot of self-confidence. My father passed away more than fourteen years ago, but ever since I was a child he always supported and encouraged me. When I began working in television, my father would drive me to work and pick me up every day. He would always tell me: "I am so proud of you! You are clever and you are beautiful!" He and God are the source of my confidence. I have a sister who resembles me; the only difference is that I am much more confident. She is a newscaster and does a medical update program for television.

What is a typical day for you?

I begin my day by reading newspapers, listening to the radio, and visiting with a few people. At nine o'clock, I go to the television station and attend a general meeting where we discuss the news and what we want to focus on that day. Then I go to the hairdresser and home for lunch. At three o'clock, I am back at work to see what is new and what has been reported. I assemble the material, have my make-up done, and at 7:30 in the evening I go on the air.

I've noticed that female newscasters in Lebanon wear a lot of jewelry and make-up — even for a morning broadcast!

We reflect our society. Lebanese women are very elegant and they enjoy keeping up with fashion. They always like to be well-groomed and well-dressed. The French have an expression: *"Tirer a quatre epingles."* Roughly translated it means "dressing up to the t's" [laughter] and that is our style!

How do you deal with stress?

We lived through seventeen years of war, which is enough to stress anyone out; especially when your job is covering the news on television. The answer to your question is: You deal with it! You train yourself to relax. Even if you are not relaxed, you have to appear relaxed. When I am on the air, I always try to appear serene. I have learned to control my nerves. The worst thing you can possibly do when giving the news is appear hassled. If people feel worried and uptight, you have to reassure them by your calmness. But when I come home, it is an entirely different matter! [laughter] On the outside, I may appear relaxed and in control but inside I am anything but that. When you are on the air, so many things can go wrong, but no matter what, you have to always appear confident and in control. If you can't pull that off, you should look for another job.

During the war was there a program or broadcast that you worked on that really affected you?

The Lebanese people had no need to pay to watch any scary movies during the war; all we had to do was look out the window or turn on the television set and follow the local news. The most frightening movie during the war was the war itself. I would go every day to work with the shells falling all around and then I would report on the fighting. Reality was much more scary than any movie.

NADIA BARRAGE

FLORAL AND INTERIOR DESIGNER

A well-composed, elegant brunette, Nadia Barrage is an acclaimed interior decorator and floral designer who has won awards and accolades in both fields. The wife of a diplomat, and the mother of four, she has traveled and lived abroad most of her married life. She is described by a client as "a dear friend with exquisite taste whom I would love to make a member of my own family."

She received her degree in interior design from the University of Pennsylvania and has practiced her profession internationally. Barrage has published numerous articles on the subject of interior design and enjoys giving flower arrangement demonstrations. She is the owner of an interior design boutique and travels extensively to replenish a wide-ranging inventory.

For the interview, we met at her home decorated with David Roberts lithographs, Persian carpets, antiques and other collectibles from her travels around the world.

*   *   *

Could you tell me about yourself?

I grew up in Beirut, attended El Aziriya (a nun's school) and then Franciscaine Missionnaires de Marie, a finishing school, where I studied French and home economics. I am the eldest of six children: we are two girls and four boys. Even though many of us live in different countries, we are constantly on the telephone with each other, and try to get together as often as possible. As the eldest, I was expected to set a good example for my brothers and sister. I was

Nadia Barrage

always very responsible from a very young age. I was the first grandchild born on both my mother's and my father's side of the family and there was always this tug between both families to take care of me. But, in spite of their attention, they never spoiled me. Instead, I was taught responsibility.

When you were growing up, what did you want to be?

I had so many dreams! [laughter] Most of all, I wanted to travel and see the world. I wanted to create: to design clothes and beautify homes. I wanted to help people feel better about themselves and their environment. I was always very good with design. After graduating, a friend and I went into business together designing dresses, which I still love to do. We supplied several dress boutiques with our creations and did quite well. I have always enjoyed a reputation for being original. I don't like to copy. I was influenced by my grand-mother and aunts, on my mother's side, who were very artistic. They never wasted a minute. Even leisure time was held to the highest standard. They were always doing or making something. I remember their hands always being busy: embroidering, sewing, knitting, making dolls for us to play with, baking cook-ies and cakes. They always seemed to be doing something original and beauti-ful, even if they were just potting plants!

What are your fondest memories of childhood?

I adored my grandmother. When I was about ten-years-old, she became an invalid and taking care of her, I felt, was my responsibility. She never treated me as a child; in fact, she always made me feel that my opinion counted. She and my aunts lived next door. When I went to visit them, which was almost daily, they would always prepare delicious treats for me and make me feel very special. They would help me with my homework or teach me a new embroidery stitch. I always left feeling I had learned something new. Often, before going to school, I would drop by so my grandmother or one of my aunts could braid my hair just the way I liked. I was a lucky girl!

You've traveled and lived all around the world. What specific qualities do you attribute to your Lebanese heritage?

My love of travel, my curiosity about people and the world, my belief that when one door closes another always opens, my adaptability, my facility with languages, and my head for business. Is that enough? [laughter] I don't know why, but you will find that most Lebanese are perfectionists. We like to do every-thing well and with style, whether it is our cuisine, clothes and fashion, enter-taining, whatever — it has to meet a certain standard of excellence. We work hard and have high expectations of life and ourselves. We are a very sociable people. We love to enjoy life!

What do you consider your best quality?

I react well under pressure. Some people crumble, I am the opposite.

Has the way your life progressed surprised you?

I was always very ambitious. Things did not happen to me suddenly, but I was ready for whatever came along. I was never insecure about what I could and couldn't do. I always felt I could succeed whatever the challenge.

Where does your confidence come from?

From my mother! When I was a little girl, whenever I did anything, she, my aunts and my grandmother would always praise and encourage my efforts. They would say: "Nadia does everything well!" When you hear that over and over again, it gives you confidence in yourself and makes you feel, in your heart, that you really can do anything!

When you were growing up, did you ever feel discriminated against or treated differently from your brothers?

No, both my mother and father wanted all their children to be well edu-cated. We were raised just as my husband and I have raised our children. There was no difference between boys and girls in the family. If anything, my sister and I were treated with more tenderness. My parents never said, "You can't do this because you are a girl." If there were any restrictions put on us as girls, it was more due to our society. For example, I never dreamed of becoming an engineer or a scientist at that time.

Coming from a conservative Lebanese family, was it difficult adjusting to a western lifestyle?

Not at all! In Lebanon, we have always enjoyed what we like to regard as the best of the East and the West. Being at the crossroad of civilizations, Beirut has always been at the forefront of change. And that is why as a nation, we are a very adaptable people. When I married and traveled to Europe and America, I was never surprised by what I saw. But I did come to realize how sociable we Lebanese are compared to other nationalities!

How did you evolve from a fashion designer to an interior designer?

It was a natural progression. Traveling as much as we did, I always seemed to be in the midst of packing or unpacking. Every couple of years, when we were assigned to a new post, I had to decorate my house from scratch. My talent was noticed by my friends and they began asking me for decorating advice. When I had the opportunity, I went back to school and earned a degree in interior design. Studying formalized my intuitive knowledge and provided me with a vocabulary. In Dakar, Senegal, I had acquired such a reputation, I was asked to decorate the new embassy. Also, I have a brother who is very dear to me. He is a businessman and developer and I have always enjoyed collaborating with him on his many construction projects. And that is how I began.

How would you describe your decorating style?

I am very comfortable with an eclectic look. I don't like to be restricted. I like to mix and achieve an element of surprise in a room. I dislike a "showroom" look. I like homes to be personalized and reflect the lifestyle of the family. When I step into a room, I like to have that feeling that everything is comfortably in its place. I like things to flow. I love it when people say, "Look what Nadia did! She mixed African art with Louise XIV antiques and kilim pillows!" Ideas come to me the moment I step into a room. I have a good eye! Immediately, I know what I must do to improve the room. I envision the transformation in my mind. Then I proceed to execute my visual blueprint. When I am working, I am not at all sociable! My thoughts are all focused on my vision and I don't like to be distracted.

Having traveled all over the world, and not having set down roots in any one place for too long, do you ever wonder who you are?

[laughter] No, I know exactly who I am and where I come from. I think, that's why I don't have trouble adjusting to new environments. I feel very well grounded and perfectly at home wherever I am, whether I am in Senegal, Saudi Arabia, Italy or Hong Kong. I have always enjoyed meeting and getting to know people from all nationalities. I am particularly blessed with being able to make friends easily. Also, I am very proud that wherever I've lived, I've always created a familiar home environment for my family. As a result, even though we moved so much, my children when they were growing up always had a sense of continuity. I would incorporate the local flavor but, at the same time, maintain familiar arrangements.

How do you like to relax?

I love to go to my flower room and be surrounded by vases of every description, flowers of every shape and color, and begin to put together an arrangement. I love selecting and combining colors and shapes. Bending a stalk in a certain way, turning a leaf, adding a bud, can result in a breathless transformation. There is a wonderful feeling of satisfaction when you complete an arrangement and step back for the final look.

How did you manage to juggle a career and a family?

I have two boys and two girls who are the apple of my eye, and a wonderful husband. Traveling so much made us a very close-knit family. With the exception of being a French teacher for two years — three of my children were my students — I was a full-time mother until my youngest was ten. As an interior designer, I've always tried to keep as flexible a schedule as possible. I had my first child in Rome; my second, in Tunis; my third, in Florida; and my youngest, in Carthage. I like to think of my family as a miniature United Nations! It wasn't easy raising a family and traveling, but somehow my husband and I managed. I remember my daughter was born two months and eight days after we arrived in Tunisia and my husband, eight days later, had to leave on a two-month trip. I was left alone with a new baby and my fourteen-month-old son. My son still couldn't talk. Every evening he would take me by the hand and together we would check to make sure all the doors and windows were secured! My husband and I brought our children up to be responsible, and to depend upon themselves and each other and that, thank God, is the way they are.

How did the war in Lebanon affect you?

It affected me a lot. I never dreamed Lebanon would ever have such a war. It was really the shock of my life. I had no idea we had so many weapons in the country. Accepting and respecting differences is a fundamental part of the Lebanese way of life. We have always been a very harmonious and peace-loving society. People of different origins and backgrounds have always coexisted and flourished in Lebanon. In fact, Lebanese of all backgrounds have always attended school, worked, and socialized together. We are a nation of entrepreneurs; war is not in our blood.

How did you cope during the war years?

When I returned to Beirut to visit my family, I was shocked by the magnitude of the destruction. From the airport to the house, I couldn't stop crying. The ruined buildings; the debris on the streets; the makeshift shelters; the unfamiliar sight of young men carrying guns; roadblocks everywhere — it really shocked me. I thought, where am I? I felt so sad for my country. When I arrived at my mother's apartment building, I stayed downstairs for about an hour to pull myself together before going up to see her.

What have you learned that has made a difference in your life?

Never limit your range of friendships. Treat everyone equally. Always be open-minded. I've learned something from every place I've lived. When you are in a developing country, you learn to appreciate the simplicity of life and to be thankful for basic things. I've learned how wonderful it is to serve people and teach them to support themselves. I've taught young girls in Africa to sew and to embroider so they could earn a living. I've worked at orphanages in Tunisia and helped start a cooperative in Afghanistan to sell the embroidery and bead-work of the local women. Those are the experiences that I really treasure. It is a wonderful feeling to know you have made a difference in someone's life — no matter how small.

SONIA BEIRUTI

JOURNALIST AND TALK SHOW HOST

The mother of twin boys and, now, the grandmother of six, journalist and television personality Sonia Beiruti exudes the confident ease of someone who has spent a lifetime in the spotlight and has had years to grow comfort-able with her celebrity status. She has published three books in Arabic, includ-ing two volumes of short stories. With her trademark short, black hair, smart slack suits, melodious laugh, and confident manner, Beiruti took Lebanon by storm and continues to do so.

For many years, Saturday evenings were reserved by entire families in order to gather around the television set and watch "The Sonia Beiruti Show," a showcase for new talent. To great fanfare, poets, musicians, singers and comedians would perform and then be interviewed by Beiruti.

My meeting with Beiruti happened by chance. On my way to an appoint-ment, I dropped in to visit novelist Emily Nasrallah. As I was leaving, she asked me to return to meet a "special friend" who would be visiting shortly. As promised, I returned and there, sitting in the living room, legs neatly crossed, manicured fingers jauntily holding a cigarette holder, and an amused expression on her face, was Sonia Beiruti.

*   *   *

If one's name is one's destiny, your surname "Beiruti," is remarkably apro-pos!

[laughter] Yes! I consider myself a citizen of the world who happens to love living in Lebanon. I love the intimacy you have with people, the constant sun-shine, and the resourcefulness and intelligence of the people. Even though Paris is the capital of the cultural world, I can't seem to stay in Paris longer than fifteen days without feeling as though I were suffocating. To exist, I need to feel the rays of the Lebanese sun.

What changes would you like to see take place in Lebanese society?

Sonia Beiruti

Many. My husband, who is a manager at CDR (the organization responsible for the reconstruction of Lebanon) is Muslim and I am a Christian Maronite. I dream about a society where there are no differences between Christians and Muslims. I have experienced the tensions between the two. When I was a child, I was brought up in Ashrafiyeh, a Christian area. Now, I live in Ras Beirut, a Muslim area. There is no difference between the people in both areas. We are the same. There is no reason why we can't all get along. I also dream about a Lebanon that is truly independent.

How did you cope during the war years?

At the beginning, I thought the war was rather droll. I did not take it seriously. I was working for a newspaper and I was constantly traveling around the city doing interviews. When I would return to the office, they would ask: "Did you pass by such and such a street just now?" I would say, "Yes, why?" They would shake there heads and say, "We heard over the radio, a car bomb just went off there!" The first year of the war, I had the curious sensation I was in a film. But after that, as the war dragged on, it became very hard to bear.

The hardest period was in 1982. I was at home in my apartment on the Cornishe Mezzerah and I remember thinking: This is what Hell is like. We were being bombarded from the air, the mountains, and the sea — all at once. It was indescribable. Sometimes at night, when the bombardment was less intense, we would go out on our balcony to look at Beirut. I remember my husband remarking as we stood there that it looked as if it were right out of a scene from Nero burning Rome! Everything around us was burned or burning and there was no water nor any firemen to put out the flames.

Even though I don't like to think about this period, I am full of pride when I think of the way the women coped. They were heroic. They made their own bread, carried water up to their apartments, removed the plants and flowers from pots on the balconies and grew vegetables and spices. We were living in the 20th century, yet we had to rely on the ways of the past. There was one woman in her early fifties that I will never forget. I saw her one morning, at five o'clock, driving an old car that was loaded with bread. Artillery shells were falling everywhere and her car was the only one on the road. I waved her down and asked: "Why are you out?" She said, "When it is too dangerous for the bakers to open in Beirut, I drive to bread ovens outside of the city and come back with bread to sell here. What can I do? I have five children and my husband was killed. He was a taxi driver. I didn't know how to drive, but I learned. Before the children wake up I will, God willing, return home to prepare breakfast for them."

So many women were ill-prepared to take on the responsibilities that fell on them; yet, when they had no other alternative, they rose to the occasion. The war obliged women to be strong because while many men left the country to find work, women were the ones who stayed behind and took care of the children. The men couldn't afford to take their families with them. It was the mothers who stood in the bread lines, who comforted and made sure the children were fed and sheltered, took them to school and picked them up under the shells.

Do you feel that you have become a stronger person having survived the war?

They say, "what doesn't kill you makes you stronger," but what a price to pay for a little strength! The destruction was enormous. Before we ever had a war, I opposed the very idea of war. I detest war and fighting for any reason. With this viewpoint, imagine how I felt seeing people killing each other for no good reason with such extraordinary violence. It was as though the "Princes of War," as we called them, were being paid to destroy our country. It was unbearable. I was offered jobs in other countries but I refused to go. I couldn't bear the thought of leaving and not having a country to return to. I felt somehow that by my staying, Lebanon would continue to exist. It gave me a certain peace of mind. I could not imagine finding myself in the position of the Palestinians — leaving one day and then discovering they had no country to return to. What horror! I was not willing to take that chance. I thought that no matter how intolerable the living conditions were, it was still my country. It hurt terribly to see people leave, even though I knew how difficult it was to stay.

Tell me about yourself.

I always wanted to be a writer. Writing was my favorite way of expressing myself. Everything that happened to me, everything that I thought about or saw, I would write down. When I was furious, I would write; when I was happy, I would write. At the beginning, I wrote in French because at school we read a lot of French literature and it was easier for me to express myself in French. But when I needed to write something that was very serious, I always wrote in Arabic. Now, I write only in Arabic.

In school, I majored in Oriental Civilization because there was no such thing as a mass media major. I started working in journalism without really knowing anything about the profession. I just had a lot of curiosity and I learned on the job. I worked in radio as a journalist for a short time, and then television came along in 1959 and I made the switch. I was very adventurous because television was still in its infancy. There were only two or three women journalists, so I was involved in a lot of cultural programs that covered a range of subjects. We were constantly improvising. Everything was done live. When there were seven or eight subjects to cover or a number of people to interview, we were always in a state of suspense as to how things would turn out.

How did you become a journalist?

I always had this desire to work. Long ago, I learned from books and those around me that a person should be independent. I was fourteen when I came to that conclusion. When you become responsible for yourself, you learn to depend upon yourself and take your work and your relations with others seriously. When I was fifteen years old, I told my mother: "I am going to teach and earn my own money. I want to be free." After three months as a teacher, I realized teaching wasn't for me. I had a friend who was a journalist and I asked him, "What should I do?" He said, "Why don't you become a journalist?" He introduced me to Said Frayha, the head of a publishing house, who was as adventurous as I. He looked me over and said, "Okay, you can work for me." Then he took off on a two-month trip. When he returned, he saw me and said: "You are still here?" I said, "Yes! Don't you read your newspaper?" He said, "I've seen articles with your by-line but, tell me, who really writes those articles?" I was furious and was about to walk out when he said, "Sit down and respond to my question in writing." I wrote him a long memo. He read it and said: "Okay, I am now convinced you deserve a salary." I worked in all sections of the newspaper: politics, art, literature, everywhere. Whatever I was asked to do, I would do. I learned the entire business — editing, research, layout — from the bottom up.

In 1962, some of my male colleagues decided to start a woman's magazine called *El-Hasna*. The idea appealed to me and I joined them. The magazine, initially, was successful but then it floundered when clergymen started complaining that we were flaunting the current laws regarding the status of women. I then worked for a number of daily newspapers and, in 1973, during a period when the United Nations was preparing for "The Decade of Women," I joined another woman's magazine as editor-in-chief. We were already reading the works of feminist writers such as Simone de Beauvoir and having serious meetings to discuss women's issues within political parties. Understandably, the owners wanted the magazine to sell well in all the Arab countries, so we had to be very careful not to appear to be too controversial. When the fighting became intense in Lebanon, the magazine's staff moved to Egypt. I was unwilling to move there permanently, so I would spend ten to fifteen days a month in Egypt, complete my work, and return to Lebanon.

Were you married at that time?

When I was very young, I married a third year medical student. I worked and he studied. When he went to Germany to continue his studies the marriage did not last. I had two children — twin boys — and I remained a single mother for six years. Then I married again in 1968. My husband and I agreed not to have children because I did not have the time to take care of a baby. I was hosting a very popular weekly show on television; I had a radio show, five days a week, featuring comedy sketches; and I was editor-in-chief of a magazine. There were many days when I would leave in the morning and come back at midnight. I rarely had time to sleep. I wrote a novella on the subject. It is about a man who has the temerity to tell his wife: "You should be an exemplary wife: take care of the children, take care of me, keep the house in order, prepare meals, and then, if you want, you can also have a career because I have nothing against career women."

As a female journalist, have you experienced much discrimination?

When I began, I was young and I worked very hard. I needed the money. It is difficult to be faulted when you work like five people at once! But there was obvious discrimination where salary was concerned. When I was appointed editor-in-chief of the magazine I worked for, I was offered half the salary a man would have been offered. Society has drilled it into our heads that it is the man and not the woman who is responsible for providing for the family. Since the war, that is no longer true. I know many women who support their parents and family. These women depend upon their salary, as small as it may be, and cannot afford to complain and risk losing their jobs. We keep quiet because the laws are discriminatory. Most people think that when a woman works, she does so to seek higher social standing or to earn a little extra pocket money. This is not the case. Many women lost their husbands; others need to work because of inflation. Before the war, twenty percent of women worked; now, almost sixty percent do. With so many women in the work force, I think things will improve. Immediately after the war, many of us thought that there were more important problems to solve and it was not the time to complain about equitable salaries. But now, our patience has run out and we are prepared to take a stand.

What kind of influence did your mother have on you?

My mother is very bourgeois. She likes things to be done traditionally and believes a woman should be taken care of by her husband. When I told her I was going to work as a journalist, she started crying and asking God, "Where did I go wrong?" She was always joking and was either extremely happy or extremely furious over little things. We were very much opposites. I loved her, but I did not want to be like her. I asserted myself by clashing with her views.

Who did you admire when you were growing up?

Simone de Beauvoir! I admired her very much because even though she came from a very bourgeois, conventional family, she was a free spirit. I also admired her way of thinking about global issues as though they concerned her personally. She was very confident, profound, tolerant — a real woman.

What kinds of interviews and programs interest you?

I am a truth seeker. I enjoy interviewing regular people. I feel I connect with them best. They have a very clear perspective on life. There is no duplicity. For example, when you interview a peddler, a fisherman or a villager, you discover extraordinary things about these people. Often, they say things that are very profound and touch you; unlike politicians, who tell you what they think you want to hear or what sounds good. When I interview officials, I approach it like a game. I am always skeptical about what they have to say.

I have always been interested in cultural programs of value. After the war, we now have a potluck of programs. We need to be more selective in what we broadcast and set standards of excellence. Everyone sings, acts, paints, and dances. We need to offer people a level of comparison so they can appreciate the leap between mediocrity and excellence.

How did you get started in television?

A colleague of mine was working on a program and he needed a woman journalist to appear on the air with him. I was in the midst of writing an article and he asked me if I would join him. I said, "Okay, as soon as I finish." I thought he was just taking me along for an audition to see if I was suited for the job, and to check if I looked and sounded good on camera. There were a few people he wanted me to interview. He told me to ask them questions about themselves and their work. I did and then I went home. My mother greeted me at the door and said, "Are you crazy?" I said, "Why?" She said, "I was at the neighbor's house and I saw you on television! Your nylons were like this, your hair was like that and you were wearing no make-up! How could you do that?" I said, "I was on television?" She said, "Yes! Don't you know where you were?"

After such a debut, television was never intimidating to me. But it can be draining. After I do a show, I usually relax by going to the beach for a swim. I adore the sea and the sun.

What are you currently working on?

We have wonderful archives at Radio Lebanon and I am making use of the material. Having gone through so many years of war, we, as a nation, have become economically and spiritually poor. I thought it was important that young and old be reminded of our past. I wanted to do a program that would showcase artists, literary figures, politicians, business people, who in the sixties and early seventies had a lot to do with Lebanon's renaissance. I wanted to show the public how these people were then and how they are today. In cases where an individual has died, I present in the first half of the program a montage featuring the original trailblazer, and then in the second half, I introduce the person, today, who continues where the trailblazer left off. The program, in essence, is an attempt to link the past with the present and provide hope for the future.

NORA JOUMBLATT

ART GALLERY OWNER

"I enjoy being at the heart of things in the cultural world," says Nora Joumblatt, a tall, slender blond, who could easily be mistaken for a high-fashion model. Joumblatt, co-owner of 50 × 70, one of the leading art galleries in Beirut, is an avid art collector. She studied fine arts in Paris at the École des Beaux Arts and the history of art at the University of Paris.

Joumblatt is also responsible for organizing the popular Festival of Beit Eddine, recommended as a tourist destination in Time *magazine's "Traveler's Advisory" section. The summer festival, which goes on for five weeks from July through August, highlights Lebanon's cultural heritage and features a wide array of music and dance by performers of regional and international renown.*

Married to Walid Joumblatt, a minister of state in the Lebanese government and the hereditary leader of the powerful and insular Druze community, she lives in the magnificent Joumblatt family home at Moukhtara, a Druze enclave in Lebanon's Chouf Mountains. Her home, built of dressed stone, is surrounded by courtyards enlivened with fountains and cascading waterfalls. The mother of two teenagers by a former marriage, Joumblatt is a talented athlete who enjoys tennis, skiing and scuba diving.

*   *   *

Who is Nora Joumblatt?

I am originally from Damascus, Syria. I come from an old Damascene family. My father, Ahmad Sharabatti, in 1928, was one of the first Arabs to graduate from M.I.T. He went into politics following family tradition. My mother is Latvian. My father was an Arab nationalist. He was imprisoned many times by the French for his political views. In 1943, he was a deputy in the Syrian Parliament and, in 1948, during the first Arab-Israeli war, he was the Syrian minister of defense. My father held a series of government positions in the fifties and then, in 1963, we had to leave Syria and come to Lebanon because of a change in government. I was nine years old at the time.

In Damascus, I went to the Franciscaines School, which was run by French nuns, and I continued to attend a branch of that school when we moved to Beirut. At fourteen, I left Beirut for Lausanne, Switzerland, where I studied A levels and O levels at the Chateau Brillantmont, a girl's school. From there, I went to Paris where I spent three years studying fine arts.

What initially sparked your interest in art?

The Orient has a very rich and varied culture and being exposed to such a culture on a daily basis can be quite stimulating. My mother also enjoyed painting as a hobby and she passed her interest in art on to me.

What is a typical day for you?

When I am in Beirut, I normally have gallery work to attend to and business luncheons. I am involved in a lot of planning activities as a member of the American University of Beirut Museum Committee. Friday, Saturday and Sunday, when I am up in the mountains, in Moukhtara, I meet with people who need to ask special favors of me. I attend openings, do social work, follow the progress of a French cultural center we created in Dar el Amar, and I like to visit schools in our area. My husband works all day, including weekends. We always have people over for lunch and dinner. We keep an open house and people are in and out all day. My husband receives hundreds of people and many of the businessmen, politicians and friends who come to see him have to be entertained and dined.

When you have a scheduling conflict between your husband's political obligations and your work, which gets priority?

My husband's political engagements come first.

How have you managed to juggle a career and family when you are involved in so many different projects?

It can be a bit acrobatic at times! [laughter] Walid and I have five children between us. Two are mine from an earlier marriage and three are his from an earlier marriage. My children live with their father and Walid's children live with us and they all see each other on weekends. I find as long as you deal with things in an open and civilized way, you can make anything work if you really want to.

How did you cope during the war years?

I think we were too busy trying to survive and trying to be there for others to really think of ourselves.

Do you consider yourself to be a patron of the arts or a businesswoman?

I don't think I am a businesswoman because if I were I would have chosen something other than art. In recessionary times, art is not a very lucrative business to be in. If you were to ask me, how is business? I would tell you, "It is not constant." [laughter] Also, I prefer dealing with the artist rather than the client — not a very good business position!

How did you decide to open an art gallery in Beirut?

I wanted to do something in my field and I thought after so many years of

Nora Joumblatt

war it was time for Beirut to take back its place and reestablish itself as one of the cultural centers of the Arab world. Opening an art gallery was something I, as an individual, could take as a step in that direction.

Art galleries seem to be springing up everywhere in Beirut. What distinguishes yours from the others?

The goal of our gallery is to reintroduce Arab artists to Lebanon. We try to represent the entire Arab world in our gallery by showcasing Arab artists. Before the war, in 1975, there was a great deal of interaction between artists from all over the Arab world and Lebanese artists. There was a real exchange of ideas and Beirut was an important intellectual center in the Arab world. The war changed that — things stagnated. As a result, now, we need to reinvigorate the intellectual milieu and bring the Lebanese people back into the Arab fold by exposing them to new ideas and movements taking place in the Arab world, which they missed out on during seventeen years of war. There is a lot of catching up to do. It is my hope that Beirut will return to the open and cosmopolitan capital it was once before the war.

Why did you call your gallery "50 × 70"?

We were looking for a name for the gallery and a friend suggested 50 × 70, which is the most common canvas size used by artists. We liked the idea because 50 × 70 represents something that is fundamental to art.

What do you look for in an artist you want to showcase?

It is important that I believe the artist has something to contribute to the art world. I look mainly for originality and for a unique style. I like art that forces you to interact with it; art that has a different vantage point so that, at the very least, the spectator will think, "Hmmm, that is interesting."

How do you deal with difficult artists?

We've had artists who have been difficult but remember we are in the Orient, a place known to be long on patience. You might say 50 × 70 operates very much in the tradition of the Orient! [laughter]

Do you trust your instincts to spot talent?

Yes, my partner and I have to. Sometimes, of course, we may be wrong. When we hesitate and are not quite sure, we consult an advisory committee made up of art critics who happen to be our friends.

Have you found yourself in the awkward position of being asked by friends to exhibit their art?

[laughter] It has happened! We try to let them down gently or we resolve the situation by exhibiting their art during slow periods.

Besides the well known artists that you exhibit, have you discovered any promising new talent?

Yes. In fact, at the end of each year we award a scholarship to a young artist who we think has promise and would benefit from additional training. We have been following a few artists and we encourage them by offering them exhibition space.

Is your husband consulted on matters dealing with art?

Yes, I think he has a very good eye. He has done a lot to beautify the Chouf area. Although my husband is a politician and a very busy man, he still makes time to pursue cultural activities. He financed and personally oversaw the creation of museums (showcasing mosaics, pottery and Roman glass) at Beit Eddine and Baalbek. He took it upon himself to renovate Emir Bashir's Palace at Beit Eddine. Whenever he had a free hour, he would go to check on the work in progress. He was involved with every detail of the renovation, including how best to illuminate the palace. I can't tell you how many times we would drive around at night to check the illumination of the palace from various distances and angles! He loves to work on projects of cultural merit — it is his passion.

What kind of art do you personally enjoy?

I enjoy contemporary art very much.

When you buy a painting for yourself, do you purchase it because you think it is going to increase in value or simply because you like it?

I suppose it is a little of both, but mostly it is because I have, as they say in

French, a *coup de coeur*! I fall in love with it. Inevitably, when that happens, the painting comes home with me!

Do you have any wall space left in your house?

Not much!

What influence has the war had on the art produced by Lebanese artists today?

The war might not be the primary subject of a painting, but often you can feel it. The pain and imagery comes through in the choice of colors, the brush strokes and the subject matter. I don't believe Lebanese artists have yet digested the war. Thus far a "Guernica" has not been created. There is a lot of creativity going on but we have not come to terms with the war and gone beyond it. We are still in the fermenting stage.

MAY KAHALÉ

PRESS SECRETARY

May Kahalé, a stylish woman with an engaging personality and a ready smile, is press secretary and advisor to the president of the Republic of Lebanon, Elias Haraoui. Kahalé, the first woman to ever hold the position of press secretary is described by a close associate as "a savvy journalist with remarkably well-honed political instincts." We met at her office in the newly renovated presidential palace at Baabda.

*   *   *

Could you tell me about yourself?

I am French educated. I attended a private Catholic high school. In college, I studied journalism and history because journalism was not considered a suitable profession for "a lady." It was revolutionary to be a female journalist! After college, I was hired by *Al-Nahar*, one of the best newspapers in the Arab world. The war broke out in 1975 just as I was getting started as a journalist. Nothing they taught us in school prepared us for covering a war. As a journalist, I felt it was important to make sense of what was happening in Lebanon. During the war, there was a time when some two hundred foreign correspondents were assigned to cover a single combat event. Later, fighting became so normal in Lebanon that eventually even major battles were ignored by the foreign press.

Did you ever feel discriminated against as a female journalist?

On the contrary, being a female journalist during the war was a great advantage. I could cover the war with much less difficulty than my male colleagues.

As a woman, I was considered harmless. I could travel freely between militias and armies and remain for the most part safe. Men, on the other hand, were often beaten and shot simply for their confessional beliefs. The war provided a big opportunity for women. For many of us it was our trump card. But it also revealed a very ugly reality. Lebanon was not all that it appeared to be on the surface: a beautiful country with brilliant sunshine, the best hotels and restaurants, wonderful beaches, and wealthy tourists galore. That image was just window dressing. It did not represent real life. Many of us were dumbfounded by the true reality of things. It was like a bubble had burst for us.

How did you come to understand the "true reality" of Lebanon?

It was through my work as a journalist that I began to realize Lebanon was not the Lebanon we had studied in books. It was not that appealing, ideal country referred to by so many of us as the "Switzerland of the Middle East." Instead, I discovered Lebanon was just a poor, little, vulnerable country fighting for a place in this world. It was this realization that compelled me to stay and do what I could. I had offers to work in Paris, London, Kuwait, and Abu Dhabi, but I chose to remain in Lebanon. I believed it was my opportunity to get to know my country better.

How did you become press secretary to the president?

Lebanon is the only country in the entire Middle East where we hold presidential elections every six years. To prepare for the election, I was assigned by *Al-Nahar* to create a pamphlet on each candidate. First, I had to determine who those candidates would be, because in Lebanon candidates for president don't announce their candidacy or campaign for president. Candidates are selected from a small pool of men belonging to the correct party and community, who over the years have attained a certain level of influence. Candidates are proposed by members of parliament who then elect the president. I was asked to state in the introduction of each pamphlet my personal view of the candidate. It was a real challenge to gather facts on prospective candidates, identify their views on issues, assess their character, and determine if they were qualified to be president; especially, in such sensitive times.

Was Elias Haraoui your favorite candidate?

[laughter] I will be perfectly frank with you. I identified and interviewed about twenty prospective presidential candidates for my pamphlets, but he was not among them!

How did you meet President Haraoui?

After the pamphlets came out, I was asked by the Lebanese Broadcasting Corporation to moderate a television debate featuring presidential candidates. This was in 1988 when President Gemayel had stepped down as president and the country was so badly divided we couldn't even hold elections. General Aoun was named interim prime minister and given the responsibility to prepare the country for elections. It was in this environment that the debate took place. Deputy Elias Haraoui was on the panel. It was the first time I had ever met him. During the debate, I was very confrontational. I asked him: "What exactly are your chances of being elected president, anyway?" He was not very pleased

May Kahalé

with the question. He informed me in a very stern tone of voice: "It isn't a matter of chance. It is a matter of who is better qualified to lead and who offers the best solutions. When I become president, I challenge you to be there to help me." After President Moawad was killed, I received a telephone call from the newly elected president. He said: "This is President Haraoui, I want you to be my advisor and press secretary. Come show me what you can do in this job." The offer was just like that — a challenge!

What exactly does your job entail?

My job is to act as a liaison between the president and the press. I help research the president's speeches, and I suggest ideas to him about things people might be interested in hearing about. We are trying to convince people that peace in Lebanon is a *fait accompli* and encourage those who left to return. We want them to know that Lebanon has a president who is strong and pragmatic. The government can't do everything by itself. We need our people back to help rebuild the country.

Every morning, I read all the papers and I give the president a briefing about the major topics of the day and what they are writing about him and other leaders. Sometimes, I provide the president with a quick profile about dignitaries who are coming to visit. Also, when certain important events occur in the Middle East, we need to respond quickly as well as prepare contingency plans. For example, if the American secretary of state comes to visit Lebanon, we have to brief the president about each member of the secretary of state's delegation and what his or her real influence is, and we have to prepare the president for meetings so he will be able to read between the lines what the Americans really mean when they discuss something.

You've been in this job since 1990. What are some surprises you've encountered that you didn't expect?

I was expecting a better lifestyle! [laughter] But regular hours are not part of this job. The first year was especially trying. We were working eighteen to twenty-hour days and we often had *les nuits blanches* [all nighters]. I rarely leave the office before 7:30 in the evening. I go home, take a quick shower, and then I have social engagements to attend. Also, the secrecy is something I did not expect. There are so many secrets in this job that I have to keep to myself. Being a journalist, that goes against my instincts!

Do you think you have an advantage being a woman in your job?

Yes, I think women can be more diplomatic. Also, I've noticed, men are more willing to accept criticism from a woman than from a man. But I also feel that I am constantly being tested and that I have to always prove myself to others. To be taken seriously, I am forced to be strong and assertive all the time. Being a woman in a position of authority is a relatively new occurrence in Lebanon. My current position was never a high profile position until I, "a woman," stepped into it.

Where does your drive to succeed come from?

My mother. She has always been an inspiration to me. She is a very strong woman who has had a hard life. Yet, she and my father managed to provide all six of their children with a good education. She was always pushing us to achieve. She was very ambitious and she made us all ambitious. All her daughters have very good careers — three are married — and my brother is a civil engineer.

Do you encounter much discrimination in your job?

Not discrimination, but surprise. People are often surprised to discover the position of press secretary to the president is occupied by a woman. In Lebanon, women are greatly respected as mothers and wives but, outside the home, their abilities are still in doubt. As a successful career woman, I have to prove myself daily and that can be very tiring. Fortunately, the president is a strong supporter of women; otherwise, my job would be extremely difficult. I remember my first major decision when I decided to arrange a press conference for the president without consulting the usual "experts." The press conference was carried live on five television stations and about fifty journalists participated. I arranged everything. I didn't ask for anyone's advice and consequently everyone predicted it would be a disaster. Fortunately, it was a success. I am sure that if that first press conference was a failure, I would now be history!

How do you relax?

I really don't. In addition to long work hours, social obligations are an important part of this job. In Lebanon, attending social functions — dinner parties, weddings, funerals — is a matter of politics. I am single so I can afford to maintain an active public life. When I turn down invitations, people think the president is unhappy with them. Rarely do they think that it is because I am simply tired! Fortunately, I don't require more than five hours of sleep. I like to read a novel before I go to bed. I try to do sports and gymnastics. If my Sunday is free, I visit my family. We are five girls and one boy. I am number four in the pecking order. I have many friends within my family and I have nine nieces and nephews so there is always a lot of family news to catch up with!

What do you think makes the Lebanese lifestyle unique?

It is the people. We have strong family ties. We are a mixture of communities. There are more than sixteen different religious communities living together in Lebanon. It is a very rich experience! There are so many different lifestyles existing side by side. We are a broad cultural mosaic with both similar and distinctive traits. Politics is what divides us. Our political offices are relegated to members of different communities. Only a Maronite Christian can be president; a Sunni Muslim, prime minister; a Shiite Muslim, speaker of parliament and his deputy has to be Greek Orthodox.

Do you think this system is wrong?

No, I think it is a useful system. It allows all communities to participate and share in Lebanon's political life.

How did you manage during the war years?

Surviving the war was an accomplishment. We did not suffer from hunger or diseases because regardless of which community we belonged to, we helped each other out in the face of adversity. With each new wave of fighting, we grew more united as a people. I believe this is what made the war in Lebanon different from wars in other countries. There was a real feeling of solidarity among the Lebanese people even when communities were fighting against each other. For example, when the Israeli Army surrounded West Beirut, which was known as Muslim Beirut, Christians from all over Lebanon sent in food and water; similarly, when Christians were thrown out of their regions, their Muslim friends received them and provided them with food and shelter.

Ironically, I believe this solidarity among the Lebanese people prolonged the war because we proved too adaptable. To survive, we accommodated ourselves too adeptly to each twist and turn that the war took. It was very difficult being shelled day and night, being nervous and tense all the time, and not being able to move freely about or sleep in peace. People are now feeling the effects of the stress on their health and even such symptoms as memory loss is an indication of the stress we endured for so long. It is hard to forget what we went through. I am constantly reminded of our ordeal by the ruins around us and the fact that many of my friends are no longer here: many were killed and many emigrated to other countries.

Do you feel bitter about what happened?

Yes, why not? So many people died needlessly. Life is too precious to be given up absurdly. We should all have the opportunity to live long, full, active lives.

What have you learned from your war experience?

I am now more tolerant of other people's views regarding Lebanon. I wasn't before the war. I was very romantic in my love of Lebanon. War teaches you to accept people as they are and to try to understand them better through communication. In the Middle East things are black and white. In journalism, we learn to see all the colors. It's very difficult to convince people that there are other colors. If you want to change people to your point of view, you have to be a psychologist and deal with each person differently. With the right approach, I am convinced, nothing is impossible.

MAY MENASSA

JOURNALIST

One of Lebanon's most respected journalists, May Menassa covers cultural, artistic and literary events for Al-Nahar, the country's premiere newspaper. She is described by a colleague as "one of those rare critics who delights in the accomplishments of others, appreciates beauty, and encourages talent." During the twenty-six years she has been with Al-Nahar, her assignments have ranged from fashion writer to war correspondent.

Menassa started out in television as Lebanon's first female news broadcaster and then moved on to journalism, writing in both Arabic and French. She is the author of several novels and a children's book on Gamal Abdel Nasser, the former president of Egypt.

A charming, vivacious woman, Menassa exudes passion, commitment, and a disarming spontaneity. Whether she is greeting a friend of long-standing or a new acquaintance, she does so with warmth and enthusiasm. In the midst of our interview, at her office in the Al-Nahar building, a former colleague, a stooped gentleman, whom she had not seen for many years, approached her desk and inquired hesitantly if she remembered him. Smiling, and with eyes twinkling, she sprang from her chair to give him a warm hug: "Of course, I remember you. Would I forget a friend?" The elderly man, visibly moved, responded: "You would not."

*   *   *

Could you tell me about yourself?

I was born July 20, 1939, in the heart of summer. Ever since I was young, I always loved literature and music. I would spend hours listening to Beethoven and Chopin. My parents never understood where this love for music came from. I enjoyed singing and I wrote poetry — very mediocre poetry I might add — but at the time I thought it was the most romantic thing in the world to do! The year I completed my B.A. degree I entered the world of television, became a news anchor, and had my own program called, "Women of Today." After television, I went into print journalism. Currently, I write about music, art, poetry, and literature. I am totally committed to my profession! Every time I write about one of these subjects I, too, become a musician, a sculptor, an artist, a poet. Sometimes poets call me and ask my opinion about a poem in progress. That gives me tremendous satisfaction. I feel I am witnessing the emergence of a new life!

What initially drew you to journalism?

The fact that with a sheet of paper at your fingertips you can travel and explore the entire world! Journalism has permitted me to have the most

May Menassa

memorable encounters. It is a passionate profession full of passionate people. Of course, it is up to you to search them out. Recently, I attended a two-hour lecture on medicine given by a brilliant medical researcher who is also a gifted sculptor. Afterwards, he allowed me to follow him to his studio and watch him as he chiseled a sculpture from a piece of rock. It was fascinating to see the different facets of this man. Only through journalism are such encounters possible.

I cannot say that journalism has been an easy profession. No! It is like you are always going to school and you have to deal with what I still call, after all these years, "*la menace*," deadline pressures! You are constantly studying, listening, reading books on art, history, philosophy, science, to know more about certain subjects. If you depend upon your own knowledge, you will soon be out of your depth. When I became a journalist, I was determined to be the best. I am not good at being second best. When I cannot be first in something, I make room for others. My profession gives me enormous satisfaction because I am engaged by the world. An occupational hazard is that I am always analyzing things, wondering what is the real meaning behind words and deeds. Yesterday, I was thinking I have become much too curious! I feel I am always listening, trying to discover what people are thinking and talking about — I even find myself listening in on the neighbors! [laughter]

How has the war changed you?

I used to love to sing and play the guitar but when the war broke out I could no longer do either. I changed. I became a sad person. The death, the destruction and the cruelty I witnessed, pained me deeply. For many years I only dressed in black. I mourned the dead and the loss of my country. The war years took up a large chapter of my life. I wrote *une cuisine libre* for seventeen years and kept a journal to pour out my reflections and feelings about the war. It was also during this period that I began exploring the great religions of the world, searching for God. I had this burning need to find Him.

Was there a single event that sparked that need?

When someone would narrowly escape death by a bullet or a shell, I always found it disturbing to hear their friends and family say afterwards: "God loves him" or "God loves her." It made me ask: Why? Does God love the person who is killed less? I began studying Christianity, Buddhism and Islam in depth. I wanted to understand religion from very close up. I wanted to discover which religion is closest to the truth.

What did you discover?

That I have this need to be overwhelmed by God. That everyone must find the truth for themselves. There is no one truth. Today, my conception of God, of Christ, of Buddha, of Muhammad, has changed. I have a relationship in my soul with God which is not based on curiosity or ritual prayer. I don't pray the same prayer over and over. I address myself to God anew each time. I have written hundreds of articles and I found that as I studied religion my writing underwent a change. In the past, when I wrote, I rarely mentioned the name of God. Now, God appears in almost every article I write. I have become more transparent, more spiritual.

The senseless spilling of blood made me want to get away from people and live alone. People were being killed for a handful of dollars, for pieces of paper, for being caught in the wrong village, for their name, for their religion — for things they had no control over. I had nowhere else but God to turn to for answers. Material things no longer mattered to me: if you took my house, I could care less; if you took the clothes in my closet, it would make no difference to me. I realize that we are all just passing through this life. From God's point of view, our lifespan is no longer than the flight of a bird. I am fortunate that I am not alone in this world. I have a thirty-year-old son and his fiancée whom I adore. I am divorced from my husband, but I am surrounded by wonderful friends and by my sisters. I feel I have so much love and compassion within me that I want to share. Hate does not exist in my heart. God has gifts which he gives to certain people in ample portions.

What gifts has He given you?

Literature is an expressive force. If you know how to write and express yourself you are a very lucky person. God gave me the gift of writing like he gave others the gift of singing. God is found where the good things are. When I hear Mozart's "Requiem Mass," I think God is here. Yesterday, I attended an international Arab music concert held in a convent. It was the first time Islamic music had ever been played in this convent along with Maronite, Syriac and Byzantine music. Musicians from all faiths congregated together to play. Afterwards, I wrote in my article: "When God is present, religion binds people together and teaches them to love one another; when politics is present, religion pulls people apart and teaches them to hate each other and all is lost."

Were you very religious before the war?

The war brought me in conflict with myself and God. I was not deeply religious in the sense that I never practiced the rituals of religion. Early on in the war there was a time I doubted that God even existed. I thought if there were a God, He would not allow such suffering and cruelty. This doubt filled me with a terrible agony. I would find myself saying out loud: "God, stop being absent! Show yourself! What is this absence?" My faith was sorely tested. Today, it is in a stable state. I have come to realize the stronger your faith, the stronger you are. Voila!

Did you lose anyone close to you during the war?

I did not lose any family members and my house was never hit. My apartment is on the ground floor and it was always the safest place in the building. When the shelling would start, everyone would come down to my apartment. At one point I had fifteen neighbors living with me. I never lost even a single pane of glass. Everyone paid for the war. I did not. Often, when I would hear about the terrible things befalling my friends, I would feel ashamed and afraid to confess my own good fortune.

Studies show that many people who held up well during the war are now suffering from mental breakdowns.

Yes, that is true. During the war, people ran on survival instinct. They had to save themselves and their children. They had to fill their stomachs. But once the war ended, the shelling ceased, and they felt they were out of harm's way, many began to experience a wide range of emotional problems such as depression, weeping for no reason, fear of loud noises, nightmares. I did not suffer too badly because I was constantly occupied. I wrote all the time. I did not have time to be sick or tired. I never had the time to even say "ouff!" The war was the most important thing in my life. Every article I wrote represented a great achievement. It was like completing a great novel! In fact, it was due to my coverage of the war that I was inspired to write two novels.

What are the novels about?

One novel deals with the exodus of Christians from their villages in the mountains. It is based on personal experience. I belong to a village in the mountains that was taken over and I was prevented from visiting it. In my novel, I was brutally honest about my feelings and that is why I have not yet published it. The displaced are now in the process of returning to their villages and I did not want to stir up old emotions. The second book is about a woman living through war who has flashbacks to her childhood. It is written in a very romantic style. I did not intend for this woman to be me but a lot of her feelings, the events that take place, and the surroundings she inhabits are largely autobiographical.

Are you looking forward to the future?

Only the present matters to me. Strangely enough, I don't think much about the future. If anything, I am afraid of the future. The war conditioned me to live one day at a time. For sixteen years "tomorrow" meant possible death; therefore, you lived only for today. Of course, not everyone is alike. There are those who have closed their doors on today because they cannot stand what they see. They spend their days saying: "How wonderful Lebanon was before the war." I don't do that. The past for me is buried. As for tomorrow, I don't feel I have a visa that allows me to enter the realm of tomorrow. I live intensively in the present — in the now. My day begins at seven in the morning and ends at one o'clock in the morning. It is a day spent working, thinking, and reflecting. Even when I am cooking, I am thinking about the article I am writing. At night, I dream a lot.

No nightmares, I hope.

A few.

What is a typical day for you?

My assignments generally include covering some kind of cultural event: a recital, a concert, a poetry reading, an art exhibit, a literary conference, a dance or folkloric performance. Then I do my shopping, go home and cook. In the evenings, I am often joined by my son and his fiancée. Friends drop in without telephoning for dinner or a drink, and we stay up until midnight discussing everything and nothing. After they leave, I go to my desk and work for an hour before going to bed. I get up early in the morning and finish my article. Then I drop it off at the office and find out what is happening that day.

Does writing come easily for you?

Yes, I love to write. Writing is like breathing for me, but that doesn't mean that as soon as I get behind my desk the ideas come! Thoughts that are in one's head are different from thoughts you put down on paper. They take another form. I put a lot of color in my articles. I am like a painter. I have tried to use a word processor but I find that I think better when I write with a pen. For me, a pen represents blue blood! I write with a Bic pen. I have tried to be elegant and write with a Parker pen, but I am always losing my pens. [laughter]

What was your first job?

I began as a television broadcaster. My first job in journalism was with *Al Nahar.* I have now been with the newspaper for twenty-six years. I headed the section on women's issues but after the war broke out, they dropped that section and I jumped into covering the war.

Whom do you admire in your profession?

I am not a jealous person but I have always been jealous of Oriana Fallaci. I wanted to be a great journalist just like her! She is the only person I have ever been jealous of in my life. Her courage astounds me.

What do you think are important qualities for a journalist to possess?

You have to be knowledgeable about your culture, curious about the world around you, involved in what you do, and able to empathize with others. As a journalist, I experience other people's lives. I get to put myself in the shoes of famous artists, singers, writers, et cetera. I love my profession. Everything I do is because of it. My professional and my private life are inseparable.

Have you ever felt discriminated against because of your gender?

During the war my male colleagues always told me that my being a woman was an advantage and they were right. I was not threatened or menaced to the degree that they were by militiamen. When I was threatened or treated impolitely, I responded without fear. I talked back and released my anger. My male colleagues could never do that without seriously endangering their lives. They would certainly have been killed. Every time I felt I was illegally stopped on the road and forced to pull over at a barrier, I would get out of my car and cause a scene. I was furious and I would vent my outrage. I would tell the Syrian soldiers they had no right to stop me in my own country. I would tell the young militiamen: "What are you doing with your lives? Why aren't you in school getting an education? Don't you know you are destroying our country. What is to become of you after the war? What type of future will you have? Go to school! Refuse to fight!" I never stopped resisting the war. I never got accustomed to the waste, the utter senselessness of war. I felt God had a mission for me and that mission was to shake sense into these eighteen-year-olds, running around with guns, who knew nothing of life. They were not even familiar with the geography of their own country. All they did was threaten and menace unarmed people. I was disgusted by their attitude. I was careless, but I don't regret my madness.

What are you most proud of having accomplished?

Writing articles during the war under very difficult circumstances. I am especially proud of my "War Journal" which covered twenty-two days of intense shelling. I remember leaving my house with my journal in my satchel to go drop it off at the printers. I traveled by foot that day because most of the roads were closed. I encountered a car along the way and the driver gave me a lift. He dropped me off in a deserted part of town because the roads were destroyed and he could not pass. He told me, "You are now in Dora." I knew the town of Dora well. I passed it all the time. But that day, with all the destruction, I did not recognize Dora. Everything was demolished. There were no landmarks: not even trees were left standing. I did not know which way to go. I was totally lost.

Then I saw two people running, carrying a coffin between them. It was such a strange sight. For a moment, I thought I was hallucinating. I grabbed my journal from my satchel and at the bottom of the last page I wrote: "In my country the dead now bury themselves." Normally, we have large processions consisting of friends and relatives who accompany the dead to their final resting place. I was deeply pained that no one was there to walk behind the coffin and pray for the dead person's soul. As though pulled by a magnet, I followed the coffin. Then I heard from far away someone yelling: "Madame, be careful! You are walking in a mine field." I froze. I did not know which way to step. For some reason all I could think of was Lot's wife in the Bible when she was warned not to look back or risk turning into a block of salt. In my twenty-six years of journalism that is a moment I will never forget. One of my novels, in fact, begins at that precise moment.

A week earlier, a colleague of mine, a photographer, had been killed in that same area. He was a brave and talented man who lived to capture "the moment" on film. When George died no one was there to capture his death. He had covered the fire that enflamed Dora when the petroleum depot blew up and he went into the flames to take pictures. When he returned to the office, his face was burned and his hair singed. I told him: "George, you take too many risks." Shortly thereafter he gave up his life on that same road. His body remained there, exposed, for four days. No one dared go near the area for fear of getting killed. The army, finally, managed to get through and return his body to his family. I was thinking of George when I followed the coffin that day.

Are you proud to be Lebanese?

I need to be proud of my government first. I want a government that works for the good of all the people; a government led by leaders and not by people who are just interested in prestige and job titles. Titles mean nothing! To love my country I have to love my government.

What is the reaction of people when you travel and they learn that you are Lebanese?

During the war I detested airports and traveling. Airport officials would see my Lebanese passport and always assume the worst. They would ask: "So, are you carrying any guns or hashish?" Even as a joke, it was offensive and humiliating. I would bristle and say, "Lebanon and the Lebanese are not like that. We are tourists not terrorists." We too were victims of a vile war and our plight was made worse by the spread of disinformation about Lebanon. Now, things have calmed down a bit. Today, you read about "poor Lebanon, how beautiful it once was." Before, we were all considered terrorists; now, we are to be pitied. I don't know which is worse!

Are you optimistic about the future?

For the moment, I have little hope. In two years maybe my view will change. In spite of everything there are still people who come here and say, "Lebanon is the most beautiful country in the world." Even non–Lebanese come here and they love it. They simply shrug their shoulders regarding the garbage, the absence of electricity and water. They say, "Here, at least, you don't have to pay taxes!" They adore the disorder and the lack of discipline. We don't even have police to stop a crime in progress! I am a law-abiding person. I like law and order. My father was in the military and he brought us up to respect discipline and the law. That is why I am so unhappy to see my country as it is today. I have always loved to swim and submerge myself in the sea, but even the sea is now polluted. I am like a tree deeply anchored in the ground. I can't go anywhere else, but if this tree could run, I would go and live in St. Paul de Vent, a village in the south of France, with the most beautiful architecture.

Why do you remain in Lebanon?

I have parents, family, a career; I have roots here and despite everything, I am Lebanese. My heritage, for me, counts a great deal. Lebanon is the source of my identity. I wish we could live up to our heritage and pursue a dialogue worthy of our past. We have always been innovators. The first vestiges of culture originated from here. We will not be thrown into the dark ages. When I see other governments meddling in our affairs, it is as though a knife were plunged into my chest. I don't want to live in another country and be considered a foreigner. I love Lebanon. If I could gather up my country in my arms and embrace and protect it, I would.

RIMA SAID SHEHADEH

INTERIOR DESIGNER

Vivacious and articulate, interior designer Rima Said Shehadeh has dedicated herself to creating harmony not only within interior spaces but among her countrymen as well. She is the inspiration for an article that appeared in Time *magazine, in 1991, under the sub-heading: "Muslim hostess gives a party to help bring her divided country together."*

I met Shehadeh in Beirut at her palatial 19th century villa as she prepared for her annual two-week Christmas open house, a tradition now in its eleventh year. Carpenters and electricians were transforming the upper floor of the villa into a Christmas wonderland. After a brief tour, Shehadeh ushered me into her office, the nerve center of the operation. Her secretary was answering telephone calls; the fax machine was spewing messages; and her daughter, Rana, an architect, who also serves as her mother's business manager, was sorting through a pile of correspondence.

In appearance, there is nothing fussy about Shehadeh. She dresses simply but elegantly, wears no fingernail polish or jewelry and minimal makeup. On the wall, facing her desk, hang photographs of vegetables from her garden in the mountains as a reminder (when things get frantic) of the simple things in life that make her happy.

*   *   *

How did you cope during the war years?
By continuing to work. Our work consisted not so much of decorating as patching up people's homes. We patched shell-torn walls, broken windows and furnishings so that people could continue to live under their own roof. Leaving was never a choice for me. When my house was shelled, I patched it up. When my roof was blown off, I replaced it. When the house caught fire, I helped put out the fire. For so many years, we were not decorating, but surviving.
Is that how you would describe the war years?
Yes, this neighborhood was a very "hot" area. This is where the war started. We had so many different factions fighting against each other. Once we were cornered by four factions; each trying to get into our garden. There was no place to hide. We have no basement. This house was not built for war. In the entire house there is only one room with two solid walls; all the other rooms have windows on all sides. This house and plot of land was my Lebanon. Had we not stayed, we would have lost our house as did so many of those who left.
But you could have also lost your life.
It is a risk you have to take. I hate cowards.
What was the worst experience for you during the war?

Rima Said Shehadeh with roses from her garden.

There were so many. I learned a lot from the war and it is a page I don't want to turn back to. I have vowed not to look back. I live for the present and the future. The past is done. I don't want to even think about it.

Do you believe religion was a major contributing factor in the war?

Yes, religion played a role. Yet, I don't understand what credit one can take if one is born Muslim, Christian, or whatever. I am perhaps more open-minded than most because I come from a mixed religious background. I have never judged people by their religion or felt superior or inferior to another because of religious beliefs. I wish everybody would mix. Intermarriage would save Lebanon. We all eat the same food, speak the same language, and look the same. The difference is that some believe in the cross and some believe in the Koran. Is that enough to kill for? At home, my grandmother, who was Christian, never changed her religion when she married my grandfather, who was Muslim, and he never changed his.

How were you raised?

We were raised in neither one faith nor the other. We were brought up simply believing in God. We celebrated both Christmas and Eid. I remember, one day, I came home from school and I told my mother, "I want to wear either a cross or a Koran." I didn't know which was mine, but I wanted to wear one because all my friends at school were wearing gold chains with either a cross or a Koran. My grandmother overheard my conversation and said: "In this house, we do not wear articles from any religion! Religion is what you believe in your heart. It is not something you wear for show." That was the end of the discussion, and I have never worn anything that shows my religion. Outwardly, you will never know what my religion is. You can only know if you ask.

Tell me about yourself. Who is Rima Said Shehadeh?

I am the wife of Dr. Najib Shehadeh, mother of two grown children, Rana and Hussein, and the grandmother of three: Ghazi, Luluwan and Talal. My father met my mother at the American University of Beirut where they were both students. My father was a businessman and my mother, Selwa Said, had many interests. She was very active in the Red Cross and was president of the International Festival of Baalbek. I had a well-rounded education and I studied Arabic, French and English. I have always been a perfectionist. I find myself always striving to do better. I believe everything that you do from the heart is always better.

Did you come from a large family?

We were three children: one boy and two girls. I was the middle child. From the age of three until the age of eighteen, we all lived at my grandparents' home. My grandmother was a teacher and she was one of the first women to be educated in Lebanon. We were very much influenced by my grandmother, a fantastic lady by the name of Julia Tahumie. She was a Christian from the mountain village of Moukhtara and in her youth she used to travel by donkey to attend school in Sidon. She came from a very simple village family and managed to educate herself on her own. She was a great orator and could lecture on any subject. My grandmother published the first magazine for women in the Arab world. It was called *Al Mara' al Jadida* [The New Woman], which she edited herself. It covered cooking, world news, sewing, women's achievements, how to deal with marriage, stories for mothers to tell their children, health and beauty tips, poetry, et cetera. She believed a country could not advance without the active involvement of women who were well-rounded and an asset to their family. She did not believe that women were meant to stay home and just bear children. Also, she was the first Christian from the mountains of Lebanon to marry a Muslim Beiruti. Considering the scandal their marriage caused, it was a successful marriage.

How did you become an interior designer?

My parents always had a lovely home. My mother loved beautiful things. She had very good taste. I inherited my taste from the women in my family. I remember when I was young, we used to live in an old house and my room opened into the living room. Often, I would wake up in the morning and find the living room completely redecorated. My mother would do, every two months, what I now do once a year for the Christmas open house! It was my mother who involved me in interior design. She was always asking me to help her with decorating ideas she had for the house. I spent a year in London getting a degree in interior design but it really takes five years of study to become a proper decorator. What I have is a good eye and experience.

When you were growing up, what did you want to be?

I wanted, quite seriously, to be Florence Nightingale! I love people, and I like to help those who are in pain or in need. At one stage, I was so good at the piano that my parents thought I would become a great pianist. They bought me this grand piano that you see in the entrance. Unfortunately, after seven years of piano my interests waned, but I am still "Florence Nightingale" during my free time!

When I was young, I didn't have time to dream. I barely had time to come home, study, have dinner, and sleep. We were continuously at school. Even when we were at home, it was like being at school. Our whole day was scheduled. We had to be doing things all the time, and we had to do them well. We were considered failures if we were not achieving, even at a young age.

What do you find challenging about your work?

The challenge always is trying to realize your vision when you are working on a project. Also, your priority is to make the client happy and, at the same time, you don't want to lose money on the project. I am very bad on the money side — that is where my daughter steps in. We charge by the job, not by the hour. Time doesn't mean anything to me when I am working on a project. It is my passion. I know, if I were working in New York, people would look down at me for not charging for every minute. In business you don't give anything for nothing. But I give a lot for nothing. If I don't find just the right table for my client and I have that perfect table at home, I will take it from my own house and put it in my client's house.

Do you work with your client's taste or do you try to influence them?

I try to incorporate their taste. I help them discover what they like and what they don't. Usually, we start at opposite ends and then we meet — not necessarily in the middle! [laughter] They either convince me or I convince them. If they have a carpet, a chandelier, or something special that they like in the house, I use that as a starting point. If a client can afford it, I always like to introduce a few old pieces because I think old pieces give a house a certain feeling of stability, history, a sense of tradition. This is especially necessary when you are decorating a new, modern, concrete house. Also, comfort and good quality are important. Comfort doesn't necessarily have to be expensive. A room should be soothing to the eye. I am a believer in good quality furniture. A house is forever and it should grow with a couple. If one doesn't have the means to buy quality pieces, you should buy one good piece at a time instead of filling up the house with rubbish and then throwing it out because you can't bear to live with it after a few years.

Who are your ideal clients?

My ideal clients are those with taste. I worked in Saudi Arabia for a number of years. I was the first female decorator there and I had to wear a veil and be chauffeured wherever I went. Many of the people who hired me to do their homes had no idea what they wanted. I rarely saw the woman or the man of the house. I was simply told to decorate a house. It was up to me to find out which prince's house I was decorating, what his wife and children were like, and what the interests of the family were. I didn't need to investigate their backgrounds but I always did. I wanted to make their home as comfortable and perfect for them as possible. To properly decorate a house, you have to go into the intimate details of people's lives. For example, do the husband and wife have separate rooms? Do they enjoy reading, watching television, or listening to music in bed? Do they both get up at the same time in the morning?

When you enter a house, what is the first thing you notice?

I look for warmth.

If I entered a room you decorated, is there any clue that will tell me: this room was decorated by Rima Shehadeh?

My cushions are my special touch. Often, I hear people say: "These are definitely Rima's cushions!" I love mixing. I am an Oriental lady and I push the Oriental look. After all, this is a Middle Eastern country and there are so many designers from around the world who come here to get ideas. I don't believe we should neglect our own heritage. I try to promote in my work everything that is Oriental, whether it is carpets, tapestries, paintings, or furniture. I know that an English spring sofa is much more comfortable than a mother-of-pearl sofa, but a mother-of-pearl mirror, bench, or shelf can add a lovely touch to a room. I am all for integrating our past with a modern look.

Has it been difficult juggling a career and a family?

I started taking my career seriously in 1970 when I divorced. My children were eight and nine years old at the time. I went to England and studied interior design. I needed to have my own source of income because I didn't want to ask my parents for financial assistance. I married a doctor, Najib Shehadeh, who believed I had talent and he encouraged me to pursue my career. He had no problems with my going to Saudi Arabia to do decorating jobs. I would travel for several months and then come back home.

How do you unwind?

I am constantly on the go. I am under pressure all the time. It doesn't stop. I even dream about my decorating projects. But I've learned to switch off during the weekends by getting away to my place in Sofar, in the mountains. It is full of family souvenirs and I have no phones there. I spend my day thinking of nothing except my radishes and roses, the snow and the dogs. From the time my son and daughter were very young, I collected pictures, paintings and letters they sent me over the years, all of which now hang on the walls of my bedroom in my mountain house. I love getting up in the morning and being surrounded by their pictures and their creations. On my last birthday, my daughter gave me something quite special — the first pictures drawn by my two- and four-year-old grandchildren. I couldn't have received anything more precious!

I have learned that with all the mishaps, the anguish and sorrow you encounter in life, it is the simple pleasures that make life worthwhile and you should take the time to enjoy them and not take them for granted. I relax when I am with my grandchildren. They distract me. My sister-in-law and I are growing six hundred roses together. My house in the mountains is an inherited house. It belonged to my grandfather, then to my father, and now to us. My sister-in-law (who was married to my late brother) and I inherited the property. She has my father's house and I have my grandfather's.

How did you start the tradition of opening up your house to the public for Christmas?

The idea originated at a time when everything was battered and broken, and there really was no longer a Lebanon on the map. I opened up my house as a nationalistic gesture to bring the nation together. Everyone is invited and anyone can come. It was dangerous when only fighters were on the streets. But the end result was well worth all the money, time, and effort I put into decorating the house for Christmas. I found it unacceptable that people who went to school together, shared the same school bench, were neighbors and friends, turned into enemies because of differing political beliefs and faiths. I wanted to do something to bring them together. I can't tell you what we had to endure during the war. At my open house, I saw so many people weep and hug each other because they hadn't seen one another for years. One woman told me: "Thanks to your open house, this is the first time my seventeen-year-old son has dared come to this area of Beirut which he once vowed never to visit in his life because of the ugliness of the war." Imagine!

GHADA SHOUJAH

BANKER

Although the Phoenicians are regarded as the original bankers, Lebanese women seldom officially participated in banking. Today, Ghada Shoujah, one of the first women in Lebanon to achieve prominence in banking, heads up the Commercial Department of Allied Business Bank, one of Lebanon's most prestigious banks. She is also a regional manager and the manager of the Hamra branch, the bank's largest branch office in Beirut.

Described by a colleague as "nice to a fault, but rub her the wrong way and you will find steel," Shoujah, a short-haired brunette with an easy laugh, is well known for her efficiency.

We met late one afternoon as the bank was closing. From the vantage point of her office, with its glass frontage, nothing on the banking floor escaped her notice. Employees darted in and out to consult with Shoujah. Several late customers were allowed into the bank with her approval.

*   *   *

How did you go into banking?

In a roundabout way! I received my B.A. in English Literature in 1974 from Beirut University College (BUC) and I produced several plays when I was in college. I could have gone into the theater or into teaching, but an opportunity came along in banking and I took it. Representatives of a bank came to BUC to interview students for banking positions. When I applied, the interviewer looked at my college transcript and said, "Ghada, you took all these courses in literature, are you sure you want to be a banker?" I said, "Yes, I want to be someone important!" He laughed and accepted me on the spot. I began as a teller and worked my way up. I started, in 1974, at Al Nashrek Bank and when Allied Business Bank opened a new branch office, in 1988, I was asked to be the manager.

Do you think the war served as an equalizer for men and women in the professions in Lebanon?

Perhaps, but I credit my advancement to hard work. Gender had nothing to do with my promotion. It was neither a positive nor a negative factor. I am very dedicated. Even when I go home, I think about my work. Sometimes, I even dream how to solve certain problems that come up during the day at work. I only relax Saturday when I go up to the mountains to spend the day with my parents. For the last five years, I haven't had a vacation although I am entitled to a couple weeks of leave every year. I have just been too busy.

My day is spent dealing with correspondent banks, the commercial department of my bank, the head office, clients and bank employees. I am responsible for fifty-four employees at this branch in addition to six employees that make up the bank's commercial department. My day begins at 8:15 in the morning and it ends anywhere from two o'clock in the afternoon to seven o'clock in the evening. When they talk about bankers' hours being short — that is a myth! Running a bank is easy; dealing with people and their money (something very dear to them) is difficult. It was especially difficult during the war because people were very agitated. I had clients who would come and spend hours telling me about their problems.

How was your bank affected by the war and the devaluation of the Lebanese pound?

Whenever there was a crisis, and there were many, we would have a run on the bank. People in a panic would come to change Lebanese currency into foreign currency. I especially remember in 1984 when the Lebanese pound was

Ghada Shoujah

eighteen to one U.S. dollar and then there was a time when it was 3,000 Lebanese pounds to one U.S. dollar. Imagine what happened to people's savings! It was terrible. I spent a lot of time at work during this period. When the shelling would start, I would gather all the employees together and we would go down to the shelter or I would send them home, whichever I thought was safer. Our work during the war meant much more to us than just a salary. It kept us focused and served as a constant in our lives when everything else was so unpredictable. Those of us who had jobs were the fortunate ones. It gave us other things, besides the shelling, to think about.

Whenever the shelling started, our greatest concern was not whether a shell was going to land on top of us, but how the shelling was going to affect our ability to get to work. In many ways, because of the danger, the war brought many of us closer together. When you spend hours together with neighbors and colleagues in a shelter, unsure if you are going to come out of it alive or not, the normal distance you maintain between yourself and others doesn't exist anymore. We became like one large family. We all relied on each other. We were in it together. When that happens, you cannot help but become closer to friends, neighbors and colleagues. Personally, I have never differentiated between religious groups: to me a Lebanese is a Lebanese. We are a strong people. If we were not, we would not have survived the war and there would be no Lebanon left today.

Are your bank customers depositing less and spending more compared to before the war?

It is hard for me to compare the spending habits of people before the war because the seventeen years of war represent a good ninety-five percent of my career! Those years are basically my only point of reference. During the war many people kept their money at home. It was too dangerous to come to the bank and they needed their money to be accessible because they were constantly moving from place to place, from shelter to shelter. It is true, many people spent their money liberally because they believed tomorrow might never come. For many years, the sign of an optimist in Lebanon was a person who, when leaving, would say: "See you tomorrow!"

When you were growing up, what did you want to be?

I wanted to be a writer. The Romantic period in English literature was my favorite period and that is why I majored in English literature. I also wanted to be a teacher, like my mother. She taught French at an English school. But my parents didn't think that I had the necessary patience for a teaching career. Apparently, they convinced me of that, too, because when the opportunity in banking came along, I grabbed it.

Do you have any regrets?

None. If I had it to do all over again, I would still choose banking. I think banking is a wonderful profession for women. I am very proud of the position I have attained. My goal is to keep moving ahead and one day become chairman of a bank.

Do you find it advantageous being a woman when you have to deal with bank customers?

Yes. I think customers feel more comfortable discussing money matters with a woman. My clients trust me. When they are upset or angry about a banking matter, it helps being a woman. Out of respect for my gender, they refrain or, at least, make an attempt to hold back their anger. In Lebanon, after the war, tempers are short and it is common for people to shout at each other when they are upset. It is a real plus being a woman under these circumstances. For example, last week, one of my clients came into my office very upset. When he saw me, he said, "Because you are a woman, I am not going to be angry with you." That type of chauvinism, I have no problem with! [laughter] People find it sometimes easier to hold back their anger rather than to be impolite to a woman. I hope that mentality continues to prevail in the Middle East!

Have your priorities changed since the war?

Life has become more sacred to me and my family more precious. Surviving the war was extraordinary. I feel blessed. I have been very involved in my work. The seventeen years of war did not provide too many opportunities for marriage. People were too busy just trying to survive. My father died in 1980 from cardiac arrest. I have a brother and three sisters. One sister is head nurse at the American University of Beirut (AUB) Hospital; another has a bachelor of arts degree from AUB and works at the Javit Library at AUB; my third sister is married and has a Master's degree in public health and lives in the United States; and my brother has a diploma in interior design and runs a woodwork shop. I am very close to my family.

MEDICINE

MAJD ARISS-TIMANI

PEDIATRICIAN

Majd Ariss-Timani, president of the Lebanese Pediatric Society, is a pediatrician at the American University of Beirut Medical Center where she has both teaching and clinical responsibilities. She instructs interns and residents, and lectures third- and fourth-year medical students. When not teaching or attending to her own private practice, she is a student at AUB pursuing a Master's degree at the School of Public Health. "Majd is one of the most disciplined and compassionate people I know," says a fellow pediatrician. Ariss-Timani also serves as a consultant with UNICEF on matters regarding community pediatric care, breast feeding, vaccination, preventive medicine and primary care recommendations. As president of the Lebanese Pediatric Society, she helps organize symposia and round-table discussions with visiting physicians.

We met, after she had completed her rounds, in a conference room at the American University of Beirut Medical Center. The mother of two daughters, she is married to a cardiologist.

* * *

Could you tell me about yourself?

I come from a family where girls were encouraged to pursue their education. We were five girls and there were no boys. My mother spoke four languages and strongly believed in the value of a good education. She would always tell us: "Your inheritance is not going to be property or money — it is going to be a solid education." She and my father raised five daughters, all of whom are university graduates and professional women. I am the middle child. My primary, secondary and intermediate schooling was at the Makassid School for Girls. My basic education is in French. I started medical school in 1959 (in a class that was 25 percent female) and I received my medical degree in 1966 from St. Joseph University. I was able to transfer from a French to an American university with ease. The Lebanese educational curriculum on the secondary level prepares you to be totally flexible in either language.

Did you always know you were going to be a physician?

My intellect has always been of a scientific bent. In intermediate and secondary school, my biology and biochemistry teacher, Dr. Samia Amaish, was a

Majd Ariss-Timani (left) and the author.

pediatrician and I remember deciding in the eighth grade that I wanted to be a pediatrician, too.

Did you remain in Lebanon during the war?

Yes, through it all. The war is now over and my two daughters are teenagers. My children tell us now: "Why didn't you leave? Why didn't you take us away from here so we could have the opportunities of children our age?" I tell them we did not want to abandon our country and we never expected the war to drag on for so long. Now, so many years later, we find ourselves without plans for the future. For so many years, we lived one day at a time. It was difficult to motivate the children and ask them to compete and study hard when we felt the war could break out again at any moment.

What effect did the war have on the children?

There were two generations that really suffered from the war: my generation and my children's. The war began when my generation was just starting out in life. For twenty odd years ours was a fight for survival, trying to raise and protect our children in a confined area and achieve the goals we set for ourselves. There was no room for fantasies or dreams, we had to limit ourselves to the basics and work hard to ensure that our children received the same educational opportunities we did.

What is a typical day for you?

When you are a mother and a physician, quiet time to reflect and to relax is a fantasy. I have always believed my children are my priority and then comes my career. I am lucky to have a husband who is also a physician because he shares and understands my situation. We have had to give up our social life entirely in order to spend time with each other and the children. My eldest was born in 1974, a year before the war, and she is now a sophomore in college majoring in biology. Ordinarily, I am at the Medical Center from eight in the morning until five in the evening, and I am on call 24 hours a day. I get up at six o'clock, prepare my daughters for school, have coffee with my husband, and see him off. He is a cardiologist and he begins his rounds at 6:30. My husband and I have been keeping this schedule since we were both interns and residents together. I am at work at eight and begin the day by doing a quick round on newborns. If it is my month for teaching, I begin at 8:30 and by ten o'clock I am either at my private clinic or I am doing clinical rounds with residents. In the afternoon, I either have a teaching clinic for residents or I attend courses at the School of Public Health.

What motivated you to become a student again?

Lebanon needs good public health planning to resolve community health problems. In private practice, you only affect the health of a few individuals, while in public health, you can make a real difference in the lives of many. That is the challenge! We need to work on preventive medicine and primary care because we are deficient in both areas. In Lebanon, seventy percent of medical care is private and the cost is tremendous. The Ministry of Health has a grant to help the needy as do several private agencies, yet a very high percentage of the population who cannot afford medical attention are not covered. Today, a woman has to work. With the escalating rate of inflation in Lebanon, her income is vital for her family's survival.

How did you cope during the war years?

I coped by concentrating on the needs of my patients and the well-being of my family. Every two to three years, there was a lull in the fighting and we took advantage of it by traveling outside of Lebanon for a week or two.

When I am here at the AUB Medical Center, the reception areas are always jam-packed. How do you deal with this constant influx of people?

[laughter] Believe me, it is much less crowded than it was before. We have now put into effect a schedule to limit visiting hours. We Lebanese are a very sociable and empathetic people. When someone falls ill the entire extended family and sometimes even the entire village comes to visit.

Was there any one patient or incident that deeply affected you during the war?

There were many. There was a patient of mine who died on his thirteenth birthday as a result of a car bomb. The news came as a terrible shock to me. The child had received a bicycle as a birthday present and he was proudly polishing it in front of his apartment building when the bomb went off. I had been his doctor since he was a baby and had seen him through so many phases of childhood illnesses. I had given him all his vaccinations, helped him through asthma attacks, corrected flat feet, saved him from pneumonia … so that he could die from a car bomb.

Did the war make you bitter?

Bitter, no. Fatalistic, yes.

What was the worst point for you?

It was 1989. No matter where you were, that year, you felt the shells. For fifteen years, I was the pediatrician at the AUB campus infirmary. I went to the infirmary every day and treated employees and students in the corridor because the shells were landing all around the infirmary. I also had to treat my patients here at the hospital and then I had to go to the medical library to teach students. We would often hold classes in front of the elevators since it was the only enclosed area. We were exposed to shrapnel everywhere else. On days when the shelling was particularly heavy, I was always amazed to see students in class. It meant that they were willing to leave the safety of their homes, at great risk, to come and learn. You really had to have a combination of bravery and fatalism to go on. You had to believe: "If I'm going to die, I am going to die even if I remain in my bedroom. So why stay at home?" That is the way we trained ourselves to think.

I sent my children out of Beirut to Sidon during this period because it was too dangerous for my husband and I to commute between the hospital and our home. Our apartment building was hit by six bombs and my car was destroyed. I slept on and off for several weeks in my husband's car, parked in the basement of a building, located near the hospital. I coped by focusing on one patient at a time, and I had some peace of mind knowing, thank God, that my children were safe in Sidon.

What have you learned from your war experience?

I have learned to be self-sufficient. When we were short of water, we found a way to recycle water; and when we were short of electricity, we installed an electrical generator. As for food, the traditional Lebanese family doesn't buy food for every day. We buy in bulk for the season and that is how we survived.

Do you think the war brought people closer together?

No, I don't think so. The war dispersed many of us. A different redistribution of the population occurred, making people more independent and selfish. If you talk about families, many have emigrated; if you talk about neighborhoods, many have changed. Families have moved and displaced families have replaced them. My old neighborhood is no longer recognizable to me.

What is it like for you when you travel outside of Lebanon?

I defend my nationality and I suffer for that. My passport exposes me to segregation and to being treated differently. Nevertheless, we Lebanese are very adaptable. If we emigrate, we quickly adjust and make a new life. The problem with Lebanon is our terrain happens to be conveniently located for many meddlers. Before, we were preoccupied with physical survival; now, we are preoccupied with economic survival. Pent-up stress is manifesting itself in nervous breakdowns, heart attacks, and ulcers. There are many families whom I look after, who have been forced to take their children out of school because they can no longer afford to pay tuition. Life has become difficult. The middle class is no longer a middle class. They have been ruined by inflation. They are frustrated and their health is suffering. My husband, a cardiologist, says he is seeing patients suffering from heart attacks in a much younger generation. The economic collapse in many ways was worse than the war itself. We have reached a point where people say: "Whoever dies is lucky. He is no longer suffering." It is the survivors who are to be pitied. I prefer to be an optimist, but it is hard.

MUNA MATTA-MUALLEM

DERMATOLOGIST

A blue-eyed brunette with a serene smile and flawless complexion, Muna Matta-Muallem is a well respected dermatologist who heads her own private clinic in Beirut. She is also an associate clinical professor of dermatology at the American University of Beirut Medical Center where she has taught since 1974.

Matta-Muallem received her B.S. in 1965 from the American University of Beirut (AUB) and her M.D. in 1969. She spent four years as a resident in dermatology at the AUB Medical Center, followed by a year as a Fellow in skin microbiology at St. John's Hospital for Skin Diseases in London. She has published numerous articles in her field and is a member of the American Academy of Dermatology, the Lebanese Society of Dermatologists, and the Medical Alumni Association of Beirut.

A regular participant in conferences held around the world on dermatology, Matta-Muallem is married to an anesthesiologist and is the mother of three. We met at her private clinic in Beirut.

* * *

Who is Muna Matta-Muallem?

I come from the suburbs of Beirut, from a family that has always regarded education as something very precious. I have two sisters and two brothers and I am the youngest. One brother is an engineer and the rest have undergraduate

Muna Matta-Muallem

degrees. We have always lived conservatively; we are not a showy family. Education is sacred with us. There were no medical doctors in my immediate family. I went into medicine because when I was growing up everyone in my family would tell me: "Wouldn't it be nice if you became a doctor?" So I grew up with that goal in mind. I was also fascinated by Dr. Albert Schweitzer. I read everything I could about him. He left quite an impression on me.

How did you decide on dermatology as a specialty?

I like dermatology because it is a particularly convenient specialty if you are a woman and want to combine a career with a family as I have done. If a family emergency comes up, I can always reschedule appointments since there are very few real emergencies in dermatology. My schedule is much more flexible than that of doctors in other specialties. Having a career and a family is never easy but with my specialty it has been manageable. Were I to do it all over again, I would still choose dermatology! Since the war, the Dermatology Society has resumed its activities in Lebanon, and we now have about eighty registered dermatologists with about half of them based in Beirut. Considering the size of Lebanon that is a lot!

How did you find medical school?

I didn't find it particularly tough because I had been preparing for medical school most of my life. Of course, it took a lot of time and work but I went straight through it. I think the experience was different than it is today: our society was much more stable. All we had to focus on was our studies. There was no other outside pressure. Now, we are coming out of a war and I feel a certain discontent and unrest in the population that did not exist before the war. I find it difficult to commute to work and even to communicate with people. Also, the AUB Medical Center was not the huge medical center it is today. Before, we were like a family living in a small community where we all knew each other.

Were you one of the first women to attend medical school, here?

Oh no! The year I graduated there were thirty-six medical students. I happened to be the only female in my class, but there were several women in the classes before and after me.

As the only woman in your class were you treated differently?

Yes, I was spoiled! [laughter] Everyone was extremely nice to me. It was wonderful. The class I graduated with was very sympathetic. I never felt unwelcome nor did I experience any extra pressure being the only woman in the class. The number of women attending medical school has changed dramatically since I graduated. For instance, twenty-nine percent of the AUB Medical School class of 1995 and thirty-two percent of the class of 1996 is female. That is quite a change from my class of 1969!

Has it been difficult being a woman practicing medicine in Lebanon?

Occasionally, a man will come to make an appointment and he will ask my secretary: "Does the doctor treat men?" But on the whole, I haven't really had a problem. In fact, in certain specialties, women seem to be preferred. For example, I am often asked by patients to refer them to women obstetricians and gynecologists. They feel more comfortable with a female doctor. Also, there are many mothers who prefer female pediatricians because they think a woman understands a mother's concerns better than a man. On the other hand, there are specialties, like surgery, where male doctors are preferred. I've never personally been discriminated against in my profession but, indirectly, you sometimes get this negative feeling. For instance, if I visit a patient with a male medical student, the patient's questions are usually directed to the male student rather than to me.

What are you most proud of having accomplished?

I am very proud of my family. I don't give them all of my time, it's true. But as a result of my outside work, when I am with them, I really appreciate being with them. My youngest is twelve-years-old. I have an eighteen-year-old daughter who is pre-med (she is majoring in biology at AUB), and my eldest son is twenty. He is in his third year of architecture school. It's not easy having a career when your children are young, but you have to keep going. Otherwise, once you quit, it's very difficult to go back, not only because of evolving knowledge but because your family becomes accustomed to having you available at home. If they are used to your working, they are better able to respect your time. I am also proud that I followed my dream. I may not have made any big discoveries in medicine, but at least I have fulfilled myself.

How have your priorities changed since the war?

I think I speak for most people who have gone through the war: We tend to take things day by day and grasp happiness whenever we can. But I am not overshooting or trying to make up for lost time. There are many here in our society who are trying to compensate for the lost years. I try to maintain an even keel. It is true, we live day by day, but I grew up in a family who always planned for the more difficult days ahead. Those days are always in the back of my mind. I try to instill in my children the idea that you have to look ahead and that applies to the way you study and the way you deal with people. You can't live wisely if you don't think tomorrow is inevitable. The only way I've changed is that I used to be very sensitive. If something bothered me, it would drag on with me for days. Now, whatever happens, I deal with it right away. Petty annoyances don't bother me as much as before. I feel I have become more mature and more tolerant. Maybe it's not due to the war but rather the natural progression of age!

What troubled you most about the war?

The violence. As a doctor I saw a lot. I still have very vivid memories of the horrible scenes I witnessed: badly butchered people brought into the hospital in masses, doctors working frantically hour after hour on the wounded, and then another car bomb would go off leaving hundreds more dead and injured. It seemed so hopeless. The contradiction of working so hard to save one life and then the devastating loss of lives in a single bomb explosion. This was repeated over and over in Beirut. It was hard to live through, let alone accept.

How did you manage to cope?

I suppose I was able to cope because I never allowed myself the time to stop and reflect. Everything seemed accelerated. I am often asked: "Why didn't you leave?" The answer is we never thought the war would drag on so long. Had we known it would last seventeen years, I don't think anyone who could afford to leave Lebanon would have stayed. What kept us going was this hope that one day soon the war would end. Our staying here had nothing to do with bravery. We had just reached a stage where we didn't have a choice anymore. Now, of course, looking back, I think we took a big risk. I had cousins who died in bomb blasts and there were more than a few times when my children and I narrowly escaped death.

What has been the effect of the war on your children?

My children have known nothing but war. For the longest time, they didn't experience any other kind of life. My eldest son was badly affected. At one stage, my husband had to take him out of the country to England for a couple of months because he was becoming very tense and nervous. I couldn't leave with my other two children because we couldn't get them visas to travel. During the bombing, instead of staying in the corridor or in the shelter, my eldest son would become hyperactive and try to go outside. The war affected us all. I may appear serene and calm on the outside but, compared to the way I was before the war, I have changed. I am a bit *survolte* [overcharged]. If I hear a loud sound, I panic. Last June, I attended a conference in New York and, afterwards, I went shopping with a friend. We were walking down the street and there was a loud bang. Immediately, we ran into the entrance of the first building we could find. There was a doorman standing there and he looked at us as though we were mad. He didn't know we had just come from Lebanon!

Did the war affect your outlook towards religion?

Yes. I no longer believe in organized religion. I believe God is in one's heart. I've become more religious within myself. I am turned off by fanatic members of all religious castes. Yet, I see a growing fanaticism in all the political parties in Lebanon. I am revolted by fanaticism because that is what started the war.

Do you worry about the children of Lebanon?

Yes, because they were brought up seeing nothing but violence. For example, when I watch a film with my children, violent scenes horrify me, but I have noticed that my children have become immune or blasé towards violence. They are used to it. A question that I have discussed with many of my friends, who are trying to raise their children the way we were brought up — to have morals and values, respect people, to be honest and always try to do the right thing — is: Are we providing our children with the right foundation to survive in this society? When you look at life, the way it is around us, I worry that they are going to suffer for being honest and truthful. Sometimes, I ask my husband: Are we raising our children right? Will they be able to survive in a society that seems to favor those who bend the rules and believe in "Survival of the fittest"?

Are you proud to be Lebanese?

I am proud of the Lebanon that existed before the war. When I travel abroad and tell people I am Lebanese, the reaction is almost equivalent to if I had said: "I am a terrorist" or something like that. I will always be proud of being Lebanese because of the past. We have always been a very sociable people. We enjoy life and mixing with people from all nationalities. When I travel, I never hide my identity. I want people to know that I am Lebanese and I hope my children will feel the same way about their nationality and their country.

INDEX